Discovering Culture: An Introduction to Anthropology

BERYL LIEFF BENDERLY
MARY F. GALLAGHER, *Montgomery College*
JOHN M. YOUNG, *Montgomery College*

D. VAN NOSTRAND COMPANY
New York   Cincinnati   Toronto   London   Melbourne

D. Van Nostrand Company Regional Offices:
New York   Cincinnati

D. Van Nostrand Company International Offices:
London   Toronto   Melbourne

Published by D. Van Nostrand Company
450 West 33rd Street, New York, N.Y. 10001

10 9 8 7 6 5 4 3 2

Preface

"A mind stretched by an idea," Emerson wrote, "can never go back to its old dimensions." His statement expresses the philosophy of this book: that true education consists not of accumulating lots of facts and definitions in a notebook, but of assimilating some important concepts in the mind. Bits of information are easily forgotten; well-understood ideas become a permanent part of a person's thought. Ideas that clarify, that explain, that help one to approach the world creatively and critically are the only things that make the hard work of studying worthwhile.

We believe that culture is one of those mind-bending ideas that make the world forever different and more understandable. This book introduces beginning students to the concept of culture and helps them use it to make sense of their own world. Unlike texts that provide a theoretical introduction to anthropology's vocabulary, founding fathers, and favorite primitives, ours offers a practical grasp of the concepts, insights, and understandings of the discipline.

We have found that an appreciation of culture and behavior is best imparted through analysis of the social structure surrounding each student, rather than through the more difficult and often fruitless process of learning complicated explanations of abstract ideas. To this end, we have included at the end of each chapter material that helps students carry out empirical studies of their own cultural system. Using this approach, the course may be structured so that the concepts of culture and cultural systems unfold week by week, with each new aspect finding immediate application in the student's own semester-long study. Based on experience rather than extensive reading, the student's knowledge will be concrete and long-lasting. Beyond these brief studies, which instructors may elect to omit, the book provides a forthright, complete, and easily grasped discussion of the main aspects of introductory cultural anthropology.

The central intellectual issue of an introductory course, we believe, is the presentation of the concept of culture and the subsequent understanding of cultural relativism. We approach this problem from an empirical standpoint; we view culture as a system of patterned elements and behaviors. Through the examples offered in the book, students can learn to compare their own observations with those of ethnographers working in a variety of cultural situations. An empirical approach, we believe, achieves better results than more theoretical methods because it involves the student in an ongoing intellectual and emotional effort. For many students, such concrete involvement is essential to learning. With this approach, a semester can suffice to provide a lasting and comprehensive understanding of human behavior and culture. For those students stimulated to continue in anthropology, the book provides all the basics needed for more advanced work. For those ending their formal study of anthropology after a single semester, it offers, in a form they can accept and assimilate, the central insights of a great and liberating discipline.

In writing this book, its authors have accumulated the usual collection of intellectual and personal debts. The former, too numerous to mention here, will be obvious to many and are better acknowledged in the references found throughout the text. The latter, less obvious to anyone but ourselves, we wish to specifically acknowledge here. It is not a cliché but a plain fact that without the patience, tolerance, dedication, and conscientiousness of the inestimable Ruth Ann Holt, this book would not exist. Our spouses, Jordan Benderly, Leonard Gallagher, and Molly Young, performed yeoman service over a period of years as babysitters, sounding boards, clerical assistants, and cheerleaders. Claudia Crawford; Arthur B. Hayes, III; Geoffrey Hurwitz; John Landgraf; John Young; Leonard Gallagher; Daniel Early; Marjorie G. Whiting; and Henry Stern provided photographs from their personal collections. Stuart Crespin drew several of the kinship diagrams. And Morris Lieff, Beryl Benderly's father, first suggested that we do this book and showed us the way to get it done.

Contents

Chapter 1 DISCOVERING CULTURE: AN INTRODUCTION
TO ANTHROPOLOGY 1

The Construction of Reality 4
The Concept of Culture 7
Culture and Reality 8
Patterns, Sets, and Components 10
Acquiring Culture 14
Culture is Shared 16
What is Anthropology? 17

Chapter 2 "DOING" ANTHROPOLOGY 25

Cultural Patterns 26
Pattern Congruity 42
Explanations in Anthropology 44
Introduction to Field Projects 50
Field Project 53

Chapter 3 COMMUNICATION SYSTEMS 55

Language Structure 57
Historical Linguistics 62
Sociolinguistics 64

Ethnolinguistics 66
Nonverbal Communication 68
Proxemics 71
Kinesics 76
Field Project 79

Chapter 4 ECOLOGICAL SYSTEMS 81

Levels of Technology 83
Technology, Environment, and Social Organization 86
Food Collecting 88
Horticulture 91
Agriculture 92
Pastoralism 93
Industrial Society 94
Conclusions 96
Field Project 97

Chapter 5 ECONOMIC SYSTEMS 98

Functions of Economic Systems 99
Division of Labor 100
Ownership 105
Distribution of Goods and Services 107
Field Project 118

Chapter 6 SOCIAL SYSTEMS 120

Social Structure: Status and Role 120
Rites of Passage 125
Types of Status: Achieved and Ascribed 128
Groups 132
Social Networks 134
Social Stratification 135
Field Project 140

Chapter 7 KINSHIP SYSTEMS 142

The Family and Household 144
Residence Patterns 148
Marriage 150
Kinship Bonds 154
Kinship Terms 161
Field Project 170

Chapter 8 CONTROL SYSTEMS   171

Functions of Control Systems   171
Bands   175
Tribes   177
Chiefdoms   180
The State   181
Aggression and Warfare   184
Field Project   191

Chapter 9 BELIEF SYSTEMS   193

Belief: A Cognitive System   195
Elements of Belief Systems   195
The Nature of Beliefs   199
How Belief Systems Work   201
Types of Belief Systems   205
Religion   205
Magic, Witchcraft, and Sorcery   211
Ideology   214
Science   215
Field Project   217

Chapter 10 CULTURE AND THE INDIVIDUAL   219

Personality and Culture   220
Normal vs. Abnormal   234
Sexual Personality   238
Art   239
Field Project   245

Chapter 11 CULTURE CHANGE   246

References   271
Glossary   277
Index   281
Types of Change   247
Approaches to Change   250
Change at the Level of the Individual   250
Change at the Level of the Society   253
Change at the Level of Culture in General   262
Anthropology and Ethics   265
Field Project   268

Chapter 1

Discovering Culture: an Introduction to Anthropology

"Come. It is time to go." The young tribesman stood in the doorway of the thatched hut, silhouetted by the first violet light of morning. He was dressed for the day—the bone ornament inserted through his nose, his wide armbands in place.

The anthropologist was on his feet in seconds. He had slept in his clothes, uncertain of when the call would come and eager to offer his friend no chance to change his mind. This was the moment he had waited and worked for since he came to the village months ago. This morning he would be taken to the place where the ancestors would one day return.

The two men moved away from the cluster of thatch houses that were taking on color as the dawn rose. In single file, they walked between the garden plots, haphazardly planted and in need of weeding. Then they plunged into the heavy tropical forest. The anthropologist had trouble finding a path in the darkness, but the young tribesman moved quickly along a familiar route. Keeping up without tripping took all the anthropologist's attention, so the clearing came on him suddenly. The young man stepped out from between the last trees. "Here we are," he said: "The place of the arrival of the ancestors."

It was a large, unnaturally shaped clearing, about the size of a football field but longer and narrower. It must have taken many men hundreds of hours to cut this long, straight gash in the forest.

"You see," the young tribesman said, pointing toward a blazing bonfire, "we will guide the ancestors with that light. They will land their planes over there. We have built a large house for their airplanes, just like the Americans did. They will see we have all they need."

There was now enough light for the anthropologist to make out a huge thatch building with a bamboo tower beside it. Except for the construction materials, the buildings were like any to be found at a small rural airstrip in the States. "You have built a hangar for their planes? And what is that tall building?"

"That is where the voices of the Americans go out to the airplanes. When we call the ancestors, our voices go out there too."

The anthropologist studied his companion's face. He had read of the cargo cults back at the university, but even though he knew the reports were reliable, they still had a comical unreality that made them difficult to believe. Yet his young friend spoke in complete sincerity. And the sincerity of the thousands of manhours of labor the "airport" stretched before him represented could not be doubted.

These primitive Pacific island people had seen the Americans come during World War II in great silver planes, bringing a wealth unimaginable to Stone Age tribesmen. They had seen the Americans drive jeeps, eat ice cream, listen to radios—all marvels that came from the sky without any apparent effort. And then the Americans had gone away, taking the riches with them.

The people had been perplexed until the prophet explained. The Americans, pale as ghosts, were the precursors of the ancestors. Hadn't the holy stories said the ancestors would one day return in their white ghostly bodies with all the riches of the world? The Americans had come to show the people how to bring this about. But in doing so, the Americans had confused the ancestors. With their powerful radio beacons and their fine asphalt runways, they had kept the ancestors from finding the tribal villages. So, the prophet predicted, the ancestors would never come unless the tribesmen showed them the way by building airports as fine as those the Americans had built.

So the men had left their gardens and forgotten to feed their pigs while they built the runway, the hangar, the radio tower, and the radio shack with its tin-can transmitter—all that now lay before the anthropologist's astonished eyes. They had neglected their gardens and the repair of their houses while they manned their airfield day and night waiting for the ancestors to arrive. They had maintained their fruitless vigil for years.

"When do you think the ancestors will come?" the anthropologist asked.

"They will come some day soon, as it is foretold."

"But haven't you been waiting a long time?"

The young man said firmly, "We have."

"And you still believe they will come?"

Now the young man smiled. "Many people wait a long time for what is foretold. The reverend at the school, he told us that the Christians have been waiting a long time too for their God to return."

The heat of the Caribbean summer was intense, and many of the people in the village were sick with stomach troubles. But this didn't explain the condition of Pierre, the anthropologist's neighbor. He had enjoyed perfect health until three days ago, when suddenly he had been overcome with a feeling of weakness and had gone to bed. Since then he had had nothing either to eat or to drink, had writhed in misery, and had spit blood. The anthropologist called a doctor he knew in the next town. The doctor examined the man and declared himself helpless to do anything.

"There's nothing wrong with him—organically, that is."

"But he's dying before our eyes," the anthropologist protested. "How can that be?"

"Ah, my friend," the doctor said, "You have never seen this before. A case of death by bewitching."

"What! Do you mean to say that you believe in that!"

"It doesn't matter what I believe or don't believe," the doctor sighed. "What matters is that *he* believes he has been bewitched. I can put him in the hospital, but it will do no good."

The sick man's wife refused to have her husband moved from the village, where the *hungan* was trying desperately to counteract the spirits of the dead in order to save Pierre's life. In tears, she told the anthropologist that a man whom Pierre had cheated had asked a sorcerer to call on Saint Expedit to send the dead to take Pierre's life. This evil man had further sought the permission of Baron Samedi, lord of the graveyards. The hungan had not begun to counteract the spell soon enough, and Pierre was probably lost.

Pierre continued to fail, despite the hungan's efforts. He took no food or drink before he died.

The anthropologist visited the doctor sometime later. He raised the question of Pierre. "Surely you don't believe he died from a spell?"

"Ah, no, from a medical standpoint I suppose I must say he died of fright. But my friend, what is the difference?"

For the young man from the Pacific Islands, the coming of the ancestors is a very real possibility. People don't spend their time cutting down the jungle with hand tools for something they do not believe in. Nor can anything be more real than the death of Pierre and the terror of his wife. Even if we call his illness psychosomatic, Pierre's fear of the spell was powerful enough to kill him. But we Americans can believe in neither the advent of the ancestors nor the power of sorcerers. We bend our backs and give up our lives for entirely different things.

THE CONSTRUCTION OF REALITY

An Indian from Central America tells us that he "sees" winged spirits roughly the size of a pineapple, which shimmer and change color and look like huge bumblebees. These creatures make the corn grow. We "know" that this is impossible, but the Indian insists that he is telling the truth. He lives in fear of these spirits. We know him as a highly respected man in his community, a man of integrity. What's more, other men in the community agree with his story. They too claim to have seen these creatures. Are they all crazy? Maybe they are drunk or on drugs. If they exist, why can't we see these creatures too?

In 1956, the United States Air Force conducted a study to determine why, in the absence of pilot error or aircraft failure, so many mid-air collisions took place between aircraft (Young, n.d.). The aircraft in question were the first jet planes; the pilots were highly experienced flyers. The study sought to determine exactly how long an object had to remain within the pilot's optical frame of reference (on the retina) before he was able to see it. Experimenters tested the speed of pilots' optical reactions by showing them geometrical designs flashed on a screen in a darkened room for varying lengths of time. They found that two aircraft flying directly toward one another at or near the speed of sound did not appear on the pilots' retinas long enough for the man in either plane to notice the presence of the other. This accounted for the high rate of mid-air collisions. They simply did not see one another.

A second and even more startling fact emerged from this study. Pilots found that by concentrating on the flashing geometric images, they could *learn to see* other aircraft at a speed faster than anyone had ever seen them before. Nothing in their previous experience or training had enabled them to learn this technique of seeing; nothing that they had experienced in their childhood or even in advanced pilot training had taught them to see rapidly enough to survive in a changed environment—that of the jet age—but they learned.

Is it possible that this somehow explains why the Central American Indians see spirits and we don't? Could it be that the spirits fly so fast that the average, untrained person can't see them?

Perhaps, however, this question is less important than a more general one: Can there be more than one reality? Is it possible, for example, that we and the Indians each know contradictory things, both of which are true?

Some Thai Buddhists believe that guardian demons like this one can affect their lives. (courtesy of Geoffrey Hurwitz)

The nature of reality is one of man's oldest philosophical questions: for millenia, arguments have raged about the ways of knowing what is real. We, as anthropologists, do not intend to enter these debates on the side of any philosophic school. What interests us is the fact that people do not agree on what they *think* is real. We are less interested here in the nature of the world than in the nature of people's notions about it.

People everywhere live in the belief that they know the world as it truly is, and they live in terms of that reality. They usually go through their lives unaware that they act inside an invisible framework, that their framework is very different from that of other people, and that it is the *framework* rather than any "true" reality that structures the things they do and the way they do them.

The framework structuring the thought of the young man in the jungle clearing includes the probable return of ghostly ancestors. That of Pierre and his wife includes the power of sorcerers to inflict painful death. The

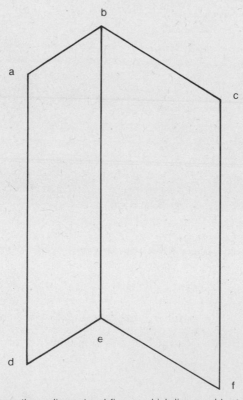

Figure 1–1. If this were a three dimensional figure, which line would appear to be closest to the viewer? *ad, be,* or *cf?*

The answer is that it depends on how you "see" reality. From one perspective, *be* appears to be closest, whereas from the other, *cf* appears closer. It is important to realize that either "reality" is equally possible, logical, "real," and, therefore, valid.

Central American Indian lives in a universe populated, in part, by pine-apple-sized spirits. These people did not imagine or invent these possibilities. Such ideas, widely shared among friends and associates, are not original to any living individual. Rather, than flow from the ordinary frame of reference of normal people. They are elements of the invisible mental framework within which each individual learns, as a child, to construct his thinking.

THE CONCEPT OF CULTURE

This invisible framework is *culture*. In any human group, every person considered normal lives within a culture and guides his life according to it. Cultures vary from group to group and make members of the same group similar to each other and members of different groups different. Culture influences people so profoundly, constantly, and pervasively that we usually do not realize it is there. As folk-wisdom states it, the fish never knows it's swimming in water. Only those outside the water can see the fish's world as it is.

When anthropologists use the word "culture" they are not referring to a specialized body of knowledge or feelings acquired in concert halls, picture galleries, or poetry readings. They do not define culture as something that some people have and others do not, or as something you gain by studying art or literature. To an anthropologist, culture is something that *every* person takes part in.

What anthropologists *do* mean by "culture" is difficult to explain succinctly. No one has ever written a simple or completely satisfying definition of culture; two famous anthropologists even filled an entire book with different definitions (Kluckhohn and Kroeber, 1963).

Therefore, it is best to learn how to feel and understand culture almost the way one would feel and understand a poem in which the meaning goes far beyond the printed words. True understanding occurs as a result of assimilation of experience. This is somewhat like learning to swim: you learn to swim by doing it and no amount of description of the process can really teach you how.

To begin to know culture, therefore, we will begin by building some sort of feeling for the concept. A definition will naturally evolve as we progress in understanding, and will change somewhat as our knowledge expands. But it will remain of the type that social scientists refer to as *operational,* a definition that lets you recognize something by the way it operates or functions. By learning how culture acts, you will be able to recognize it and to evaluate your experiences with it, and thus you will begin to achieve an understanding of it.

CULTURE AND REALITY

We will begin by using the following definition: A culture is a way of constructing reality.

This may seem, at first, like an outlandish statement. Most people believe that reality is concretely "out there," and that it is the same all over the world at all times. The first lesson in learning to see culture is learning that reality (in the sense we intend) is inside the mind as much as outside the body—that we do not see except with the specific vision that we have.

People who have experienced altered states of consciousness, whether through drugs, Yoga disciplines, or sense deprivation, sometimes bring away the knowledge that reality appears different if the mind is different. They find that basic, perceived experiences, such as time and space, colors, and the feel of their body, seem different—*in fact are different*—when the mind is different. The signals coming to these people from the outside world—the light rays, sound waves, the pull of gravity—have not changed. All the signals coming to the mind and body are the same; only the mind's way of receiving, organizing, and interpreting them has changed. The mind in an altered state of consciousness receives the same signals as before, but it builds a different reality from them. That is why people have so much difficulty talking sensibly about this type of experience: the concepts of our language do not readily encompass the experiences of altered consciousness. People try to expand the English language with new words and phrases to describe their expanded experience, but rarely do they succeed.

Such experiences have shown many people that multiple conceptions of reality are possible, although most people do not generalize the experience along philosophic lines. Nor do they usually draw the more important and far more fruitful conclusion that the "real" reality to which they return is every bit as much a construction of the mind as is the temporarily altered one.

Our seemingly cavalier dismissal of the good old solid, workaday reality beyond our temporarily distorted senses may disturb some readers. Surely reality is really out there, they may argue, the same at all times and in all places. But if someone can only see through a pair of eyeglasses that make everybody appear two feet tall, does it really matter that to other eyes people are twice as tall or more? Each of us can see only with the eyes he or she has. We can see only the reality we have learned to see. If members of a group generally agree about what is really out there, it may be that they are looking through the same distorting eyeglasses.

Social scientists disagree about the extent of the mind's influence on the shaping of reality. Some, such as Claude Levi-Strauss and Noam Chomsky, believe that certain basic conceptual structures are inborn, and that therefore all people construct reality from shared basic concepts or elementary units. Others give inborn concepts much less weight and believe that man's leeway in constructing reality is very wide indeed. Only future research will resolve the question. Scientists do agree, however, that the leeway is wide; much wider than most people imagine. It has indeed been shown to be true that people living in different cultures live in very different worlds.

A Hindu construction of reality

The Hindus of India, for example, live in a universe that passes through enormously long and recurrent cycles of time. For them, history does not progress relentlessly forward from the past into the future. Rather, it cycles back on itself. The earth, in this traditional view, achieves no permanent progress because periodically the entire world system ends in a cataclysmic disaster, only to begin the whole cycle once again. Likewise, humans and all other living creatures pass through a series of cycles. Each living being undergoes a number of lives, taking the form of various creatures such as insects, animals, people of differing kinds, and possibly even gods. The exact position of a being on the ladder of life depends upon its behavior in past lives, and the behavior in each life determines the position in future lives. Thus, the entire living world consists of beings similar in their essence but graded according to spiritual worth and power.

As strange as these concepts may appear to us, Indians believe them as firmly and as unconsciously as Americans believe that time and the world move inevitably forward, that each historic moment is unique, that each living thing passes through only one earthly life, and that human beings differ inherently from animals. Like ourselves, Indians see confirmation of their beliefs in the world around them and base other aspects of their thought and behavior on these beliefs. Indians may not eat meat, for example, because they believe that animals possess souls similar to human souls. Nor has Indian culture ever shown much emphasis on history, despite its extreme intellectual sophistication in some other areas; Indians believe that the particular events of human lives are of no consequence. Important deities have passed through multiple lives and are worshipped in several forms: a well known example is Shiva, who is Krishna in one different incarnation, Rama in another.

Thus it may be argued that the Indian and the American live in drastically different worlds. Moreover, these two worlds are not the only possibilities. Many other culturally valid images of reality exist, as different from ours and from the Indian's as these two are from one another.

PATTERNS, SETS, AND COMPONENTS

Although people of different cultures live in different worlds, no person lives in a random world. That is, no culture's image of reality lacks order. The human mind has the ability and the need to classify the innumerable phenomena of the environment into systems. This ability appears to develop as a part of the child's developing intelligence. Some scientists say that the propensity to classify is a product of the mind's inability to handle extremely large quantities of signals or data; that the structure of the nervous system requires the mind to simplify before it can understand. Our knowledge of the nervous system is still too limited to enable us to ascertain the validity of this hypothesis. But, for whatever reason, man strives to classify phenomena and to build a systematic world. Therefore, the realities that people build are systematic—they work according to patterns. They are composed of a finite number of items, and the items are classified and arranged according to rules.

The physical phenomena of the world are infinite. No two objects or events are ever exactly the same, and most differ from one another in more than one way. Man takes the individual things he perceives—what we might call items of experience—and in order to make sense of them, he groups them into categories. These groups of components, the categories or sets, are divided from one another according to particular criteria or definitions. For example, all the people in your anthropology class may be grouped in a variety of ways: by sex, height, age, religion, eye color, grade point average, or any of a number of other criteria. All the students studying anthropology with you compose one set, opposed to all those studying anthropology in other sections. All those studying anthropology in your college compose one set opposed to all those not studying anthropology.

Obviously, the particular categories into which one actually divides a range of items will depend, in part, upon the usefulness of the division. Sex may be a useful division of an anthropology class if you are planning to have a party. Grade point average may be useful for assigning honors work. Age may be useful if you're trying to convince your classmates to vote for a certain candidate for political office. Some categories one can think of have no use at all—it makes little sense to divide up a class according to shoe size or number of letters in the members' last names. But, useful or not, all these categories are equally possible, equally logical, and equally inherent in the range of items. The particular categories arrived at will vary according to the criteria used, but the only differences between categories are the criteria applied and the reasons for applying them.

Because people live in many different environments and situations, the criteria they find relevant vary widely. Living in a temperate climate, for example, most Americans use a number of categories to classify precipitation. Rain differs from snow and hail by being entirely liquid. The latter two differ from one another in shape and degree of hardness. We distinguish different rates of rainfall, such as showers and downpours, and of snowfall, such as flurries and blizzards. Once it is on the ground, we distinguish ice from snow. Skiers distinguish a few further categories of snow such as powder and packed snow.

People who live in Arctic environments, however, where survival depends upon careful exploitation of a precarious environment, make many finer distinctions among categories of ice and snow. There is ice that will support a sled and ice that will not; ice too slippery for snowshoes and ice where snowshoes are safe. There is snow firmly enough packed to be cut into building blocks and snow that is too powdery; snow on which a sled can pass easily and snow on which it will bog down; and many other highly relevant types. An American from one of the contiguous 48 states, viewing the Eskimo habitat, sees only a wasteland of ice and snow. An Eskimo viewing the same panorama sees a variety of ground conditions and materials as different to him as concrete, macadam, blacktop, and gravel are to us.

Cultures can thus be viewed as elaborate systems for dividing the people, things, and ideas of daily life into categories and for dealing with the categories. The differences between cultures at this level might be illustrated by the differences between two games—chess and checkers. They are very different games, but they both begin with the same components: a board divided into squares of two colors and two sets of differently colored pieces. Checkers divides the two large sets of pieces—black and red—into two subsets—singles and kings. The patterns for relating the sets, the rules of the game, are relatively simple. There is one pattern for singles and another for kings.

Chess, on the other hand, divides the two color categories into a larger number of subcategories—kings, queens, rooks, knights, bishops, and pawns. Each subcategory has its own particular pattern of movement that relates it to the other sets. The differences in the categories and rules of chess and checkers make the two games very different.

Cultures are vastly more complicated than board games, and no culture uses categories or settings as simple as those we have just described. But the games clearly illustrate the influence of choice of categories over a culture. The entire difference between chess and checkers, games of vastly different emotional and intellectual texture, can be explained by differences in the sets into which the pieces are divided and the patterns that relate the sets. Likewise, a difference in the sets by which a culture divides its people creates drastic differences. A society that distinguishes slaves from free men, for example, is vastly different from one that recognizes only one category of liberty. A society that largely disregards age difference among adults is vastly different from one that divides people into formal life-long groups according to date of birth. Some African societies, for example, recognize a number of formal age sets, each composed of all the men born within an approximately five-year period. The sets maintain a concrete identity throughout the lifespan of their members, and men may not progress to pursue new activities or gain new privileges appropriate to a particular age group unless their age set has officially advanced to that stage.

Looking at culture in terms of sets or categories helps us to understand why people behave the way they do. People everywhere have difficulty understanding why people in other places or other groups act differently from themselves. What most people fail to realize is that everywhere people act in what they believe is a reasonable manner. It is only that the culture of each particular group of people defines "reasonable" for them in different ways. Eating caterpillars, for example, is not considered reasonable in our society—only children or crazy people would do it. Among Yanomamö Indians, however, caterpillars are an easily accessible protein feast. At one time, anthropologists suggested that so-called primitive people act differently from our "civilized" selves because their mental processes differ from ours in some basic way. Scientists wondered whether the logic that governed the thinking of people in complex societies might overtax or confound the mentalities of people in simpler societies. Perhaps, they wondered, primitive people think according to different principles because of some inherent, or genetic, difference. Indeed, they wondered whether primitive people thought at all.

Years of contact with people all over the world have conclusively shown, however, that "primitive" people think as reasonably as we do *in the terms of their own cultures.* The mental processes do not differ, but the foundations on which the mental processes are built may. To return to our chess and checkers example, the distinction we make between a black single checker and a black chess knight is not inherent in the piece. Any agreed upon pebble, coin, electric fuse, or salt shaker could serve as a knight in a chess game; the horse's head on the standard piece merely serves to remind the players that the piece is to *act* as a knight. The piece's actions follow from the rules of the game (or in cultural terms, the patterns of the culture), not from any inherent nature that requires it always to move at right angles.

Likewise, if people reason from and react to a differently constructed reality, their behavior will be different. If the eye, the mind, and the emotions have been trained since infancy to divide the world into certain categories and then to deal with them in certain ways, reasonable behavior will follow the patterns of a lifetime. Thus, two people raised in different cultures will act "reasonably" in different ways, even in the same situation.

Japanese prisoners of war, for example, "reasonably" disclosed all they knew about their army's battle plans (Kluckhohn, 1960). American prisoners of war, on the other hand, "reasonably" endured torture rather than make the smallest signs of cooperation with their captors. The Japanese way of dividing the world excluded the possibility of an honorable soldier being captured in war: an honorable soldier either conquered or died trying to. Since no prisoner could reasonably expect to return to an honorable place among his own people, he ought to cooperate with his captors in order to win a place and a new life among them. Americans, on the other hand, did not perceive a prisoner of war as different in any significant way from a soldier in battle. He owed the same loyalty and bravery to his country and would be justly rewarded when he was finally liberated.

Similarly, in certain Muslim societies it is considered reasonable for men to require their wives, daughters, and sisters to shun the company of men outside the family, spend most of their lives out of sight behind walls, and cover themselves with tent-like garments from head to toe when they venture onto the street. Women "reasonably" accept these restrictions on their freedom of movement, flee in modesty whenever an unrelated man approaches, and ignore entirely the possibilities of friendship with members of the opposite sex.

In contrast, men in our society "reasonably" encourage their wives, daughters, and sisters to work outside the home, attend school and social events, move about with almost unlimited freedom, mix freely with men, and, on certain occasions, to wear in public the scantiest possible garments. In most Muslim societies, a woman in a bikini would humiliate her husband, her father, and her brothers by allowing other men to admire her beauty. In our society, a woman in a bikini is often a source of pride to her husband, whereas the admirable Muslim wife, covered from head to foot, would be a source of embarrassment or humiliation.

These contrasting customs derive from different constructions of reality. To the Muslim, men and women are drastically different beings, unlike in character, interests, moral strength, intellectual endowment, capacity for discipline, and many other attributes. Women are believed to possess strong sexual drives that they lack the strength of will to control. If left to themselves, they would fall into perdition and lead unfortunate males there with them. Men, therefore, for their own protection and that of their womenfolk, maintain a strict and jealous division of the sexes outside the home. Our belief that men and women are essentially similar in many respects and that it is the male who possesses the stronger sexual drive strikes the Muslim not only as immoral, but even more basically as untrue.

A cultural system thus consists of a particular construction of reality and

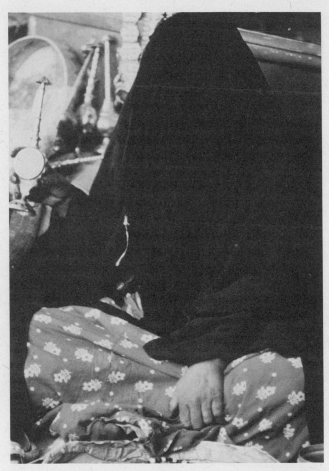

This is how many Muslim husbands wish their wives to appear in public. (courtesy of Claudia Crawford)

of the behavior that flows reasonably from that construction. It contains not only ideas, but actions; not only mental categories, but patterns of behavior and the products of that behavior.

ACQUIRING CULTURE

If cultural differences derive from reasonable behavior based on different assumptions, then it follows that cultural systems are learned rather than inborn. Despite individual disagreement on the degree of innate patterning of the human nervous system, no scientist seriously suggests that the details of cultural behavior such as language, belief, skills, and customs are anything but learned. Cultural systems pass from generation to generation through a process of learning. Every person spends a substantial portion of his life learning a share of his culture.

Any individual, if he begins early enough, can learn any culture. An individual's genes do not predispose him or her to learn any particular culture. The ease with which immigrant families become "Americanized" within a generation or so shows the possibilities of cultural learning. Thus, the particular construction of reality that guides a person's life results from his early training. Once set, the system is virtually impossible to remove completely. But for every individual there is a time in early childhood when he can easily learn whatever culture is presented to him.

Ethnocentrism

Once set in a person's mind, a cultural construction of reality becomes integral to his view of the world. People who look through the eyes of their own culture and do not suspect there are other realities of equal validity show the attitude we call *ethnocentrism.* That is to say, they evaluate their own life, and those of all other people, by a single fixed standard. In a shrinking world with an expanding population, ethnocentrism prevents people from communicating and working together, limits the richness of many lives, and can cause much misery and conflict. Ethnocentrism is the belief that one's own way of seeing and doing things represents the only natural, true, sensible, and moral way; ethnocentric individuals often believe that anyone different from themselves is savage, ignorant, bad, or just plain stupid. If one's own way of life represents truth, then all others must represent falsehood. The goal of overcoming ethnocentrism by *understanding why* others behave, think, and feel the way they do is at the core of anthropology.

The example of the prisoners of war provides an interesting case in point. The Japanese astounded their American captors by their willingness, indeed their eagerness, to cooperate in any way they could, even to the extent of spotting targets for United States flyers. For a people willing to go on suicide missions for their emperor, their behavior seemed bizarre indeed. It enhanced an American view that the Japanese, although fanatics, were basically treacherous and cowardly. The American prisoners, on the other hand, dumbfounded their captors by their implacable stubbornness. To the Japanese, any man so lacking in pride and courage as to allow himself to be captured alive should be incapable of resistance. This only enhanced the Japanese view that Americans are uncouth and barbarous.

Cultural Relativism

Learning to think anthropologically means learning to look at people's behavior in their terms rather than in ours. The Japanese prisoners acted in a way that would be treason *if Americans had done it.* In our culture, morality spans situations: what is right at home is equally right in a prisoner of war camp. Loyalties to country are permanent; collaboration with an enemy breaks the moral tie with the homeland. For the Japanese, however, morality is relative to the situation; one acts in a manner appropriate to the present circumstance. The break with one's duty came at the moment of the capture rather than at the moment of collaboration. Therefore, once taken prisoner, cooperation with the captors was the most appropriate behavior.

This insight makes much of the moral overtone of the behavior drop away. In a cross-cultural situation, the most appropriate judgment is generally relative rather than absolute. The standards of one culture rarely apply to behavior in another. To combat ethnocentrism, therefore, we adopt the attitude of *cultural relativism,* which seeks to apply to any situation only the criteria that are appropriate and to understand behavior in the context of the culture in which it occurs.

Now that we have told you that ethnocentrism is bad and something that you ought to avoid, let us start you on this process of understanding by examining ethnocentrism to find out why it is such a natural and nearly universal attitude and in what sense it can also be regarded as good. As soon as people are born, they begin learning about their culture. They learn how to talk and how to behave properly towards other members of the society, they learn what is good and what is bad, when and what to eat, how to make a living, and many other habits of their culture. In short, they become *enculturated:* they learn how to be acceptable members of their society. It is necessary to the maintenance and the continuation of a society that most of its members be ethnocentric, perceiving their own society's major activities and beliefs to be good, proper, and important. Otherwise they would not participate in their society's patterns, and the society would cease to be a functioning system.

CULTURE IS SHARED

A cultural system is not just any system of constructing reality. A lone individual who invents or discovers a novel way of constructing reality has not ordinarily originated a culture; usually he becomes a cultural reject, a person branded as strange or dangerous by those around him. An original interpretation of reality only becomes a culture when a group of people accept it and organize their lives according to it. Individuals like Joseph Smith, the founder of the Mormon church, and Muhammad, the founder of Islam, among others, developed radically reconstructed realities. Unlike many others who have tried, Smith and Muhammad were able to convince substantial numbers of their neighbors of the correctness of their new realities, and to convince them so completely that they were willing to leave their former lives and live according to the newly revealed reality. These prophets, therefore, were able to establish societies based on their new realities. They transformed their visions into functioning cultures.

Society and Culture

In an unavoidably circular set of definitions, a *society* may be defined as a group of people organized according to a cultural system, and a *cultural system* as the way of life of a society. Although these definitions serve well enough for the small, simple, isolated societies that anthropologists studied in earlier times, they are a bit misleading when used for large, complex societies like our own. Within complex cultures there are *subcultures* associated with specific subgroups that come together recurrently or have some kind of group identity. The subculture is a variant of the larger culture of which it forms a part. The *subsociety* is a small sample of the members of the larger society. To the extent that they do in fact form subcultures within the larger cultural system, these groups organize themselves according to a specific interpretation of reality that may vary from those of other groups in the system. The differences may not be basic ones; often they are a difference in emphasis. An athletic team, for example, organizes itself according to a different perception of reality (different beliefs, values, and actions) than a religious order or a symphony orchestra. Although quarterbacks, monks, and concertmasters share many elements of the general culture in which they live, their particular subcultures separate them. Each indicates by his actions that he perceives certain goals as valuable and that his particular array of knowledge is different from that of the others. These groups make different classifications of reality. The ideas, values, knowledge, and emotions each group shares are different: therefore, their patterned behavior arising from different constructions of reality is also different.

WHAT IS ANTHROPOLOGY?

Learning that the cultural dimension exists in human behavior is a bit like learning that a range of phenomena exists beyond the range of our vision. You have probably seen ultra-violet "black lights" and x-rays and experienced other special kinds of sight—through a microscope, for example—that let you see things that are present but invisible unless you know how to look for them. Anthropology is a special way of seeing, too. It lets you see the hidden structures that support and determine much of daily life. But unlike ultra-violet lights and x-rays, it does not depend on special equipment. A trained eye and a curious mind are all you need.

Anthropologists use their special sight to look into the world of man. The term *anthropology* comes from two Greek words, "anthropos" and "logos," meaning the science or study of mankind. Anthropology tries to understand and comprehend *everything* about man—what he is, where he came from, what he thinks and feels, and why he acts the way he does. Because anthropology attempts to do so much, it is not easy to define. Anthropology is the newest of the social sciences, and since its inception in the 1860s it has largely been regarded as the study of the old, the exotic, and the obscure. Through the years there have been numerous attempts to define the essential nature of anthropology. Some of these explanations are trivial, such as, "Anthropology is what anthropologists do." Others try to be funny, saying, "Anthropology is the study of nude people by lewd people."

Subfields of Anthropology

One of the more serious ways of trying to establish the basic identity of anthropology is to list its areas of interest. As taught in the United States, anthropology consists of four subfields. *Physical anthropology* is concerned with human biology; with man as a physical being. It has two main interests. One is to illuminate the processes of human evolution, showing where, when, how, and why *Homo sapiens* developed. It accomplishes this primarily by studying the skeletal remains and artifacts of modern man's ancestors and the physical and behavioral characteristics of man's fellow primates. The other concern of physical anthropology is to describe and explain biological variation, or the physical differences that exist in and between contemporary human populations.

Cultural or social anthropology deals with the description and analysis of cultures and societies in all their variety. *Ethnography* is the term used to refer to the systematic description of different cultures. *Ethnology* refers to the comparative theoretical study of these cultures and societies. The cultural anthropologist compares the various ethnographies, constructs and tests hypotheses, and thus develops theories to explain observed differences and similarities in peoples throughout the world.

Archaeology is the subfield of anthropology that provides an important time depth to the testing of cultural and physical hypotheses. Archaeologists concern themselves with man's past cultures, reconstructing them

Archaeologists carefully excavate the Thunderbird Site, Front Royal, Virginia. (courtesy of John Young)

from remains dug from the ground. This field has developed many highly sophisticated methods of excavating materials and dating, classifying, preserving, and analyzing them in order to learn about human life in the past. Although archaeologists expend a great deal of effort developing techniques of excavation and preservation, they do so for the larger purpose of reclaiming materials with a minimum of damage so as to permit reconstructions of past cultural systems and to learn about cultural processes.

The fourth subfield of anthropology is *linguistics*. Anthropological linguists study all of the world's languages. They have developed a large body of highly technical methods for analysis and description of this important aspect of culture. Linguists are concerned with the origins of language, the historical derivations of languages, and their changes over time. They investigate the structure of languages, and show how languages differ. They are also interested in the nature of language, how it is used, and how it influences social life. In many respects, linguists' concerns overlap with those of cultural anthropologists.

Characteristics of anthropology

This listing of the subfields of anthropology gives some idea of the breadth and depth of the discipline, but little idea as to what sets anthropology apart and makes it different from other social sciences. The distinguishing marks

Field worker examines early Andean Indian skull. (courtesy of Arthur B. Hayes, III)

of anthropology derive not so much from its subject matter—indeed, there is little or nothing that can be regarded as strictly anthropological—but rather from its approaches, concepts, and methods.

There are three outstanding characteristics of anthropology as a discipline. In the first place, it is uncompromisingly and systematically *comparative*. Any hypothesis or conclusion must be checked to see if it applies to all people, both in space (in all parts of the world), and in time (throughout history). For example, a currently popular hypothesis states that war is inevitable because man is by nature an aggressive and violent creature. In order to test such a statement, an anthropologist looks at the total variety of cultures, those that currently exist and those that have existed in the past, in order to determine if all of them show patterns of warfare. Upon finding that some societies completely lack a history of warfare and violence, the anthropologist then attempts to determine which sociocultural factors are commonly present in warlike societies but absent in non-warlike societies. In other words, in what other respects do warlike and non-warlike societies differ? Ultimately, the anthropologist hopes to discover factors that can explain and predict the presence or absence of warfare in all societies. An understanding of war would include knowing which factors cause wars and which, though not in themselves causes, are present at the onset of wars.

Unlike many other disciplines, anthropology seeks to transcend the values and viewpoints of contemporary American or Western culture. It inherently opposes a narrow or ethnocentric outlook. For example, many Western economists base their models on the view of man as a rational economic being, consciously deciding how to expend the least amount of energy in order to attain the greatest possible pay-off. Given this view of man, how can the potlatch of the Indians of the Northwest Coast be understood? Potlatch was a ceremony in which these Indians gained prestige not by accumulating wealth, but by destroying or giving it away to their enemies.

It is for comparative purposes that archaeology, with its time depth, is so important, and it is partly for comparative purposes, also, that anthropologists have spent so much time studying the geographically scattered "primitive" societies. The whole world is the testing ground for anthropological theories. Each culture has its own reality, its own view of the world, which must be taken into account if one is ever to understand and explain the behavior of man.

A second outstanding characteristic of anthropology is its use of a holistic approach. *Holism* is a universalist approach to man. In order to solve a particular problem, the anthropologist will use any and all sorts of pertinent information: psychological, biological, geological, linguistic, environmental, demographic, or social. In this regard anthropology differs from most other disciplines, which tend to emphasize one or perhaps two sets of causal factors. Human behavior is in fact very complex; the anthropologist uses whatever analytical tools seem appropriate to gain a complete understanding of a phenomenon.

In studying the nature of sickle cell anemia, for example, anthropologists have used data from genetics, bacteriology, ecology, cultural history, and linguistics. By using information from many fields, anthropologists have demonstrated that the gene that causes sickle cell anemia, and therefore death, in persons who have two of these genes (*homozygous* form) persists in human populations because it offers protection against malaria to persons who have only one gene of this type (*heterozygous* form). Only by tracing the movements of populations in several regions in Africa from historical, cultural, linguistic, and biological evidence could this case be made convincingly.

A third notable characteristic that distinguishes anthropology is its *methodology*. Cultural anthropologists study human behavior in order to learn why people act the way they do. They attempt to learn to think like the people they study, to understand the culture from their subjects' standpoint, to see the world as the same array of components and sets, and to form the same patterns.

Anthropologists thus try to *participate* in the culture, to learn its components and sets well enough to duplicate its patterns accurately and convincingly. But because they are not native to the culture, they can never forget their own system of sets and patterns. Thus, while they try to participate in a culture, they also *observe* themselves and others and try to record *objectively* the culture they see. The field anthropologist strives for a double sight: the insider's view balanced by the outsider's view. This special anthropological way of studying cultural behavior is called *participant observation:* learning about a people's way of life by immersing oneself in it—by participating in day-to-day living while at the same time attempting to observe, describe, and analyze the people's behavior objectively.

Participant observation has been the traditional fieldwork technique of cultural anthropology since Bronislaw Malinowski went off to live with the Trobriand Islanders during World War I (1915–1918). Though the ideas behind this technique are simple, participant observation, in practice, is not as easy as it sounds. People are individuals, regardless of what society they belong to. No two people do things exactly alike, and no one lives by the rules all the time. Some rules, in fact, might not even be meant to be followed, although everyone will insist that they are, when talking to outsiders. Thus, there are various levels of rules or systems: things people say they do; things they say they should do; things they really do; ways they bend the rules without actually breaking them; ways they break the rules and get

Anthropologist John Young develops rapport with an informant. (courtesy of John Young)

away with it; and the ways they feel about all this. To understand a culture, one must know the deviations, exceptions, and individual quirks as well as the rules themselves.

Participant observation also reflects anthropology's dual nature as both a scientific and a humanistic discipline. Through the stress on participation and getting the insider's view, anthropologists of necessity become personally involved with their subjects. They show a humanistic concern for the people they study, and through their attempts to understand and describe people's behavior they help give outsiders a rich appreciation for other people and other ways. Nevertheless, with its stress on observation, anthropology attempts to fulfill the requirements of a scientific discipline. Anthropologists strive for objectivity and accuracy. They often actually count, for example, the number of times specific behavior patterns occur and under what circumstances; they use this data for empirical studies that integrate their observations into general laws of human behavior.

Understanding anthropology requires understanding its dual nature. Perhaps two inelegant but useful terms borrowed from linguistics will help. *Emic* refers to the array of categories (and their systematic relationships) through which the bearers of a particular culture perceive the world. *Etic* refers to the array of categories (and their systematic relationships) used by Western social scientists to explain the world. In other words, the emic

23

view is the insider's, the participant's, view, and the etic is the outsider's, the scientific observer's, view. Pierre's emic view of his death, for example, is that he died from the power of the sorcerer; the anthropologist's etic view is that he died from physiological effects of fear, induced by his belief in the sorcerer. Both views are valid under the proper circumstances, but anthropology requires that they be clearly distinguished from each other because they derive from different methodologies, consist of different kinds of data, and lead to different types of knowledge. Together they facilitate a complete understanding of a culture. Anthropology's uniqueness lies in the fact that it encompasses them both.

Chapter 2

"Doing" Anthropology

Anthropology has always striven to be an inductive science; that is, one that derives its principles from specific observations and its theories from concrete facts. So far in our discussion, however, we have established anthropology's basic concept mainly in theoretical terms. We must now translate this understanding into an operational approach that will permit us to study the functioning of culture.

People live, and anthropologists work, in a world of innumerable specific actions. Theories have meaning only insofar as they illuminate the relationships of particular actions. To be an anthropologist is to learn about the forest by categorizing and comparing the trees.

We have mentioned that members of different cultural groups see the world differently. Their different cultures teach and continuously reinforce structures of perception that bear no necessary relationship to those of other cultures. Acting on their culturally influenced perceptions, groups of people create distinctive ways of life. Each of these perceptual systems and its concomitant galaxy of behaviors, which together we call culture, also appears to function as an internally consistent system. This is probably related to innate features of the human nervous system, which appears to have the tendency to simplify and organize experience. It follows from all this that a group's behavior relates logically to its perceptions and that the perceptions can be understood, to a certain extent, by studying the behavior.

CULTURAL PATTERNS

Understanding a culture, therefore, requires detailed attention to everyday behavior: the way people speak and act tells us about their system of perceptions. Anthropologists doing fieldwork take pains to observe accurately what people say, to whom, and in what tone of voice; how and where they arrange themselves and their possessions; what happens when they gather in groups; the order in which they speak, seat themselves, greet each other, or stand. These observations, though highly particular, are full of meaning: specific actions, though in themselves trivial, are not random. The challenge lies in discovering principles that make what appear to be mere reflex actions operate as patterned elements. For example, the simple observation that American students do not rise when their teachers enter the room, although students in some other cultures not only rise, but also bow, carries deep meaning in terms of the various systems of authority, relations between the generations, and the nature and place of knowledge in society.

Cultural patterns may be said to exist at two levels: the behavioral and the perceptual. In the natural course of things, we can only directly observe behavior. But although we cannot read people's minds, we can attempt to deduce their concepts from their actions, the outer signs of inner states. If we watch people as they eat, sleep, work, rejoice, grieve, learn, play, and get along with their fellows, we can learn something of what they think about these activities and why they do them. The behavioral level of culture is real and concrete, while the perceptual level is largely an assumption. But the assumption that this perceptual level exists has proven so powerful in explaining behaviors and so fruitful in producing insights that we accept it as having the force of fact.

Whether or not anthropological research allows us to penetrate into what people really think is a question that anthropologists have generally answered pragmatically. We can never know if our images of what people think truly mirror their thoughts. But in practical terms, the question makes no difference if our understanding permits us to explain and predict why things happen. Anthropologists have succeeded in understanding the perceptual and behavioral systems of some other cultures well enough to act within them. In most sciences, the ability to reproduce results and to predict behavior, whether of a human group or an atomic particle, is the ultimate test of theoretical soundness. By these tests, anthropological research has produced many acceptable results.

We can now see that the implications of the assumption that culture is patterned go much deeper than merely allowing us to say that people act in ways their culture teaches them. Because behavior proceeds according to certain rules, it is reasonably predictable. Past experience in a culture teaches its members (and knowledgeable outsiders) generally what to expect in the future. Furthermore, experience teaches people to evaluate their perceptions of themselves and others in terms of the pattern or of possible deviations from it. To take a very simple example, experience in American culture teaches the types of dress and decorum appropriate to a funeral, and how they differ from those appropriate to a wedding. This knowledge permits a person to predict what he should wear and how he should act at each of these two occasions, and, moreover, to form an opinion of the motives or intelligence of those who act at either in a manner appropriate to the other. Such knowledge, of course, remains specific to the cultural milieu that generated it. Thus, appearing at an American wedding in a bright red bridal costume would carry a meaning entirely different from the meaning it would carry in Japanese culture, where red is a traditional color of brides. We must learn the patterns of each culture separately.

So, in order to understand what members perceive, we must learn about patterns of behavior—an understanding of which we can gain only by careful analysis. The word analysis gives us a clue to both the structure of behavior and the technique we can use to comprehend it. *Analysis* means breaking down the whole into its parts, and that is precisely the first step: to break down the behavior pattern into the significant units that compose it.

The term *pattern* means, most simply, a phenomenon that is repeated. We speak of a design imprinted on fabric as a pattern because it appears over and over again throughout the material. Thus, shirts may have a plaid or a striped pattern, or perhaps a pattern composed of flowers, cars, or boats. In the same sense, items of human behavior may be said to be patterned if they are repeated by different members, or perhaps by the same member, over and over again in the same basic way.

The marriage pattern of a culture is an example of a type of behavior frequently studied by anthropologists. We see that in American culture the same basic pattern of behavior occurs over and over again. This pattern always consists of the same elements—one wife and one husband in every instance, repeated like the colored stripes on the shirt.

Nowhere in American culture do we permit this pattern to vary—it is as inviolable as the stars in the American flag. But just as other countries have other flags, so do they have marriage patterns different from ours. Some cultures allow a man to keep more than one wife at a time. In such cultures, you can observe many cases of this behavior, and you will find that the members repeat its elements in the same way. Many men in the culture desire more than one wife, and given sufficient resources, they will behave in a way that reflects this desire. Not everybody finds a spouse in our culture, but the generally accepted practice is to follow the ideal behavior pattern.

People strive to meet culturally patterned standards. (courtesy of Henry Stern)

Those who deviate from the ideal know that they are doing so. A further important point is that both polygamy and monogamy are varieties of the same larger category of marriage patterns. Anthropologists further categorize marriage patterns as part of the larger system of social organization.

To summarize, anthropologists recognize behavior patterns by their repetitive nature. But often an observer may have difficulty assigning a single bit of behavior to all the various patterns that involve an individual at one time. We might, for example, observe a Dani man in the highlands of New Guinea as he breaks ground for a new garden. He is involved in a subsistence activity, or pattern, since, as a result of this labor, similar to that of other men of his group, he will derive food for himself and his family. But the food he raises will be distributed according to his society's system of social organization—that is, in this case, to individuals belonging to his own family, but not to other individuals classified as friends. He is therefore also involved in behavior we may classify under social organization. As the farmer works, a friend passes by, on his way to sanctify a guard tower. He stops, they exchange greetings, and as the friend leaves, he accepts a few stalks of grass from our farmer. He will use them in a religious ceremony to sanctify the tower. The farmer has thus participated in three patterns at once: subsistence, social, and religious. Where does one begin and the other end? How can we isolate one pattern from all of these others in order to study it?

The answer to this problem lies in an understanding of the *participant observation method* used by anthropologists. The trained investigator, through participation in the culture and observation of the behavior on a continuous basis, learns to distinguish the random inclusion of unrelated elements from the essential elements in the pattern under study. As he observes members' daily behavior over a period of time, and as the result of frequent comparison, he becomes aware of the elements repeated over and over again in the same way.

Patterns and time

Because all cultures exist in time and space, the anthropologist may first notice patterns in the use of these two infinite extensions, one of the visible world stretching from horizon to horizon and the other of the flow of events stretching from memory to expectation. Many cultures deal with time and space as series of finite units. The units differ in both form and content, but all cultures require the behavior of members to be patterned according to temporal and spatial categories. Meals, for example, generally occur at certain times and not at others. Breakfast in American culture, for example, does not occur after noon; even if it occurs after 10 A.M., its nature changes slightly and the meal category becomes brunch.

A further dimension of time is timing, or rhythm—the rate at which activities take place within the pattern or the rate at which they change. Activities follow their own proper rhythms for members of a culture. A business discussion in American culture, for example, begins after a few minutes of pleasantries about the good or bad qualities of the weather, mutual acquaintances, one's pleasure at being with one's companion, and the health of the respective spouses and offspring. But spending as much as even a quarter of an hour in this manner with an associate who is not also a personal friend marks one as an unbusinesslike person who wastes time. In the Middle East, on the other hand, business discussions often follow lengthy social overtures that may range in detail over the beauty of one's surroundings, the amiability of one's host, and various points of philosophy and include the consumption of numerous cups of coffee. Sometimes business matters do not intrude until the second or third meeting. To stint these courtesies marks one not only as ill-bred, but, more importantly, as untrustworthy and unsuitable as a business partner.

Every American teacher and most students know that classes have their own rhythms, according to their various types. But all share a generally similar rhythm that may be represented like this:

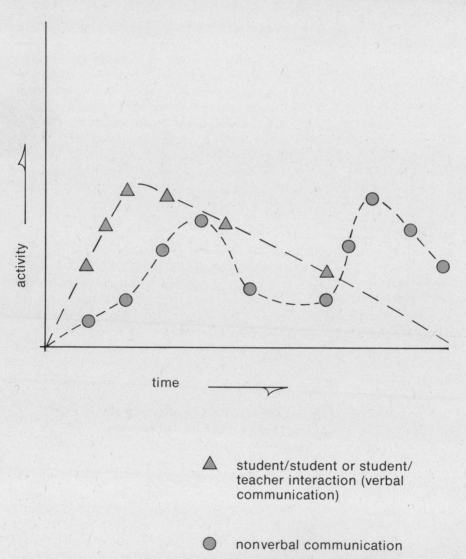

△ student/student or student/
teacher interaction (verbal
communication)

● nonverbal communication

Figure 2–1. Students signal the approach of the end of class by nonverbal communication.

The rhythm of activity builds for about ten minutes. Conversation, concentration, and cogitation reach a medium high level, as does restless shifting and crossing and uncrossing of legs. After the initial build-up, the activity level remains fairly stable for the next 30 to 40 minutes, but abruptly reaches a new high just before class ends. The "end of class dance" of shifting around in seats, rattling papers, rearranging books and jackets and closing pens signals to the teacher that the pattern is approaching its end.

A class is not a very large group as societies go, but larger groups also operate according to timing or patterns. A common category of such patterns is the cycle of the agricultural year. Throughout the world, changes in rhythm take place as a function of planting and harvest times. A graph of a North American agricultural society might look like this:

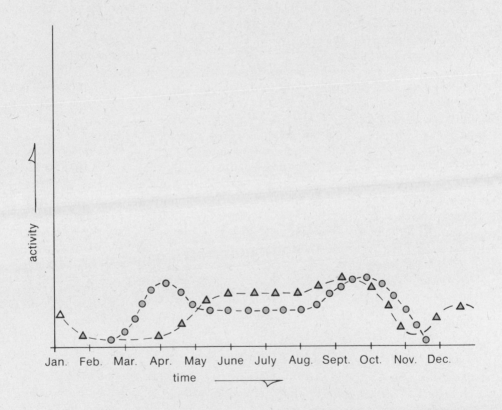

△   social activity (dances, weddings, "husking bees," hayrides, etc.)

○   planting/harvest cycle

Figure 2–2. The relationship of social activity to the planting/harvest cycle.

This annual rhythm governs the behavior of the members of the culture as they do their work and as they observe the special days of their religious and social life. The Cree Indians of the southeastern United States, for example, used to celebrate a major activity of their religious calendar, the Green Corn Ritual, at the time of spring planting. This ceremony not only insured a successful crop but provided a special time for choosing a spouse and for mourning all the dead of the preceding year as well.

Annual cycles need not, however, hew closely to the agricultural seasons, and may sometimes even conflict with them. The Muslim calendar, for example, which controls an elaborate series of feast days and fast days, follows the moon rather than the sun. Unlike many lunar calendars, it lacks a correction for the discrepancy in the lengths of the lunar and solar years. The months of the lunar calendar thus revolve through the solar calendar every 33 years. Every year, therefore, holy days fall at a slightly different season, over decades changing from winter to summer or from rainy season to dry season and back again. *Ramadan,* one of the great observances of Islam, entails a month of fasting during daylight. No food, drink, or smoke must pass the lips of the faithful while enough light exists to tell a black thread from a white one. But as it circulates through the seasons, the Ramadan fast falls at times of heavy work and at times of natural rest, at times of great heat and at times of cooling breezes. The requirements of the observance never vary, however, and the faithful suffer greatly in some years, bringing in harvests on empty stomachs and sweltering through long scorching days in the fields or desert without a drop of water. This syncopated rhythm has held for over 1,300 years. Like members of all cultures, Muslims see the rhythmic pattern to their lives and consider it natural.

Patterns and space

Place, or space, is also perceived and evaluated by members as part of a pattern. Some aspects of space, such as terrain, climate, and geography, lie generally outside the control of human or cultural activity. The specific boundaries vary, because some technologically advanced cultures can move mountains and change the course of rivers and some religiously audacious cultures believe they can affect weather; but in general, the principle holds.

Space always includes a realm that can be modified by man according to the needs and beliefs of his culture. Thus, physical modifications such as the construction of villages and cities, campsites and gardens, serve the needs of various groups. In some cases, boundary lines divide otherwise unaltered terrain into the territories of specific groups. National frontiers, for example, may take the form of fences, walls, or barricades, or they may just as easily exist as imaginary lines running through trackless jungles. The *watan* (home territory) of a Bedouin tribe, while lacking what we would recognize as formal boundary markers, is distinguished from apparently similar stretches of desert by commonly agreed-upon landmarks.

In most cultures, some spaces are set aside for ritual purposes such as prayer and burial, and others are reserved for specific types of behavior such as eating or sleeping, socializing or being alone. Many cultures reserve specific spaces for the exclusive use of one or another of the sexes.

As we have already observed, there usually is a close relationship between the various patterns that compose a culture, and thus the culture's overall tendencies generally find expression in its treatment of space. Japanese culture, for example, shares with other Eastern cultures a philosophy stressing concepts of "centering" and "oneness." A traditional Japanese house appears barren to Westerners, almost devoid of furniture. The main

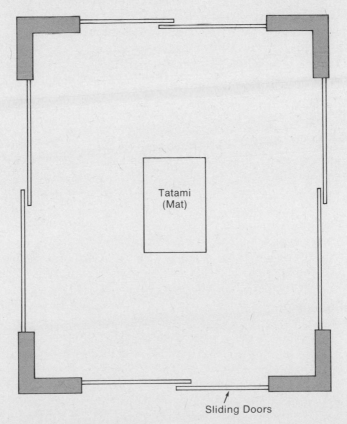

Tatami
(Mat)

Sliding Doors

Figure 2–3. Japanese room.

article of furnishing, the *tatami,* or mat, is stored in a closet when not in use. When using the room for eating, sleeping, reading, working, or chatting, the Japanese generally choose the center, and observe no restrictions on what type of activities must take place in the particular room. Here we see the concepts of "centering" and "oneness" expressed spatially. The Japanese expression of these concepts might look like Fig. 2–3.

Western cultures characterize space differently. Their ideas about the proper use of space might look like this:

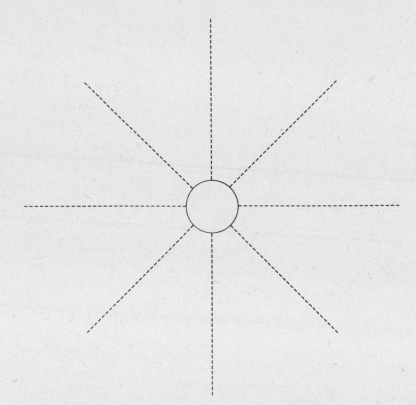

Figure 2–4. French spatial pattern.

or like Fig. 2–5.

The first of these, Fig. 2–4, is the French spatial pattern. Emphasizing the centralization of power, it extends to social organizations as well. The most important spot (and the highest status) in a French government office is the center of the room. In a French classroom, the student with the highest grades sits in the place of honor—the center. The city of Paris and

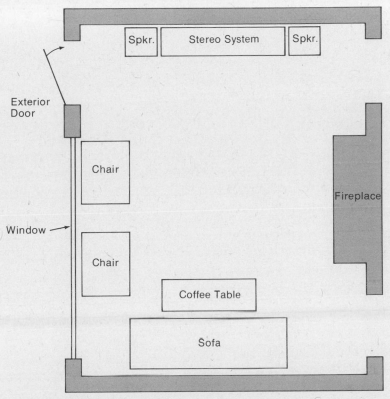

Figure 2–5. American living room.

the city of Washington, D.C. (designed by a Frenchman) express the same idea. The important functions occupy the center, with lesser functions radiating concentrically from it.

American spatial patterning looks more like Fig. 2–5 and breaks a large space into smaller units that roughly replicate it in shape. The center has no special importance in American rooms. Except in dining rooms, the major pieces of furniture tend to hug the wall, with the center left open.

Rules of selection, order, and number

Perceptions of time and space may provide basic structure to behavior patterns, but do not suffice to tell a person the behavior expected of him. Knowing where and when is not enough: concrete knowledge as to what, how much, and in what sequence—information we may refer to more succinctly as selection, number and order—is also needed.

If we assume that every culture has developed a repertory of skills and objects that enable its members to carry on their daily life, then every situation in which members find themselves requires choosing from this repertory. Proper selection combines with proper time and proper place to create a pattern. If a hungry American finds himself in a place called his kitchen at a time called 7 A.M. on a weekday morning, he may select from a variety of available foods, procedures, utensils, and companions. But chances are he will select the elements he has learned as appropriate to this time and place: eggs, orange juice, bacon, coffee, a frying pan, and his wife and children. He will probably not select wine, a T-bone steak, caviar, cherries jubilee, and his boss. Although equally nourishing and possibly as congenial, the second selection of components is inappropriate to the pattern known as breakfast.

Rules of selection determine which components of the culture's inventory can be included in a given pattern. Since almost any human activity can be defined as either a pattern or a set if it lasts for a perceptible period of time, takes place within an area or "place," and recurs periodically, it can be seen that the number of possibilities available to any one member is enormous. Within the patterns, furthermore, the selection of sets and of components making up the sets may also be large. Thus, an American's breakfast may consist of orange juice, eggs, toast, bacon, and coffee. But it may just as easily consist of grapefruit, oatmeal with milk and cocoa, or stewed prunes, french toast, and a glass of milk. We can see that breakfast appears to consist of three sets: fruit, main course, and beverage. Fruits may come raw, cooked, or in the form of juice. Main courses contain protein and starch, and beverages are hot, except for milk and orange juice. The sets of acceptable breakfast foods do not, however, include all foods with the characteristics we have described. Watermelon, for example, is not an acceptable fruit. Spaghetti and meatballs or a cheeseburger, although consisting of protein and starch, are not appropriate.

So far our discussion of sets has concentrated on things, but we must keep in mind that behaviors also form sets. The entire process of eating breakfast, for example, may be seen as a set of the overall eating pattern of American culture. This pattern consists of three large sets of behavior: breakfast, lunch, and dinner (or breakfast, dinner, and supper in some parts of the country) and a residual set called snacks.

Within the remembered life experience of an adult member, incidents, events, and sets of behavior may number in the millions. The problem of proper set selection is further complicated by the fact that before a behavior may be performed in the context of a pattern, it must be modified or transformed to fit its particular context.

Take the pattern of greeting behaviors, for instance. A child learns to greet his parents almost as soon as he learns to distinguish between his own

The eating pattern in Borneo is different from that familiar to Americans. (courtesy of John Landgraf)

self and others. But he also learns that this behavior must be modified if the person being greeted is someone other than mother or father; that is, another component of the set of greeting behaviors must be used. If the other person is brother or sister, the greeting doesn't have to be modified very much. But if the other person is not a family member, then the greeting must be altered considerably. Furthermore, if we look at the greeting set of this child after he has grown to young adulthood, when he is attending his first dance, for example, we can see that it has expanded considerably. For this person to display the same behavior he used as a child welcoming his parent would be incongruous indeed. Yet, if we compare the two events, we may find enough significant similarities to identify them as modifications of the same pattern called "greeting behavior." If a person in a situation that required greeting behavior performed a subsistence behavior instead, he would be corrected by others present.

Beyond an appropriate selection of elements, a properly executed pattern depends on appropriate order and number. Thus, our breakfast eater will select his orange juice before his bacon and eggs, and will save his coffee for last. *Rules of order* determine the sequence of appearance of sets in a pattern or the sequence or use of components in a set. Breakfast precedes lunch, which is followed by dinner. Dinner, in our culture, begins with the soup and ends with the coffee and dessert.

Rules of number limit the number of components in a set and the number of sets within a pattern. For example, most of us consider one or two eggs, two to four strips of bacon, one or two cups of coffee, and one or two pieces of toast to satisfy the rules of number in a breakfast. Three eggs is not out of the question, but a dozen violates our sense of "rightness"; that is, the rule we obey in reference to the breakfast set of subsistence patterns. We would also consider two breakfasts in one morning inappropriate. Nor do we use a different eating utensil for each type of food—one fork, one knife, and one spoon are considered to be sufficient. The participants form a set that also follows rules of number. Except during celebrations or in cafeterias and other institutionalized eating places, we seldom find more than half a dozen people eating together, and even in cafeterias the table size usually limits the number of participants to four or six persons.

Sometimes a cultural preference for a certain number appears to run through a variety of the culture's patterns. Authorities have suggested that in American culture such a number may be three. Although not the only pattern number, it seems to be the most preferred. Alan Dundes (1968), a noted anthropologist and folklorist, suggests that this preference for doing things in sets of three structures much of American behavior without our being consciously aware of it. According to Dundes, this "three patterning" appears in the telephone dialing system, education, religion, and the military; even space and time are conceived of by Americans as being three dimensional.

Components, sets, patterns and systems

To summarize the points of this chapter so far, we will learn to understand culture by studying patterned behavior. The first step is to isolate a piece of repeated behavior; it can be something as large as the propensity of people in the culture to marry and live in families or as small as the way they greet each other on the street. The bit of behavior in question is a *pattern*. This pattern is composed of a number of *sets,* each of which is a category of people, things, actions, or ideas. The individual people, things, actions, or ideas composing the sets are *components*. In carrying out a pattern, a member of a culture chooses the particular sets appropriate to the pattern, and then, from within each set, he selects the particular components he will use.

It is important to remember that the difference between a pattern and a set often depends upon the decision of anthropologists as to what they will study, rather than upon the characteristics of the behavior itself. Breakfast, we have seen, can be either a pattern in itself or a set within the larger pattern of daily eating, depending on the scale of the study.

Most anthropologists group the patterns of cultures into several large and very abstract analytical categories generally called *systems.* These relate to analysis of the culture itself rather than to analysis of the specific behaviors composing it. We will soon make this clear.

Analysis of a cultural pattern

Any analysis begins with a body of exact data; only if the original observation is correct will analysis yield the correct constituent parts. Data consist of descriptions of actions, objects, and environments. For example, an anthropologist might have recorded the following:

> Chandra seated himself at the leftmost end of the bench. Lal seated himself to Chandra's right after Chandra had sat down. Mohind squatted on the ground after the other two had seated themselves, although two-thirds of the bench remained empty. When Baldur arrived, Lal and Mohind stood. Lal moved away and Baldur seated himself to Chandra's right. Then Lal seated himself to Baldur's right, and finally Mohind squatted near the half-empty bench.

This simple sequence, repeated in various forms and with various personnel dozens of times a day, expresses an Indian villager's concepts of social space and its relationship to social rank. As we will note in later chapters, these concepts reverberate throughout the culture, affecting religious beliefs as well as organizing seating in village lanes. But for now, we will regard the sequence simply as an example of a cultural behavior pattern, the basic building block of any study.

Each of the men in the sequence belongs to a universe of people consisting of the 500 or so residents of the village. Each of the men has obviously learned the rules of dealing with his neighbors. But he has probably not learned rules of dealing with the *specific* others he met on the bench. That is, Mohind was not taught as a child that when you meet Chandra, Lal, and Baldur you act in such-and-such a way. To learn behavior as a specific body of instructions relating to each particular individual would be impossible: no one could remember 500 different canons of behavior for each possible situation. It is both highly inflexible and unnecessary.

What Mohind and the others learned was how to act toward the various *types* of people they would encounter in the village. Each of the 500 people shares with some others certain characteristics that, in many social contexts, override their particularity. Thus, Mohind learned to react in terms of sets such as men and women, younger and older, relatives and non-relatives. And most important to our understanding of the bench sequence, the incident shows that he learned to treat people as members of various sets called *castes*. Castes have several features, of which the most germane to our example are that some rank higher than others in ritual and social position, and that members of lower castes show deference to members of higher castes. Among the ways in which Mohind's caste shows deference to its betters (in this case, the castes of Chandra, Lal, and Baldur) is by keeping the head lower at all times: thus Mohind squatted on the ground while the others sat on the bench.

Mohind's training also included learning methods of differentiating the various types of people in the village so that he could place each individual in the correct set. Distinctions between men and women and between young and old are easy to make. That of relative versus nonrelative hinges on the fact that Mohind knows all his relatives or, in a rare case of doubt, can consult his father or another senior kinsman who knows even those from distant villages. To distinguish members of various castes, Mohind uses such clues as name, place of residence, and relatives' identities. In addition, there are articles of clothing and ornaments that only members of certain castes may wear; from Mohind's standpoint, for example, any man who wears a special piece of cord called the sacred thread is his superior.

Thus, in Mohind's perception, the village is composed not of 500 individuals, but of 500 individuals divided by various criteria into sets, or categories, distinguished along certain dimensions. If a new individual arrives, Mohind attempts to fit him into one of the categories of which the world of people is composed. A resident of a nearby village is relatively easy to place. But even a more challenging case, an American anthropologist, does not present insurmountable problems. Easily distinguished by his physical appearance and dress, the anthropologist belongs to the caste *Americans,* which, if Mohind thought about it, might seem to be a subcaste of the *English.* The English are a strange caste; they have high political and economic status but follow defiling customs such as eating beef. For this reason, despite their high status they rank low on the ritual scale and thus are not fit to offer food to a respectable man of caste like Mohind.

If we watched Mohind as he went about his affairs in the village, we would see him greet many of his fellow villagers by name because he knows them as individuals. But even as he does this, he places them in their appropriate sets and tempers the greeting to the situation. Thus, he greets one man, a caste fellow, with a jovial slap on the back. He greets another, whom he has known just as long and as well, with a deep nod and a respectful inquiry after his health. He greets a third, an untouchable, not at all, although the man nods and greets him.

To return to the somewhat technical language we have been developing in this chapter, in his daily life Mohind sees a large number of different individuals; in this case, the *components* of his perceptions. Using his knowledge of the relevant dimensions of classification, he sorts them into their respective *sets.* In this manner he is able to elaborate his behavior into appropriate *patterns* of action. Thus, for Mohind and his neighbors, their patterns of daily behavior, and ultimately the entire system of their lives, coordinate tolerably with their perceptions of reality.

We say *perceptions* rather than perception because the mental universes of Mohind's neighbors are similar, but not identical, to his. Chandra, for example, differentiates fewer caste distinctions in the range near Mohind's caste, but more at the upper end near his own. And Chandra views all but one of the castes in the village as his inferiors, although to different degrees. Thus, as Fig. 2–6 shows, Mohind's sets look different from Chandra's.

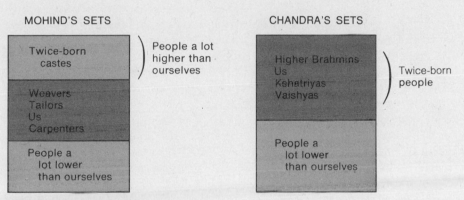

MOHIND'S SETS

Twice-born castes

) People a lot higher than ourselves

Weavers
Tailors
Us
Carpenters

People a lot lower than ourselves

CHANDRA'S SETS

Higher Brahmins
Us
Kshatriyas
Vaishyas

) Twice-born people

People a lot lower than ourselves

Figure 2–6. Mohind's sets and Chandra's sets.

Chandra's patterns of behavior, how he acts towards others in the village, thus reflect his different perceptions. But, because the village is a relatively well-integrated cultural system, Chandra's and Mohind's different patterns coincide nicely.

Thus far, we have discussed sets in this Indian village in terms of a single behavior pattern—seating oneself on a public bench in a village lane. Naturally, villagers take part in a large number of other behavior patterns. Some of these might, in fact, include seating oneself on a public bench. At the wedding of Mohind's son, for example, which Chandra attends as an honored guest, seating of guests on a bench is merely a small part of a much larger behavior pattern; seating in this case is merely a behavioral set of the wedding pattern. The wedding ceremony itself is merely a set of the culture-wide marriage pattern. So we see that patterns, as we have used them, are not absolute divisions of reality, but analytic categories to aid us in understanding a particular sequence of events.

When he acts as father of the bridegroom, Mohind uses a somewhat different group of sets. Although people retain their caste identities, they also fit into special sets such as members of our family, members of our new in-laws' family, servants assisting with the festivities, ordinary guests, honored guests, and neighbors who are helping out as a favor. Another whole group of sets comes into play in the gift exchanges that surround the wedding of a child: people we must give gifts to, people who give gifts to us, people who have to give gifts to our new in-laws (and at the wedding of whose children we will have to return the favor), and so forth.

Thus we see that sets also are not absolute divisions of reality, but merely called to consciousness when necessary. Some, of course, are salient in all or nearly all situations in a particular culture. Castes are an example of these, as are the two sexes. Patterns, as we have seen, can be viewed most productively as analytical devices rather than as permanent units of behavior. If for purposes of study we wish to isolate a certain aspect of behavior, for example, the etiquette of seating arrangements, then that becomes the pattern in question. If, on the other hand, we wish to study the functioning of a village market or a religious observance or a marriage negotiation, then these become the patterns in question, and the relevant sets will be determined by the situation.

PATTERN CONGRUITY

In nearly every behavioral situation, the culture of the individual who is doing the behaving recognizes an ideal way of performing. When confronted by a greeting situation, for example, an individual selects the proper set from his inventory of greeting sets and goes through the process of greeting. As the member performs this behavior, he also evaluates it in terms of how well he has chosen. By the way in which the person being greeted responds, the greeter can gauge his performance and may elect, if necessary, to modify the set before it is completed in order to more nearly achieve the ideal. The better the fit between the ideal performance and the real performance, the more satisfaction one derives from the performance. A set or pattern that completely satisfies the rules of order, number, and selection would be considered perfect, or *congruent,* whereas patterns or sets that are less well performed (as measured against an ideal performance) are termed *incongruous.* Another term frequently used to describe a congruent pattern is that it has *integrity.*

People do not perform behavior patterns in a vacuum. Usually they perform them before the eyes of watchers, who send signals about how they think the behavior is carried out. Every culture has a repertoire of reactions to good and bad performances. In ours, a good performance rates handclaps, cheers, praise, kisses, tickertape parades, handshakes, backslaps, grades of A, raises in pay, and any of a number of other familiar expressions of approval. A bad performance, on the other hand, may be greeted with snickers, catcalls, sarcasm, "tsk-tsk," or loss of a job, among other things. Depending upon the degree and nature of the transgression of the pattern, these reactions may include incarceration or commitment to a mental hospital. Even a person who is entirely alone will react to the quality of his performance. A good performance will cause a feeling of self-satisfaction; a bad performance, a feeling of anxiety.

What people react to in evaluating behavior is the congruity of the performance—how well it fits the relevant behavior pattern, whether the proper pattern was selected, and whether it was well executed. If the actor concludes, either from his own observations or from the signals sent by others, that his behavior is incorrect, he often adjusts it to fit the pattern. He may perceive that his timing is wrong and slow down or speed up. He may observe that the time is wrong and apologize for being late. He may observe that the people, objects, or environment are wrong for performance of the pattern.

Small corrections go on all the time. People see others staring at them and conclude that their clothing is awry; a quick, furtive tug at the skirt or zip of the fly may solve the problem. People sense that they are not welcome, and so they leave. People perceive that they have committed a breach of courtesy—what the French call a *faux pas*—and stammer a courtesy. The meaning of this expression is interesting, by the way, because it underlines the point we are trying to make here. It means *false step*.

Sometimes, however, incongruities are deliberate. In these cases they may serve symbolic or aesthetic purposes, with the actor exploiting the feelings of outrage, anxiety, or discomfort his behavior produces. The tactic of civil disobedience, whether applied in India or the American South, uses deliberately incongruous behavior to make a moral statement about the social pattern in question. Particular departures from a well-known pattern—a bride going barefoot, a teenager embroidering the flag on the seat of his or her pants, or, in a case from Sri Lanka, members of untouchable castes donning previously forbidden undershirts—make a statement about the relationship of the actor to the pattern.

Incongruity is also often an important element in humor. Through a carefully constructed situation of incongruity, the comedian builds a high level of tension in his audience, which is then released in laughter. For this reason, understanding the sense of humor of a people requires an intimate knowledge of the patterns of its culture. This is the reason that jokes usually do not translate well, even between cultures that use the same language. Perhaps, for example, you have seen the famous British humor magazine *Punch* and have been puzzled to discover, along with many other Americans, that the celebrated cartoons just aren't funny. It isn't that they are not very funny, but that they are not funny at all. The reason you don't "get" them is that you don't have what they assume in the reader; that is, a sophisticated understanding of British social behavior. When we say British humor is "dry," we mean in part that it concerns itself largely with patterns of hierarchy and social relations entirely foreign to Americans.

EXPLANATIONS IN ANTHROPOLOGY

Anthropologists spend a great deal of their research time trying to learn about behavior patterns. They watch and imitate, ask questions, hang around and listen, hoping to learn what patterns a cultural group considers congruent. If their feel is good enough, they eventually become able to replicate the patterns; to laugh at the jokes and actually to *feel* that they're funny. But anthropology is not an etiquette course; the point is not merely to learn what behavior is appropriate in a given cultural situation. This material will, of course, appear to some extent in the research report (called an *ethnography* if it describes a culture), but is not in itself the reason for the research. Anthropologists want to find out not only what behavior is congruent, but *why*.

In order to understand what follows, you must keep in mind that this "why" is not a totally open-ended question. Anthropologists are only interested in certain types of answers. If, for example, they ask, "Why do the Indian villagers sit on the bench in that fashion?" they do not want to be told, "Because of the way the upper leg connects to the pelvis," or "Because of the gravitational forces exerted on their bodies by the earth." They want to be told something like, "Because the caste system in the village requires that deference be shown to members of higher castes." In short, they want an answer that relates the particular piece of information to the *sociocultural system* under discussion. To an anthropologist, pieces of behavior take on meaning in relation to cultural systems.

A systems approach

You might imagine yourself trying to find your way around a strange city. Each of the many buildings, trees, streets, parks, and monuments you see as a separate item tells you something about the city. But only when you study a map do their relationships become sufficiently clear so that they take on a meaning in relation to the whole. This is the difference between approaching a culture as a series of facts or phenomena and as a system. This difference is one of the most crucial in science; without a systematic appreciation of its data, a science inches from landmark to landmark, discovering each as haphazardly and unexpectedly as a stranger locates the monuments of an unfamiliar town. Once equipped with a clarifying system, a science, like a newcomer with a map, can move more rapidly between known and unknown destinations and even predict what landmarks it is likely to find along the way.

The recent revolution in geology is an example of such a change. The introduction of the theory of plate tectonics (that the earth's surface consists of huge plates) vastly increased the predictive power of the science. It binds a number of previously unrelated pieces of knowledge, such as the location of earthquakes and the nature of the ocean floor, into a coherent system that explains phenomena; it permits geologists to reason from what they know to what they don't know because it describes the probable relationships between the known and the unknown.

The basic feature of any system is the relationship between its parts, the arrangement of its items into some consistent and predictable order. The Greek root of the word *system* means *putting together;* presumably things put together are not placed at random.

The relevance of these observations to our concerns is twofold. First, as we have already begun to demonstrate, culture itself is systematic, or at least appears to function systematically. Secondly, anthropology's method of approaching culture is systematic. The elements composing a cultural system and each of its constituent subsystems are bound to each other by consistent and discoverable ties; the anthropologist attempts to search for them in an orderly fashion.

The system's approach to behavior, one of science's most productive tools, makes several basic assumptions about the behavioral phenomenon under investigation. One of these is that no object or event can profitably be studied without an understanding of its context, the situation in which it occurs. The second is that the nature of the object will change if its context, environment, or situation changes. Biologists, for example, assume that the behavior of a cell will change as the temperature or pH of its medium changes, or as the number or type of other nearby cells changes. Likewise, an anthropologist observes that behavior changes in a changed environment, and that the change is often systematically related to the nature of the environment. Thus, for example, if we took our four village bench-sitters and placed them on a city bus, their behavior would be quite different. All of them would probably be wearing Western-style clothing. Probably none of the lower-caste men would defer to Chandra; he would just take the empty place next to Mohind, who would be sitting on the seat.

So radical a change in behavior alerts us to the fact that the different environment has somehow changed the rules, as indeed anthropologists in urban India have found. Unlike village life, where everything falls under a single large body of rules, city life has broken into two distinct segments:

public life and domestic. Thus, in their own homes, each of the four men would observe caste rules fairly close to those pertaining in the village. At work or in public, however, new patterns and new sets apply.

Emics and etics

What distinguishes an anthropologist from the author of an etiquette book is the fact that the anthropologist maintains a double vision of the culture he is studying. He wants to learn what it means to be a proper Indian villager, Hopi, or Yanomamö to make sure he understands their culture and to assure the continued acceptability of his presence among the people. But at the same time, he never forgets that what he is studying isn't the way life *is* (which is what the etiquette book author studies) but the way life *is here.* In short, he never relinquishes his outsider's view, his consideration of this culture *in comparison* to other cultures. The entire enterprise draws meaning from the assumption that by comparing cultures to one another the truth about them can be obtained.

Perhaps an example will make this point clearer. The same anthropologist who made the observations about the Indians sitting on the bench probably would also have in his notebook a substantial number of incidents involving cows. The anthropologist's notes would show that Indians use cattle as their major draft animals, gather cattle dung for fuel, and consume milk in a variety of forms. He or she also would have observed that Indians generally manifest an unusual reverence for cows and express aversion, even horror, at the thought of killing one; if they belong to any but a few of the respectable castes, Indians never, under any circumstances, eat beef.

When the anthropologist asked various individuals their reasons for acting this way, he or she would receive answers such as, "We cannot kill the cows—to do so is forbidden. They are too sacred." Or, "The cow has a soul of great purity; were I to kill her, I would defile myself." Or, "The cow is the giver of milk, the source of all purity." In short, the villagers act in congruence with their image of reality, a reality according the cow a sacred spiritual stature.

If you were to ask an anthropologist why people treat cows with such reverence, you would get quite a different answer. This question has been debated for years, and no theory about sacred cows is uncontroversial. A provocative answer, however, is that of the anthropologist Marvin Harris, who answers *not* in terms of the content of the villager's beliefs, but rather in terms of cultural ecology, showing why such beliefs exist in that particular society and how they relate to the physical environment. Marvin Harris (1975) argues that because of its sacredness, the cow is accorded protective behavior that serves various positive functions in the Indian agricultural

system. First, he argues, cattle are essential for plowing, the basis of agriculture. In a climate of alternating monsoon and drought, and of alternating
periods of relative plenty and near famine, the prohibition on cow slaughter
safeguards the precious draft animals from their owner's recurring temptation to kill them for meat. Secondly, the cow forages its own food from waste
material inappropriate for human consumption or from wasteland inappropriate for agriculture, so that in fact the cow "costs" the farmer nothing.
Thirdly, the cow produces "for free" valuable resources of dung (used for
fuel) and milk that would otherwise require very costly and scarce substitu-
tions. In this formulation, the "reason" for the villager's behavior is that

An important pattern in Bolivian Indian religion involves the sacrifice of a llama. (courtesy of
Arthur B. Hayes, III)

it supports important aspects of their ecological adaptation to their environment.

Which answer is right, Harris's or the villager's? Both are, but from two different standpoints. The emic view is the insider's view, which reflects the psychic reality of daily life. The etic view is the outsider's analysis of the functioning of the culture as a system. The anthropologist attempts to cultivate the ability to see from both points of view simultaneously; this is the double vision we spoke of in the last chapter.

The anthropologist, of course, isn't the only scholar who can ask questions about the sacred cow. The historian of religion, for example, might investigate the development of the concept and the symbolism surrounding it. The agricultural economist might try to find out the exact monetary value of the cow's contribution to the peasant household. No one but the anthropologist, however, is likely to ask this set of joined, yet opposite questions: "How do the people act?"; "Why do they act this way in terms of their own perception of the situation?"; and "Why do they act this way in terms of my perception of the culture as a functioning system?"

Cultural systems and subsystems

Our previous definition of culture must now be expanded, or at least refined, to accomodate some of our new insights. Culture is, in this enlarged usage, not only the particular patterns of perception and related behavior, but the system of relationships between these patterns. In practice, the operational definition of culture used by anthropologists is more elaborate still; culture is seen as a system of related subsystems, which in turn organize the relationships among cultural patterns. Such subsystems include those organizing communication, resource allocations, social interaction, reproduction, and ideology. The remainder of this book will discuss many of these systems in detail. If you keep in mind that our definitions of culture are really just abstractions used to help explain the phenomena of behavior, they won't seem so forbidding. Anthropologists used to waste a good deal of time arguing about what culture *really* is and what it *really* consists of. But other sciences long ago discovered that debating what energy, for example, is *really* composed of, does not lead to very productive results. It is more valuable to study how energy operates.

As we mentioned in the previous chapter, we will not devote much space to considerations of the evolution or other strictly physical aspects of man. It is useful to note, however, that the relationship between culture and the human species is far from accidental. Although our knowledge of the behavior patterns of other primate species is as yet insufficient to judge whether they possess the capacity for, or any of the aspects of, culture, it is obvious that for the human species at least, culture has been an inherent feature at least since man passed out of the stage of *Homo erectus* (an extinct ancestral species) into *Homo sapiens* (our present species). Strong evidence exists that the demands of culture may have influenced the evolution of ancestral people and thus helped determine the present characteristics of our species.

In any case, culture's relationship to our physical survival can be plainly seen. It provides the means by which groups of people organize themselves to gain subsistence. It is the medium for development and transmission of skills. Without the training, tools, and protection culture provides, human survival would not be possible.

A model of sociocultural systems

In constructing models of the relationship among the systems composing a culture, many anthropologists have emphasized the fundamentality of the systems of subsistence and exploitation of the physical environment. In a formulation owing much to Radcliffe-Brown and ultimately to Karl Marx, Harris (1975) suggests that the cultural system is composed of three levels. Of these, the most basic is that of technology and environment, which includes such features of a cultural system as its skills, its material objects, the opportunities offered by its environment, and the demographics of its population (the distribution of people in space, and by age and sex). The second of Harris's levels includes the systems governing the social organization of the group—its family and political structure, its distribution of rights and honors, its mechanisms of social control. Above this, Harris sees the level of ideology and ideas, which governs what people think, feel, believe, and know. Each of these levels is, according to Harris, progressively less basic to the physical survival of the group, but all are tied together in a relatively unified and functional whole. Tied together in function, they are also bound by causality. The power to cause change, however, is not evenly distributed among them: Harris believes that changes in the technoenvironmental level are more likely to precipitate changes in the higher levels than vice versa.

The subtleties of these relationships need not concern us now, for we will discuss them later in more detail. As we begin to explore the reality of culture and to discover its characteristics, it might be helpful to remember that our knowledge comes from what we can see: the patterned behavior of people in groups. From the infinite possibilities of human action, each group has selected a narrow range of behaviors. People act in their varied ways because from the different perspectives from which they view life their actions are reasonable. Moreover, it is also important to remember that, although we will investigate the great systems that compose culture as if each were a distinct entity, they remain facets of a single phenomenon, as do the different colored faces of a jewel as it is turned in the light. The unity of cultural expression begins in the unity of man's mind and nervous system.

INTRODUCTION TO FIELD PROJECTS

As we mentioned early in this chapter, we hope to transform the concepts of social group and patterned behavior into *operational definitions;* that is, definitions that allow you to recognize the phenomena and act on them, or at least interact with them. Operationalizing these concepts will permit you to undertake field work in a group of your own choosing. Through guided observations and participation, you will learn to identify the various major systems that compose a culture and to understand something of their inter-relationships.

The first step in any field project is choosing a group. Field workers choose particular groups for a variety of reasons: convenience, familiarity, relevance to a particular theoretical concern. In this case it is well to keep the special requirements of your project in mind and to make convenience the paramount consideration. It is best to work on a project of this kind with a group that you have ready access to and that you can observe conveniently over the weeks. Anthropologists studying far-away or exotic people frequently spend months mastering a language and gaining the confidence of their prospective informants. A year in the field full-time is the generally recognized minimum for a worthwhile ethnography of a foreign community. Obviously, a college student with many other activities and obligations can't spend weeks or months on a project for a single course. Think carefully, therefore, of groups you might already belong to or could readily join. It could well be that the people you work, live, play, or worship with can provide the material for a fascinating study. Combining this project with another of your interests will drastically reduce the time needed to gain entry and establish rapport.

Excellent student papers have described workplaces such as supermarkets, offices, libraries, even a mental hospital; religious groups of all sizes and denominations; extracurricular groups such as the school newspaper staff, the baseball team, or the orchestra; purely social groups such as clubs or fraternities; and residential groups such as dormitories and communes. For the sake of objectivity, it's best not to study your own family, but someone else's may be fair game if you can observe them enough.

Groups worth studying don't necessarily come complete with titles and membership lists. Well-known professional anthropologists have studied the men who hang out at a particular street corner, the bums in a local skid row, and the regulars at a neighborhood bar. Circles of friends might also prove profitable; "crowds" like, for example, the famous Algonquin circle or the Bloomsbury group have as concrete an existence as any club with formal membership and dues. The people who follow a particular line of work or participate in a particular recreational activity, even if they don't have any formal group identity, might provide a perfect focus for your study. Is there a certain place where truckers, for example, congregate? Do the habitues of your favorite bowling alley fill the bill?

For the sake of practicality, we'll define a social group for our purposes as any five people who meet recurrently. The purpose of the meetings is less important to us than the fact that they take place; over a period of time any recurrently meeting group develops many aspects of a culture. For purposes of convenience, it is best that the group meet at least once a week so that you will be certain to have sufficient opportunity to observe and to question. Be sure to pick a group you don't mind spending time with.

Once you have chosen the group you intend to study, you'll have to give some thought to approaching the members and gaining their cooperation. If you have chosen a group you already belong to, you won't have to spend time gaining their confidence and making yourself known to them. It is generally wise, however, to tell people frankly and honestly what you are doing. In that way you will jeopardize neither your standing with your friends or colleagues nor your semester's work in anthropology. Keep in mind, however, that anthropologists have heavy moral obligations to their informants. You must protect the privacy, and particularly the identities, of your informants: many anthropologists use fictitious names for people, places, and institutions. You should not divulge material your informants want kept secret. Remember that material you uncover might in some circumstances be used against members of your group. You must use judgment in what you tell and how.

If you are not already known in the group you intend to study, it is best to enter through the good offices of someone the members like and respect. Many anthropologists have found, for example, that the introduction of the priest, the town fathers, or the family elders smooths their way immeasurably. In many cases, people will simply have nothing to do with an outsider who arrives unintroduced. One field worker found it impossible to accomplish anything until the people were assured that "God and the President of Mexico" approved of his project.

As with any new relationship, rapport between the field worker and his subjects takes time. If you must establish rapport at the outset of your study, be sure to allow sufficient time for it. Unlike most relationships, however, getting to know this new group has a specific purpose outside of merely enjoying their companionship. This may make you uneasy; you may feel you are in some way "using" your people. Honesty goes a long way to ease these feelings; if people understand the purpose of your project, you will not be exploiting them. Don't forget that attention from a sympathetic outsider can be very flattering. A student working with a small religious sect was once astonished by the openness and hospitality of their welcome. He eventually learned that they believed he had been sent by God to bring word of their religion to outsiders! The same student later ran into serious difficulties when his group decided (despite his denials) that he was a candidate for conversion. Honesty about your purposes includes telling them you are working on a school paper and only a school paper; that probably no one but your professor and some classmates will read it; and that you are interested in learning about them, not in becoming like them. If they cannot accept these conditions, you are better off knowing at the outset so that you can look elsewhere.

To get your study under way, you can begin to catalogue some of the patterned behaviors of your group. Are there certain behaviors that always occur in given circumstances? Do certain activities recur? You will need to begin a list of these patterned behaviors and also to attempt to break them down into their constituent sets and components. Keep in mind that the members of the group probably are not consciously aware of all the patterns in which they take part. As the semester progresses, we will discuss in turn many of the large systems that compose culture; you will learn to identify behaviors within your group that fall into these major divisions of culture.

Gathering information raises a final point. How should you keep records? In general, it's best to keep an inconspicuous notebook with you all the time and to record your observations as soon as possible without disrupting the flow of behavior. Many people find note-taking disconcerting. Others don't mind at all. You'll have to use your judgment. But do remember that details only stay in your mind for a matter of minutes or hours at best. Within 24 hours you'll have forgotten, on the average, 80 percent of what you have observed. Observing and then forgetting wastes time and effort. Therefore, record while things are fresh in your mind.

FIELD PROJECT: WHAT IS CULTURE?

DISCOVERING PATTERNS

Earlier in the chapter we stated that "we can never know if our image of what people think truly mirrors their thoughts." This limitation is unimportant, however, if our understanding permits us to *explain* and *predict* why things happen. A little later we said that one of the characteristics of behavior patterns is that they are *repeated,* either by the same individual or by other individuals within the cultural system. The reason for anthropologists' interests in observing and describing behavior patterns centers on the need to understand them and thereby deduce the mental sets of the culture being studied. Once this has been accomplished, the anthropologist, like a member of the culture in question, can understand and predict the behavior of the members of the cultural system.

A. In order for you to study behavior patterns, you must take these basic assumptions into account and realize that what you perceive as a pattern may be different from what the group being studied calls a pattern.

1. First, you must arbitrarily choose a "piece" of behavior to observe. A good kind of pattern to study is a greeting pattern. An example of this might be the way the boss in an office always smiles, says "Good morning," removes his hat and coat, sits down at his desk, arranges pencil and paper, and so on. Or perhaps you have noticed that a particular type of customer will always go first to the rack with the dresses, next to the shoes, and finally to the jewelry department before noticing your presence and saying "Good morning." Each of these examples may be called a pattern.

2. Next, divide the pattern into sets. Again, this is an arbitrary decision on your part, but it is based on your observation that the behavior in question seemed to stop and start over again rhythmically (several times). The sets of the boss's greeting might be divided as follows:
   a. enters office
   b. smiles, says "Good morning" to employees
   c. removes hat and coat, hangs them on rack
   d. sits at desk, arranges pencil and paper

3. Now divide the sets into their basic components. In set b, for example, the components might be (1) boss and (2) employees, whereas

in set **c** we could list (1) hat, (2) coat, (3) rack. Set **d** includes (1) desk, (2) pencil, (3) paper.

4. Now that you have collected and described a behavior pattern, you, as an anthropologist, might want to determine some other things about it. Some of the questions you might be tempted to ask would concern pattern congruity—that is, rules of number, order, and selection. In the case of the "boss's greeting pattern" you would want to know whether you could substitute some components for others without destroying pattern congruity. In set **d**, for instance, could a pen be substituted for the pencil? How about a fork? What if the boss arranged two pens, or three, or sixteen? It is important to realize that *there are limits to the amount of change that can take place before the pattern becomes incongruous.*

5. Collect at least three variants of the greeting pattern or other pattern you have chosen. Break them down into sets and components and answer the following questions:
   a. Which sets do all three have in common?
   b. Which components do all three have in common?
   c. Which components appear to be indispensable?
   d. Are the sets or components arranged in the same order or in a different order in each pattern?
   e. How many components are there in each set?
   f. Do all sets have the same number of components?
   g. Does time and/or place have any effect on the pattern?

6. Collect a cartoon or other example of American humor (a joke, and so on) and assume that it is an example of an incongruous pattern. Answer the following questions:
   a. Is this pattern incongruous because of improper number, improper order, or improper selection? Explain.
   b. How would you reword or redraw the pattern to make it congruent?

Chapter 3

Communication Systems

It is no accident that "communicate" and "community" come from the same Latin root. Their bases share the same meaning: "bound together," "being one." Other words with the same root, "common," "communion," and "commune," only enhance the idea of sharing, unity, and commonality.

Anthropologists appreciate this insight of the ancient Romans: community and communication are intimately bound together; neither is possible without the other. Communication is one of the most important glues holding cultural systems together. Without the transmission of ideas, information, and emotion, the complex lives of people in a cultural system would not be possible. Man communicates on many levels; his communication is complicated, subtle, detailed, and abstract. No other creature is known to have developed a communication system of such scope.

Many animals living in groups communicate. Man's communication system, however, seems to have surpassed the communication systems that occur among other species in their natural state. Recent research with chimpanzees indicates that the linguistic capabilities of some other species are far greater than had previously been imagined. Nevertheless, man's ability to control very sophisticated levels of communication is so much a part of him that it appears to have influenced his evolution.

People generally think that spoken language accounts for the bulk of human communication. We do transmit a large portion of our thoughts, ideas and knowledge in sentences, but the old saying, "actions speak louder than words," is also true. Complex systems of communication surround language, involving not only what is said but the way it is said. Accent, expression, and word choice tell much about the speaker and how he feels about what he is saying. Complex systems of communication exist wholly apart from language proper; elaborate codes of facial expression, body movement, and spatial arrangement, both conscious and unconscious, continuously transmit vast quantities of information.

Much of man's ability to communicate comes from his ability to use symbols. A symbol, at its simplest level, is an arbitrary thing that stands for something else. For example, the cross stands for a complex of religious ideas and beliefs; the flag stands for a complex of historical tradition and patriotic beliefs; a flashing red light stands for danger requiring a full stop; and a uniform stands for a particular rank in a particular organization.

A symbol can be thought of as a kind of shorthand for something that exists concretely. Your college's seal stands for the grounds and building, the teachers and students, the traditions and activities that make up your school. Sometimes, though, a symbol serves to make concrete something that only exists as an abstraction. The word "honesty," for example, stands for a complex of notions rather than for anything you could point at. In this case, it is shorthand for a body of ideas shared by most people who speak English.

Science knows very little about how people learn the crucial concepts that one thing can *stand for* another, and that something concrete, like a word, can stand for an abstraction. Helen Keller, the famous author who was blind, deaf, and mute well into childhood, wrote that she discovered this when it suddenly became clear to her that the marks her teacher was making in one of her hands were the same as, or at least were meant to stand for, the water splashing over her other hand. Miss Keller appears to have understood in a flash this most crucial lesson of human communication. Once she understood, though, she realized that everything in the world must have a symbol—a name that stands for it—and that by understanding this concept she had been admitted to the great community of people who use those names. She realized that she could communicate.

The creation of symbols obviously implies the creation of sets. Every individual thing in the world cannot have its own individual name: the names would be too numerous to remember or use. Instead, every set or class of things has a name. As we have seen in our introductory discussion of culture, different systems may divide the world into different sets. Learning how to communicate, therefore, involves more than learning names and how to relate them to the things they stand for. It also involves learning the sets that a particular system uses.

LANGUAGE STRUCTURE

Languages are *systematic* and *arbitrary.* That is, they work according to rules, and there is no particular reason for those rules to be as they are, except for reasons internal to the language. These two features of language make communication possible by restricting the number of sounds to a quantity that speakers can learn and handle and by ensuring that speakers consistently associate the same meanings to the sounds (symbols) they emit. They force a high degree of repetition in both structure and vocabulary so that new information comes in quantities that people can absorb.

Languages are systematic and arbitrary in many dimensions. No language, for example, ever includes more than a small proportion of all the sounds the human vocal equipment is capable of producing. Each language, too, arranges the sounds it selects in ways that bear no necessary relationship to its environment or to other languages. Moreover, languages are arbitrary and systematic in their methods of combining elements into utterances that have meaning, in the divisions they make in reality, and in their grammar. Linguistics, the science of language, has developed into a highly technical discipline with specialized and complex techniques for studying the ways languages use sounds and organize them into meaningful units.

Phonemes

Probably the simplest way of grasping something of the essential nature of language is to approach it through the dimension of sounds. Every language consists of a collection of sounds that its speakers arrange and rearrange to make utterances. All languages include sounds that some others do not. This fact explains, in part, why nonnative speakers have accents; they often fail to master the sounds in a new language that do not appear in their own mother tongue. Thus, every native English speaker who has studied French has struggled with the "r" formed back in the throat and with the short "u" formed far to the front of the lips. Few native French speakers, on the other hand, ever master the various English forms of "th". German and Hebrew require guttural sounds formed deep in the throat that English speakers do not include in their speech. Some South African languages use a group of clicks or pops interchangeably with other sounds that English speakers consider "normal" in speech.

In addition to selecting different sounds, different languages classify sounds, or combine them into sets, differently. This concept is somewhat harder to grasp, but is well worth spending a little time to consider. The human vocal equipment is infinitely flexible; it can create a vast number of sounds that differ along a large number of dimensions. In order to be usable, however, the sounds must be grouped into a finite number of sets. Each language recognizes a fairly small group of these sets, each of which it considers to be the "same" sound. Take for example, the "t" sound in the words *water* and *tin.* Though English speakers consider them to be the same, if you say them carefully you will notice that the "t" in *tin* is accompanied by a little puff of breath—in technical terms, it is aspirated—while the "t" in *water* is not. In another example, the "k" sound in *key* and the "k" sound in *caught* are formed in different parts of the mouth—one toward the front and one toward the back. The science of phonetics (which describes sounds, among other ways, by the manner in which they are formed), recognizes that these two sounds are different. Every English speaker believes, however, that they are, in an important sense, the "same" sound. English speakers know *key* and *caught* start with the same sound and the difference in their manner of formation is an unimportant coincidence.

Although English speakers do not distinguish between these two sounds, an Arab hears a difference in the beginning sounds of *key* and *caught.* He will insist on the correctness of his hearing as strongly as he will insist that *pin* and *bin* begin with one and the same sound. Thus, Arabs speaking English often show a perplexing difficulty in understanding some things Americans say, and in getting Americans to understand some of the things they say in English.

This problem is not limited to Arabs. A Colombian woman, for example, was hard put to understand why Americans became embarrassed when she bragged that her brother was in jail. After all, it had been difficult for him to get in. He had worked hard and passed many long examinations to attain this honor. Only a small number of those who applied were admitted. But gradually it dawned on Americans what she was talking about. Their faces would clear and they would smile. "Oh," they would say, "You mean he's at *Yale,* the university! "

"That's what I said," she would insist. "Jail! "

There was nothing wrong with the woman's ears, or with those of the Americans. The problem was that they had stumbled over the existence of different *phonemes.* Phoneme is the technical term for a set of sounds considered to be the same in a given language. It is the smallest unit of sound recognized by the speakers of a language. The differences between the phonetics of the sounds that form a phoneme are not usually recognized within a given language. That is why the South American woman could not hear the difference between "jail" and "Yale." "J" and "y" are members of the same phoneme in Spanish. In linguistic terms, they are *allophones* of that phoneme, or one of the sounds that compose a phoneme. Likewise, in Arabic, "b" and "p" are allophones of a single phoneme, as are the two different "k" sounds or the two "t" sounds in English. The fact that speakers of different languages cannot hear the difference between sounds that other languages consider to be absolutely distinct is thus a matter of training in phonemes.

As babies learn to speak, their parents and other adults around them help separate out the sounds that are correct from those that are not, and teach them to group the sounds into correct sets. Thus, a child in an English-speaking country learns that *bet* and *vet* begin with two different sounds. But a child in a Spanish-speaking country learns that these two sounds are the same.

A pair of words such as *bet* and *vet* forms a technical test for phonemic difference; they are what is called a minimal pair, or a pair of words that differ only in the single sound in question. The fact that English-speaking people universally recognize that *bet* and *vet* are two different words, while Spanish speakers universally believe they are the same, proves that in English "b" and "v" belong to two different phonemes, and that in Spanish they are allophones of a single phoneme.

In English, the tone, or pitch, of an utterance does not change its phonemic identity, but in Chinese, tone is phonemic. Two words, identical except for the pitch at which they are pronounced, may form a minimal pair. During World War II the Americans used Navajo, a complex tonal language, as a secret code that the Japanese were not able to crack.

The speakers of every language learn the system of sound sets that their language recognizes. They group the multitude of sounds that people make, the allophones as well as the individual variations of the allophones, into their appropriate phonemes. Learning a language not only entails attempting to learn new sounds, but learning a new system of phonemes as well, and retraining the ear and the mouth to function according to the new sets.

Morphemes

Sounds (or marks on paper) are only important linguistically insofar as they have meaning. Languages therefore have rules for grouping their phonemes into meaningful combinations that their speakers recognize as words or phrases. The rules of combining sounds differ among languages in a number of respects. Specific rules, for example, govern the order in which sounds may appear in words and in which sounds may adjoin one another. English, for example, does not permit the sound represented as "ng" to start a word. English speakers, in fact, find this very difficult to pronounce, while speakers of some African and Indochinese languages do not. Spanish words, on the other hand, cannot begin with "st" or "sp"; English words frequently begin this way.

Native speakers of a language intuitively know which units of speech have meaning. They know, for example, that *child* is such a unit, whereas "ild" is not. Native speakers also recognize that *children* is such a unit of speech but, at the same time, they know that it is both different from and similar to *child*. They can also recognize that *man* and *men* bear this same relationship, and that *girls,* similarly, has two units of meaning—the word itself and the element that makes it plural. One could separate out the units of meaning in the following manner. *Children* = *child* + plural (in this case "ren". *Men* = *man* + plural (in this case "e"). *Girls* = *girl* + plural (in this case "s").

What the native speaker would be trying to describe is the *morpheme.* The morpheme is the smallest unit of a language that has meaning and is grammatically significant. It is not exactly the same thing as a word, because "ren," "e," and "s," which are not words, all express the same meaning. They are, in fact, *allomorphs* of the same morpheme—in this case, the English plural morpheme, which also includes among its allomorphs "–en" (as in oxen), "o–en" (as in women), "ice" (as in mice), "ee" (as in feet), and a silent (as in sheep). Allomorphs are grouped together because they share both a common meaning and a common function in the grammar of a language. Another example would be "in–" and "un–", allomorphs of a morpheme that acts as a prefix and means "not."

In most languages, morphemes are either *bound* or *free.* Bound morphemes must appear attached to another morpheme, while free morphemes may appear alone. Thus, "child" is free and "ren" is bound. Other bound morphemes in English include those that change the tenses of verbs—for example, "–ed" in *flaked* and "o" in *spoke.* Free morphemes may appear alone *or* in combination with other morphemes.

A language, therefore, consists of a collection of phonemes that compose the allomorphs of its morphemes (although some sets consist of only one member).

Grammar

Languages also contain rules for combining morphemes into acceptable (or, in linguistic terms, grammatical) groups generally recognized as sentences or complete utterances. Such systems of rules, or grammars, exist within all languages; often, in fact, a number exist within a given language, and even within the usage of a given individual. For example, the grammars of regional or minority forms of English differ somewhat from that of standard English. Southern dialect, for example, recognizes a second person plural ("you-all") that does not exist in most other American dialects; it appears in a different form ("youse") in some northeastern dialects. Black English forms its verbs according to a system different from that of standard English. Even within daily life, individuals use more than one grammar. In a formal speech or lecture one might use a number of grammatical forms ("whom," for example) that do not appear in informal conversational speech.

Linguists have attempted to develop descriptions of grammar for thousands of years. The first great grammar, Panini's study of Sanskrit, was completed about the fourth century B.C. For centuries, linguists and grammarians attempted to describe English in terms of the great classical grammars based on Latin. Because English does not function like Latin, however, these descriptions have been unsatisfactory and incomplete. They have nevertheless been very influential, and most people have learned a Latinate English grammar in school. Other linguists have attempted to develop grammars in terms of the frequency or relationship of morphemes.

Transformational grammar
The most modern development in grammatical studies, based on the still-controversial work of the linguist Noam Chomsky, seeks to explain how grammatical sentences are produced, rather than why they are grammatical. Chomsky has been a leader in the attempt to develop the so-called generative transformational grammar. This system, based on modern symbolic logic, seeks to develop rules that will generate, or derive, all grammatical sentences, and only grammatical sentences (of a given language). Chomsky postulates that a similar system exists in the heads of all native speakers of a given language because they can both understand and create wholly novel sentences. Chomsky observed that children do not learn language by simply repeating exactly what has been said to them. Rather, they internalize rules about language production and actually create new combinations. A sentence such as "My great-aunt Florence, a noted deep-sea diver, makes a wicked tangerine wine" is instantly recognized and understood by all English speakers, but it is probably wholly novel in human history. No previous theory attempted to explain how this sentence could be produced and understood.

Working at the level of the morpheme, generative grammars create groups (or strings) of words and word fragments that represent all the morphemes of a sentence but do not necessarily resemble a grammatical utterance. Some morphemes are silent, as we have seen, and often morphemes at this stage appear in positions different from those they would take in a grammatical sentence. This complete representation of all morphemes of a sentence is the so-called *deep structure* that Chomsky believes all native speakers understand. In an often-quoted example, speakers of English intuitively know that the following two sentences are different.

The boy is eager to please.
The boy is easy to please.

Although they appear superficially similar, the sentences differ greatly in meaning. The relationship between the boy and the pleasing is opposite in the two sentences. In the first the boy does the pleasing; in the latter, the pleasing is done to him. The difference exists at the level of deep structure rather than at the level of speaking or writing, which Chomsky calls the surface structure. The rules for moving from deep structure to surface structure are call the *transformational* rules because they govern the transformation of one string into another. Unfortunately, to delve much more deeply into generative and transformational grammar requires a highly technical background in symbolic logic and linguistics. It is sufficient to note at this point that the concept of deep structure is a highly controversial one. Does the deep structure actually exist? What use is it in understanding language? Chomsky believes that despite their surface differences, languages share universal features and human minds are genetically predisposed to learn language.

HISTORICAL LINGUISTICS

Although language is highly structured, it is not ordinarily static. Languages used in daily life tend to change constantly; only the so-called dead languages, used for special purposes by people who don't speak them daily, tend to remain relatively unchanged. In living languages, evolution occurs gradually and on a small scale. The English of Beowulf, of Chaucer, and of Shakespeare all differ from the modern form so greatly that they are difficult to understand today. There was, however, no sharp break in the development of our modern language. Words in older forms of English are like snapshots of the language at specific moments in time. Snapshots of a child taken at five-year intervals will show drastic changes; from day to day, however, the change is so small it is barely noticed.

Living languages change in several ways. Most people notice the addition of new words to the language. "Afro," "splash-down," and "Ms.", for example, were not widely used ten years ago. More difficult to perceive are gradual changes in structure, because they are slower. "Whom," for example, has essentially passed from conversational American English. "Their," in a special quasi-singular use, as in "Everybody had their ticket," has become well established.

Changes at the phonemic level also occur gradually. Pre-Norman English, for example, did not distinguish "f" from "v." Spanish gradually came to replace "f" with a silent "h" in some uses. For example, the word for "son" changed from "fijo" to "hijo." Thus, languages grow and change in all their systems. Although it is difficult at any moment to tell when a given type of variation becomes a concrete systemic or structural change, the slow accretion of cases can ultimately become a qualitative difference.

As languages grow and change, they sometimes split into branches that evolve in independent directions. American English, for example, is obviously descended from the English of the seventeenth and eighteenth century British Isles. Separated by an ocean for several centuries, however, the two forms of English have evolved along different lines, and have become, by the late twentieth century, markedly different.

Such a process of evolution, if it lasts long enough, can even produce wholly separate languages from a common base, as in the cases of French, Portuguese, Spanish, Italian, and other languages descended from Latin. Studies of the process of evolution of languages can be used to determine historical relationships, movements of peoples, and to establish dates of various events.

This type of study in historical linguistics led to the discovery that all of the languages of the Indo-European family, including nearly all the languages of the European continent were originally one language group called "Proto–Indo-European." This changed, through the mechanisms of diffusion (or slow spread) and migration, to become the mutually unintelligible languages now spoken by Germans, Indians, and Persians and others.

To study relationships between languages or forms of the same language, historical linguists use a technique known as *lexicostatistics,* or *glottochronology.* The method is based on the assumption that the basic core words in a language, the terms for such items as members of the family and common foods, change at a relatively constant rate that is slower than the rate of change of less basic words. The linguist Morris Swadesh (1971) postulates that the rate of change in the basic vocabulary is about 19 percent every thousand years. Calculation of the percentage of cognates (words that are similar, for example, mater [in Latin], mère [French], mother [English]) shared by the core vocabularies of two languages can provide a rough index of time. Thus, a comparison of core vocabularies can demonstrate if a relationship between two languages exists, and, by counting the number of cognates, linguists can indicate how long ago the split between the two languages occurred. For example, two daughter languages of the same mother will have about 66 percent cognates in their core vocabularies after 1,000 years.

SOCIOLINGUISTICS

Patterns in the use of speech should not be confused with patterns of language structure. Patterns of speaking vary in different socio-cultural contexts, and the study of these differences is often referred to as *sociolinguistics,* or the ethnography of speaking (Hymes, 1962). In studying patterns of speaking we are not concerned with grammatical correctness, but rather with contextual appropriateness. Thus, we investigate the rules prescribing which words (of several grammatically correct utterances) are appropriate for a particular context. For example, certain highly descriptive four-letter words referring to a person's origins, his activities, or his bodily functions are perfectly acceptable, often even preferred, when, in the company of one's peers, but these same words evoke considerable protest when used in the presence of one's elders. Sociolinguistics studies the patterns of speech habits that are implicit in ordinary behavior.

Forms of address

Forms of address provide a clear example of some of these implicit cultural patterns of speaking. In English, one may address a complete stranger with a polite and deferential "pardon me, sir" or a cruder, noncaring "hey you." Both forms are grammatically correct and both might be used by the same individual, but in different circumstances.

Forms of address may reflect differences in age and sex, and in social, economic, political, religious or ethnic status. Roger Brown and Marguerite Ford (1961) believe that terms of address are determined by the relationships between the speakers. If the relationship is one of equality, then the terms of address are reciprocal—first names for an informal, intimate relationship or title and last name for a more formal, or business, situation. Nonreciprocity in terms of address means that the status relationship between the speakers is a markedly unequal one. For example, if, on the first day of class, a professor walks into the classroom and introduces herself as Dr. Withit, but calls the students by their first names, what is she communicating about the nature of the student-teacher relationship? What is the difference if she introduces herself as Ima Withit? or Ms. Withit?

> Once last year as I was leaving my office in Jackson, Miss., with my Negro secretary, a white policeman yelled, "Hey, boy! Come here!' Somewhat bothered, I retorted: 'I'm no boy!' He then rushed at me, inflamed, and stood towering over me, snorting 'Whatd' ja say, boy?' Quickly he frisked me and demanded 'What's your name, boy?' Frightened, I replied, 'Dr. Poussaint, I'm a physician.' He angrily clucked and hissed, 'What's your first name, boy?' When I hesitated he assumed a threatening stance and clenched his fists. As my heart palpitated, I

muttered in profound humiliation, 'Alvin.' He continued his psychological bru-
tality, bellowing, 'Alvin, the next time I call you, you come right away, you hear?'
I hesitated. 'You hear me, boy?' My voice trembling with helplessness, but following my instincts of self-preservation, I murmured, 'Yes, sir.' Now fully satisfied
that I had performed and acquiesced to my 'boy' status, he dismissed me with,
'Now boy, go on and get out of here or next time we'll take you for a little ride
down to the station house!' (Poussaint 1967: 53).

Topics of conversation

Appropriate topics of conversation are another interest of sociolinguists.
Learning the correct grammar of a language is one thing, but knowing
when a particular subject may be broached is something quite different.
Americans consider lunch an excellent time to negotiate business deals, but
a Latin American would be offended if business matters were to intrude on
a meal. A person might discuss financial problems with a close relative, but
be very annoyed if a chance acquaintance at a bus stop inquired about his
yearly income. Topics of conversation thus may vary according to the relationship between the speakers as well as according to the circumstances
of their meeting. A person of higher status, for example, might broach
topics a lower-status person could not—the quality of one's work, for example.

Boundary maintenance

Speech patterns often serve as a means to define and maintain the boundaries between human groups. In the United States these patterns will vary
according to class, region, ethnic group, or even occupation group. Clifford
Geertz (1960) has shown that in some areas the choice of vocabulary paral-
lels the class divisions of the country. In Java there are three sharply divided socioeconomic classes—peasants, townsmen, and aristocrats—and
each uses a separate vocabulary. The basic level, the discourse of peasants,
is learned and used in the home by all Javanese children, regardless of
class. If a child is born into a townsman or aristocratic family, however, he
will eventually be taught one or both of the other forms of discourse so that
he can converse more elegantly. Then, depending upon the speaker's social
class and the social occasion, different words are used to convey the same
meaning. These sociolinguistic variations thus identify immediately the
social class of the speaker and serve to inhibit movement between classes.

Sociolinguistic variation is found in all stratified societies. In order to
really understand another group of people, it is extremely helpful to know
the culturally derived rules that underlie these patterns of speech use. They

provide the outsider with valuable clues toward understanding the values of the society, such as the joking patterns appropriate with some individuals in certain circumstances but not with others, or cultural attitudes toward the aged.

ETHNOLINGUISTICS

Language is, as we have said, composed of patterns, sets, and components, both in its structure and in its sounds. But language is also itself a subsystem, a part of a culture, and language traits are learned just as other cultural traits are learned. In addition to studying the inner nature of language, linguists sometimes examine the relationships between a language and other aspects of a culture—a study known as *ethnolinguistics*. To what extent do the traits and characteristics of a particular society influence the vocabulary and structure of its language? And, conversely, does the language also influence the culture, and thus actually determine the way that individuals within the culture view and respond to their environment?

Cultural influence on language

It seems both logical and obvious that the vocabulary of a society's language reflects its culture. One would expect that objects, experiences, or events which are important to a society's culture would receive appropriate elaboration in its language. Thus, the Eskimos, whose livelihood and existence depend on a proper reading of their icy environment, have a "snow set" that contains over thirty words, each describing a slightly different snow condition. The Aztecs of central Mexico, who lived in an environment where snow occured only rarely, however, had only one element in their snow and ice set.

Even within a single society, there are often regional or subcultural variations in vocabulary. Thus, only people who work with computers may know the expressions "software," "floating point," "Do Loop," "ALCOL," and "TECO," while only those within a black ghetto subculture know and use the terms "hype," "gas-head," "blood," "spook," and "handkerchief-head." Again, this is only common sense—language, like culture, is adaptive, and should deal effectively with those aspects of the environment that are important to a group's survival.

There are numerous examples documenting the influence of culture on vocabulary, but evidence of cultural determination of language structure is not nearly as complete or convincing. Does the cultural system in fact affect the *structure* of the language? Harry Hoijer (1951) is an anthropological linguist who thinks it does. He has studied the Navajo, a nomadic group of Indians in the Southwest, and has noted that their verb categories emphasize the reporting of events in process, or "eventings," as he calls them. The Navajo, through their verbal categories, perceive the world as filled with objects forever in the process of becoming, and activities forever in the process of occurring. Thus, according to Hoijer, the structure of the Navajo language reflects the ongoing movement that has been a cultural experience of the Navajo for centuries. Though this example seems reasonable, other anthropologists have found evidence contrary to this; namely, specific societies in which grammar does *not* parallel cultural concepts or experiences. The general consensus is that although culture often seems to influence the vocabulary of a language, it seldom seems to influence the grammar.

Linguistic influences on culture

Assuming that culture influences language, does the reverse hypothesis also hold—that language determines or influences people's thoughts, perceptions, behavior and experience? This intriguing idea has been labelled the *Sapir-Whorf hypothesis,* after the linguist Benjamin Lee Whorf and his teacher, Edward Sapir. Sapir (1931: 378) claimed that,

> It is quite an illusion to imagine that one adjusts to reality essentially without the use of language and that language is merely an incidental means of solving specific problems of communication or reflection. The fact of the matter is that the 'real world' is to a large extent unconsciously built up on the language habits of the group . . . We see and hear and otherwise experience very largely as we do because the language habits of our community predispose certain choices of interpretation.

In this view, language is seen as a cultural filter between man and the real world that both facilitates certain perceptions and hinders the formation of others. Sapir felt that the grammar of a language actually forced the individual's life experience into preconceived categories. As an example, let us take the differing number of words for snow and ice among the Eskimo and the Aztec. Since the Eskimo language has so many words in its snow and ice set, an Eskimo speaker talking about his environment is predisposed to notice whether the snow is mushy, hard, icy, or granular in order to chose the correct term from the many possibilities available to him.

This is not to say that the Aztecs did not perceive differences in types of snow or that they could not have combined their words productively in order to communicate the various attributes of snow and ice. Indeed, each and every language seems to be capable of expressing *any* concept. Rather, the Sapir-Whorf hypothesis claims that in some languages it may be easier for speakers to think or talk about certain things because their language provides readily available means for doing so. Though any concept can be encoded in any language, it is done with ease in some and with great effort in others. Thus, we most frequently perceive reality and assimilate experience according to the categories of our linguistic code.

Benjamin Whorf, Sapir's student, was interested in relating the *grammar* of a language to the world view, or the culture's perception of reality. He was particularly interested in the ways a language may structure conceptions of time and space for its speakers. He contrasted Hopi with the European languages he called Standard Average European (S.A.E.) and discovered that S.A.E. objectified time and spoke about it in spatial terms. Events can be located in time just as they can in space, for example, "at that point in time." European languages thus speak of *long* and *short* intervals of time such as "three hours long" or a "stretch of time"; their speakers think of a time period like "ten months" as being like a series of ten similar objects all lined up in a row. English grammar encourages its speakers to think of time as a divisible rod consisting of past, present, and future; a division that, not coincidentally, corresponds to the English verb tenses.

The Hopi, however, do not refer to time in spatial terms. For the Hopi, time is not a quantity or a motion, but rather an intensification of actions that are occuring. Hopi lacks anything corresponding to past, present, and future. Its tenses distinguish events that have become manifest from those still in the process of becoming manifest. Thus the Hopi language emphasizes repetition that is not wasted but accumulated—events are stored and intensified. By contrast, in the S.A.E. usage time is "spent," "saved," or "borrowed." Whorf thinks there is a connection between this implicit view of time and European fascination with time clocks, records, bookkeeping, hourly wages, calendars, and so on (Carroll, 1956).

The emphasis within the field of linguistics is now on linguistic and cultural universals rather than differences. Noam Chomsky, the leading researcher in linguistic phenomena, has suggested that Whorf was so concerned with surface structure that he ignored the deeper level on which all languages are of the same universally human character. As our world becomes smaller it is necessary to have an appreciation of what people have in common, but it is also good to remember that different languages may have important effects on what people perceive, on what people think, and on how people act.

NONVERBAL COMMUNICATION

People communicate by using time and space, other human beings, and material culture as well as language. The changing relationship between these variables, as perceived and evaluated according to the rules of a particular culture, conveys information. Thus it becomes a basis for predicting the subsequent behavior of others and for deciding how one should behave. These relationships may be viewed as communication systems or subsystems within a larger cultural system, and as such may be analyzed by a method similar to that employed for the analysis of verbal communication systems. The linguists' model of the structure and function of language may thus be extended to other, nonverbal, communication systems.

Linguists divide units of verbal communication according to their sound and meaning and the unconscious rules used for structuring them. The smallest units of sound are classed as phonemes; the smallest units of meaning as morphemes. In the case of nonverbal communication systems, we are still dealing with units of meaning, but not with units of sound; the basis for perception has expanded to include visual, and other, modes of perception. Thus, the linguistic model must be revised if it is to include these other, nonverbal, models of perception.

We can organize units of nonverbal communication systems in the same general way that archaeologists classify tools developed by man during his evolutionary history; that is, units of nonverbal communication include *physiological tools,* which are available to man through the manipulation of his own body and the modification and evaluation of the bodies of other members of his cultural system, and *material tools,* which are any material items produced or used by man. These nonverbal tools aid man in his attempt to communicate.

A typical nonverbal communication system might involve a member of American culture entering the home of a friend, John Smith. The visitor immediately perceives a particular setting involving people and things in a spatial arrangement, and predicts his own and others' behavior based on this initial communication. As communication continues, he may or may not alter his prediction in response to changes in the posture or location in space of the people and things initially perceived.

If we are to find out just what message he received, we will have to first examine the units of perception and the meaning of the system. Some of these units are material, such as chairs, a table, a television set, curtains, books, and a picture of the late Chairman Mao. The attributes of these, such as color, texture, size, design, subject matter, and so forth, also fall within the category of material units. If the room is occupied by people, perhaps family or friends, the person entering perceives their presence, posture, and attributes (height, weight, hair color and style), and these units are also part of the message. A third component of this message is provided by the arrangement of the people and objects in space. That is, the relationship defined by the amount of space or area between and surrounding people and objects is part of the message, and the basic unit of communication is the space itself.

All of these units—material components and their attributes, people and their attributes, and space—combine to make up the message. These non-verbal messages transmit as much, or perhaps even more, information to members of a cultural system as do verbal communications. The major difference between these communications systems is the mode of transmission and reception.

The relatively new subdisciplines of anthropology that study these non-verbal communications systems are *proxemics,* the study of the relationship of space and spatial patterns to material components and persons (or *members*); and *kinesics,* the study of the relationship of body posture to space and materials in terms of the messages that these arrangements communicate. While proxemics, kinesics, and linguistics all concern the study of communications systems, the method of investigation used for determining patterns, sets, and components of communication, and the rules for their use, differs for each. The linquist assumes that he is dealing with a linear and essentially uni-dimensional quantity. He understands verbal communications to have initial, medial, and terminal components, and classifies them according to their phonemes, morphemes, and grammar.

In proxemics, however, the sets and patterns may be multi-dimensional. Some spaces are perceived and evaluated as linear, but even a long corridor is measured in terms of vertical space as well as horizontal and linear space. If we refer back to the example of the Smith family at home in their living room, we can begin to see how the linguistic analogy functions and how we must modify it to understand the special case of proxemics.

In the same sense that we defined a morpheme as a set of sounds (phonemes) that has a cultural meaning, we may say that the living room is a set of material items and people located within a space that is meaningful to a member of the cultural system. If we alter the arrangement of sounds, we change the meaning of the morpheme, and in some cases the morpheme may even cease to have meaning. The same is true of the living room—altering the size and shape of the space or the position of material objects or people may alter the definition of the space and, in some cases, produce a result so incongruous as to destroy any meaning. The Smiths sitting close together, laughing, means something quite different from the Smiths facing in opposite directions. It becomes important, therefore, to discover exactly how far one may go in altering a spatial situation and the material components within it without changing or destroying the meaning of the setting. For example, all the furniture piled in a corner does not permit the space to function as a living room, but such an arrangement might communicate that the Smiths are moving.

PROXEMICS

Anthropologists have discovered a number of different types of spatial relationships within the spectrum of human cultures. These are based on the aforementioned variables; specifically, the relationship of space to material culture and the relationship of space to members.

Space: status

Space relates directly to membership or status: the amount and kind of space accorded a member of a cultural system reflects his status in the structure of the system. In many cultures, individuals (or *members*) who occupy a high status use more space than those who occupy a less favored position. In our own culture, we see this in the size of houses, yards, and the number of enclosed spaces (house, garage, shed, porches). Vertical space also serves as an indicator of differential status. The high status of a priest in relation to the congregation permits the elevation of his territory; that is, the altar and pulpit, above the heads of the parishoners. In the case of residence, high-status dwellings frequently occupy the highest geographical area of a town, and penthouses are the elite of apartment house dwellings.

Space: territory

Like other animals, man acquires, marks off, and protects his territory. He does this in a culturally-patterned way at both the group and the individual level. His ways of defining space form a system of communication that informs other individuals about his thoughts, feelings, and intentions.

Group territorial markers are chosen from a cultural system's inventory of ideas, material objects, and body tools. In some cases, markers exist solely as ideas, either in written form or in the memories of the members. In complex societies, these include local, state, or national government boundaries that exist primarily in the abstract as lines drawn on maps, coordinates of latitude and longitude, and other symbolic references to spatial divisions. More often, however, territorial boundaries consist of material components corresponding in location to lines drawn on a map, such as a fence with a sentry box occupied by a member of the system in the person of a sentry who regularly marks and remarks the boundary of his group's territory.

Individuals may mark off personal territory in a similar fashion. The anthropologist E. T. Hall (1961) distinguishes at least four separate areas of individual territoriality. He believes these "distance zones" in American culture vary according to the kind of message and the relationship between the individuals in question and their activity. Hall defines these distances as follows: *Intimate*—from physically touching to 18 inches; *Personal* —from 1½ to four feet; *Social*—from four to 12 feet; and *Public*—from 12 to 20 feet or more. The type of behavior exhibited within each of these zones relates directly to the social definition of the zone and varies according to culture. For example, in American culture Hall's intimate zone is reserved for activities of the most personal sort. Only lovers or the closest of friends approach as close as 18 inches or less; such closeness often carries sexual overtones for American adults. Partly for this reason, Americans tend to find crowded places offensive. Latin Americans, on the other hand, do not reserve Hall's intimate zone for such personal relations; the ordinary conversational distance is much closer than Americans are used to and they enjoy crowds more. Thus, they often find us "cold" and "unfriendly" and we often find them "overfamiliar" or "pushy." In analyzing cultural use of space, Hall's spatial zones may be thought of as being roughly analogous to the linguists' definition of morpheme in that it is a unit of proxemic communication that has meaning. This meaning depends on the material articles or types of people that occupy the zones—components analogous to the linguists' phoneme.

Although, as we have seen, the boundaries of culturally significant spatial zones may exist solely in the minds of members, they may also be marked by items of material or physiological culture. That is to say, objects and bodily postures may communicate the locations of boundaries. Items of material culture used as boundary markers may be close enough to touch the skin of a member or they may range in distance up to 20 feet or more.

Space becomes more "public" and less "private" the farther it lies from the individual to whom it "belongs." The exact point at which the change from the private to the public zone occurs varies between cultures and between situations within a given culture. It can often be deduced, however, from the markers people use to communicate such changes in the meaning of space. One way that people may mark off their zone—a method they share with some animal species—is to deposit wastes along its boundaries. Man, as a cultural animal, generally uses cultural rather than bodily wastes. These deposits may be waste only in terms of the specific activity being performed and may regain value as functional items when the activity ends.

You might observe on campus, for example, several students gathering

These Arabian women create a private space in a public place. (courtesy of Claudia Crawford)

A group of students uses cultural waste to define its boundaries. (courtesy of John Young)

to play cards. They place their books, purses, and maybe a spare jacket around the periphery of the game before they begin to play. During the game, members may leave and return with cokes, food, and cigarettes and they likewise deposit these or their containers as territorial markers around the periphery of the game. A member or two may leave to attend class and reclaim his or her temporary waste (books, purse) from the periphery, leaving a gap in the group's marker. Other members may move their bodies or possessions in to fill the gap if they wish to communicate that the group is closed. If, on the other hand, they wish to recruit new members, they may leave a spot open to indicate this. When they leave, many of the markers may stay behind—an empty cup, cigarette butts, and a crumpled cigarette pack—perhaps to be used by another group that later occupies the same space.

The area of anthropology that has traditionally concerned itself with the study and measurement of proxemic relationships between material and physiological culture is archaeology. Archaeologists frequently have only the "waste" left behind by members of an extinct prehistoric cultural system from which to interpret the activities, number and status of the members, as well as their relationships with members of other cultural systems of the same period and periods preceeding and following it.

The methodology developed by archaeologists to cope with the problem of interpreting these relationships is similar in many aspects to the methodology of linguists. Here an analogy may be drawn between the *structure* of a verbal or written communication and the *spatial relationship* between material components of an archaeological site. Smaller units, such as the foundation of an adobe or stone structure, a hearth, or the place set aside for a particular activity such as tool-making, may be analogous to the linguists' morpheme. Individual components, such as tools related to the specific activity of the group being investigated (and without meaning outside of this context), may be understood in the same way as a phoneme. Just as phonemes are defined as a class of sounds that vary slightly from sound to sound within that class but are understood to be the same by members of the cultural system, components of material culture may vary on an individual basis but still be classed as the same article by members. For example, there is a great deal of individual variation among different styles of coffee cups in American tableware, ranging from the styrofoam cup used at picnics to the elegant bone china cup used at a formal dinner. Nevertheless, both are classified as cups.

The archaeologist James Deetz (1967) proposes a strong parallel between the study of language and the study of material culture. At a certain archaeological site, for example, he was able to distinguish three types of arrowheads: one with straight sides and a straight base; one with sides notched near the straight base; and one with similarly notched sides, but with a curved base. Although he cannot be sure from his archaeological data, he assumes that the notching and curving had meaning to the users of the arrowheads since these characteristics are generally related to hafting and thus connote functional differences. To classify these arrowheads, he proposes that the concept of the *facteme* be used. A facteme is the minimal class of attributes that affects the functional significance of the arrowhead. Thus, for example, two arrowheads identical except that one is notched and one is not, form a minimal pair for the facteme of notching. This facteme, according to Deetz, may well have consisted of several allofacts (analogous to allophones) such as round notches, triangular notches, and square notches.

To reconstruct the functional significance of the material objects found at a site, archaeologists find it useful to study their proxemic relationships. James N. Hill (1968), an American archaeologist reporting on the analysis of an archaeological site in eastern Arizona, bases his analysis on the assumption that the use of space by the prehistoric occupants of his site was patterned rather than random. He further assumes that by comparing the spatial regularities observed at this site with ethnographic information from other cultures it may be possible to deduce the *behavioral meaning* communicated by the materials found at the site. For example, he notes that some items have *functional* meanings (that is, they are associated with certain economic, social, or religious activities) that may reflect the composition of *social segments* (that is, specific items may have been used by men, women, hunters, priests, and so on).

KINESICS

The components of body posture and appearance, like components of space or material culture, also relate directly to territoriality and status. The art of placing one's body on a particular spot or within a given area may be considered a claim to territory, and even in a complex society modern man marks a territory by traveling over it. Just as a salesman has a "territory," so does the commuter who travels from suburbia to the city and home again. The area immediately adjacent to the route he travels is considered his. He may travel this route with a number of other commuters who also share this territory.

In addition to the material, linguistic and proxemic components of the message "The Smith family is at home in their living room," the actual presence of the Smiths and their physical and material attributes are components of the total message. We have already mentioned that the amount and quality of space separating the Smiths from each other and from the articles of material culture has cultural meaning, signifying the status and relationship of members to one another. The presence of the Smiths does not have a static message however: we must take into account that they are constantly changing their posture, gesturing, and otherwise changing aspects of their appearance by widening their eyes, blushing, or rhythmically tapping their feet.

Kinesic, or body motion, behavior is made up of different types of components that are, like verbal language, culturally determined. The number of combinations of body signs of which human beings are capable is virtually infinite. It is estimated that some 20,000 different facial expressions are possible. Dr. Ray Birdwhistell (1970), the leading specialist in this field, has isolated 32 of these components, which he calls *kinemes,* within the American cultural system. These include three kinemes of head nod (one nod, two nods, or three nods), two kinemes of lateral head sweeps, one head cock, and one head tilt. Add to these the number of gestural possibilities inherent in the lateral sweep of an arm from fully down vertically to fully extended vertically, and it becomes possible to appreciate the capabilities of this type of communications system. According to Birdwhistell, kinemes, like phonemes, are combined by members of a culture into larger units, *kinemorphemes,* that have meaning. Birdwhistell suggests that kinemorphemes are in turn combined to form *complex kinemorphic constructions* that, like verbal sentences or phrases, may have only a four- or five-second duration.

Researchers in kinesiology are not yet able to categorize all the components, or kinemes, used by any one cultural system. There are, however, some types of kinesic behavior that may be hypothesized as generally char-

Gestures and postures are culturally specific. Americans can easily interpret pointing, touching, and placing hands on hips. (courtesy of Ruth Ann Holt)

acteristic of many cultures. These types of behavior involve rhythmic changes in posture and position of the body parts. Rather than attempting to differentiate the significance of finger movement versus arm movement, these researchers merely record the fact of the movement itself.

One way kinesic elements are used is to add stress or emphasis to an oral communication. A common example is that of a parent scolding a child—shaking a finger while saying "Bad boy!" emphasizes the significance of the communication. Striking a desk or table with the fist while saying "No, I won't!" adds a similar type of emphasis, as does raising an eyebrow or winking in conjunction with a vocally expressed comment or opinion.

Another category of kinesic behavior might be termed positive/negative reinforcement. Positive/negative reinforcement is commonly performed by gesturing either in rhythm or out of rhythm in the context of spoken communication (together with some form of kinesic behavior). In a silent film made of a classroom situation in which Margaret Mead was conducting an observation report, the following sequence of kinesic behavior was recorded. (The people involved in the kinesic communication in the film were Mead, a female student in the front row, and a male life insurance sales-man. The sequence lasted approximately five seconds.)

    a. The life insurance salesman is attempting to sell Mead an insurance policy.
    b. Girl in front row crosses leg, left over right.
    c. Life insurance salesman glances in her direction.
    d. Girl tugs down skirt.
    e. Mead tugs down *her* skirt, pats her hair.
    f. Girl pats her hair.
    g. Mead gestures with her hand and finger (right hand clenched, index finger extended).
    h. Girl swings left foot up and down in *exactly* the same direction in time with Mead's finger.
    i. End.

The precise meaning of this communication between Mead and the girl is not directly discernable but may be categorized generally as positively rein-forcing, or agreeing.

Disagreeing behavior is out of rhythm with the speaker's movements. Every classroom teacher is familiar with the shuffling and foot tapping that occurs whenever students disapprove of his or her behavior or comments, or when the end of class approaches. If the teacher should happen to keep the class past the normal allotted time, this negatively reinforcing, or disa-greeing, behavior becomes more intense until someone verbally disagrees, informing the teacher that the class has been kept too long.

FIELD PROJECT: COMMUNICATION SYSTEMS

I. VERBAL COMMUNICATION

A. *Structure in language: morphemes, phonemes, grammar*

1. Find a member of your cultural system who is a native speaker of, or has studied extensively, a foreign language (that is, an informant).
2. Learn to pronounce a phrase (a pattern) in his language.
3. Discover which units have meaning (morphemes) by segmenting the phrase in different ways. Pronounce these segments (sets) and ask your informant whether or not these segments have meaning.
4. Can you discover any phonemes (components) that are not used in the English language?

B. *Historical linguistics*

1. Interview a person who has been a member of your cultural system for a long period of time. Ask this person what changes he or she has observed in the language. These may be changes in terminology (vocabulary), or changes in the pattern of speaking (who speaks to whom, different topics of conversation).

C. *Sociolinguists*

1. Collect a list of terms that form a special vocabulary relating specifically to the type of cultural system that you are studying and to its material and physiological components. Does everyone in the cultural system know and use the same terms?
2. What are the terms of address commonly used in your cultural system? What variations do you find? What facts about the social system do these reflect? What do they indicate about the possibilities of change within the system?
3. What are the appropriate topics of conversation for different members and/or for different situations?

II. NONVERBAL COMMUNICATION

A. *Proxemics*

1. Draw a map showing the entire territory of your cultural system.
2. Draw a floor plan (to scale) showing the proxemic relationship of articles of material culture to each other and to the position of the members.
3. Use Hall's classification of space (intimate, personal, and so on) to deduce relationships between members by measuring distances between components and members.

4. Compare the size and shape of the area in question to other spatial arrangements with which you are familiar. Is the behavior of the members similar in similar spaces? In what ways?

B. *Material Culture*

1. Describe several of the material components present in your cultural system by listing their attributes (size, shape, material, design).
2. Do different components share similar attributes? What are they?
3. Hypothesize that the components that share attributes are components of the same set.
4. How many different sets are present in your cultural system? Are they located within the intimate, personal, social, or public zone of the member?
5. What can you say about the different statuses available within your cultural system based on an observation of the material components?
6. How do members mark their spatial zones with items of material culture?

C. *Kinesics*

1. Observe the members of your cultural system and determine the postural requirements of their status. Do they normally sit or stand, or are they in constant motion?
2. Which parts of their bodies do they move most often?
3. Can you isolate a gesture that is repeated over and over by different members of the cultural system?
4. List several ways that members punctuate their verbal communications using kinesic components.
5. Can you isolate any instances of kinesic agreement or or disagreement?

Chapter 4

Ecological Systems

The vast majority of people surviving past childhood have spent the bulk of their time working to get "necessities." Culture cannot exist without providing sufficient calories to sustain the physical health of individual group members, adequate shelter to protect them from the elements, and the other goods and equipment deemed essential for a decent life. Obvious as these observations may seem, it is important to remember that culture not only mediates between the individual and his experience, allowing him to derive meaning; it also mediates between the human group and its environment, allowing the group to derive subsistence.

Physical anthropologists have called culture the adaptation of the human species. They define the term, in the technical sense employed in evolutionary studies, as the specialized means used by a species to derive life's requirements from a given ecological niche. Just as birds use their wings, keen eyesight, and sharp claws to find food in trees or mid-air, men use the knowledge they have acquired, the skills they have learned, and the tools they have made to find food in a variety of circumstances. The analogy is meant precisely: excellent evidence exists that tool-making traditions and control of fire existed among man's ancestors before they crossed the final threshold to *homo sapiens* status, and that it was the possession of this technology that influenced the further direction of evolution. Unlike other animal species, which depend on modifications of their bodies to enhance their adaptations, man now depends primarily on cultural learning and equipment to extend his abilities.

Every population of organisms lives in a dynamic relationship with its environment. Before its elevation to superstar status, *ecology* was an ordinary technical term meaning the study of that relationship. A population, if it is to survive, must meet its needs from the resources provided by its environment. The population, however, by its presence and its life processes, affects the other species present as well as the inanimate objects composing the environment. For this reason we say the relationship is dynamic. Thus, for example, a population of birds feeds on a certain type of insect, seriously influencing the numbers and distribution of members of the insect species. The insects, in turn, pollinate one species of vegetation and feed upon the foliage of another; the survival chances of each of these species are affected by the insect. A change in any of these species affects the others. A blight on the foliage plant may spell hard times for the insects, which in turn reduces the amount of pollination and also depletes the diets of the birds. A rise in the market for bird feathers might lead to a marked increase in the number of birds killed by man. The insects multiply rapidly, defoliating one type of plant but increasing pollination of the other.

Each species has, through a lengthy process of evolution, developed mechanisms that insure survival under a specific range of circumstances; changes in these circumstances influence, for good or ill, its chances of survival. Man, as an animal species, lives within these limitations. Man's ecological niche, however, differs markedly from that of other animals. It is physiologically narrow, but ecologically vast. That is, man can only exist within a narrow range of body temperature and caloric and nutritional intake. He exists, however, on every continent and in all but a few geographical and ecological circumstances. Man has lived in tropical, temperate, and arctic zones, in deserts, jungles, and grasslands, on the tops of mountains and at the bottom of the sea, even on the face of the moon. Possibly no other species except the cockroach has so large a geographic range. No animal—mammal, reptile, or fish—occurs naturally in so many environments. But, of course, no other animal has culture.

The secret of man's success is technology. By technology, we mean all the devices man uses to achieve his purposes in the material world: all the tools he makes, all the skills he learns in using them, all the knowledge that tool-use implies. Some anthropologists like to refer to *Homo sapiens* as *Homo faber* (man the artisan) because they believe that the purposeful and systematic use of tools to extend the individual's power is the mark of the human species. Although some other primate species are known to use found objects such as sticks or bones to achieve short-term goals such as reaching a banana or extracting termites from a termite hill, they do not appear to have developed *traditions* of tool-making and tool-using. This is a crucial point. What appears to distinguish man is the transmission of technical knowledge across generations and the accumulation of experience over time. Ordinarily, a person learning a skill, whether it be arrowhead making or computer programming, does not set out to invent the skill by himself. Rather, he seeks instruction from an expert who shows him how it is done. Any given worker at a craft may develop an innovation that improves the product and may pass this along to others. It is rare, however, for an individual to invent a whole new technique. Even scientists famous for their discoveries have actually built on the work of many predecessors.

If each individual working to learn a skill stands on the shoulders of the masters who have gone before, it is obvious that symbolic communication plays a significant role in technology and distinguishes it from the occasional use of an object as a tool. Particular craft traditions are generally strongly tied to particular social or cultural groups. Archaeologists, for example, can distinguish prehistoric peoples and follow their travels, invasions, and development by the differences in their pottery styles.

Learning the technology of one's people is a large share of the work of youth. In our society, young people learn to read; type; drive cars; keep their wits about them in supermarkets; run sewing machines, adding machines, saws, scissors, pocket calculators, and all the other things they will need to know in order to control their society's technology. In other societies, young people learn to handle bullocks and hand plows, saddle a camel, bake bread on a dung-fired stove, distinguish the tracks of a wounded giraffe from those of a healthy one, know when roots have reached the point of maximum juiciness, or whatever they will need to know in order to live in the jungle, desert, or mountain village in which their people find themselves.

LEVELS OF TECHNOLOGY

Technologies exist at all levels of complexity, and social scientists have classified them as "primitive" to "advanced," or "simple" to "complex." It is unfortunate that this classification carries certain overtones of superiority or inferiority to ethnocentric Westerners, who tend to evaluate other cultures on the basis of their technological advancement. The development of material culture bears no relationship to complexity of social organization, value systems, or art forms. Probably the most complex kinship system known to man developed among the Australian aborigines, who possessed one of the world's simplest technologies. Anthropology students ordinarily need to do advanced study in social organization before they grasp the workings of Australian marriage classes, a system so involved that it can only be accurately charted in three dimensions. Every illiterate aborigine, however, carried the system in his head and used it with perfect ease. It cannot be convincingly argued, furthermore, that the technologically advanced societies have developed more satisfactory explanations of the mystery of death or the meaning of life; more humane treatment for widows, the aged, or orphans; or more moving symbolic interpretations of life than have the less advanced societies. The so-called great religions all developed among peoples with relatively simple technologies.

A limited or simple technology in no way implies limited knowledge or skills. Most simple technologies depend on vast bodies of extremely detailed and subtle information stored in the memories of illiterate people. Hunters and gatherers, for example, must know in detail the habits and signs of many species and the developmental cycles, structures, and uses of hundreds of plants. Nomadic herdsmen must know in detail the topography and flora of large ranges of territory and must also be keen students of both weather and veterinary medicine.

Two famous examples from the Eskimos, possessors of one of the sparsest but most sophisticated technologies on earth, demonstrate this point. Living as nomads in one of the most difficult of human habitats, the Eskimos use their wits in place of cumbersome equipment. For hunting polar bear, for example, the Eskimos combine knowledge of animals and engineering skill to construct a fiendishly effective little device. A thin piece of bone is sharpened at both ends, then wound into a tight spring. This is placed between two pieces of meat that is then frozen solid. The hunter places this bait in a spot frequented by the intended quarry. The bear smells and swallows the meat, which is then melted by the animal's body temperature, releasing the spring, which snaps open, piercing the bear's stomach walls with its sharp points. The hunter, with no danger to himself, merely waits for the huge beast to bleed to death.

With the same ingenuity and knowledge of animal habits, the Eskimos devised a means of protecting the family's valuable sled dogs from attacks by hungry wolves. A shiny knife is placed in a snow bank at wolf-eye level. The object catches the eye of a passing wolf, who goes to investigate. He licks the knife, cutting his own tongue or mouth. The taste of blood encourages the ravenous animal to continue licking until he is covered with his own blood. The wolf's companions smell the blood and, hungry themselves, attack their own pack-mate. As the injured wolf defends itself, others become wounded, and a general melee ensues in which the starving wolves kill or weaken each other.

Technologically simple societies require highly developed skills. This Guatemalan Indian woman will perform many operations to transform the fibrous yucca leaf into a garment like the one she wears. (courtesy of Daniel Early)

Technologically simpler societies exploit the resources of their environment more fully than do advanced societies, as can be seen in this photograph of a Mexican market. (courtesy of Daniel Early)

TECHNOLOGY, ENVIRONMENT, AND SOCIAL ORGANIZATION

It is the joining of technology with environmental resources that produces the salient features of an ecological system. Thus, for example, Arabian nomads wandered for centuries over lands containing the vast oil supplies that are presently transforming their country. Only the technology of the internal combustion engine and oil drillings transformed a geological feature into a cultural fact.

Moreover, whether they are whittled tree limbs or microprinted transistors, the tools used by men and women are embedded in social and cultural systems. Human relationships, as well as tools and skill, are needed if a group is to make a living, and the social arrangements a group adopts tend to be related to its environmental resources and available technology.

Rhoades and Thompson (1975), for example, observed that marked social similarities exist between the German-speaking villagers of the Swiss Alps and the Sherpa villagers of the Himalayas, who inhabit very similar mountain environments. Both groups earn their living from the same combination of field agriculture and animal herding. Both groups also organize their social life around nearly identical property and governmental arrangements. For groups of such divergent cultural origins to resemble one another so closely illustrates the effect of environment on social organization.

Because of this relationship, a change in technology can drastically change both the resultant ecological balance and the social organization. Arabian Bedouin society, which most people regard as the quintessential desert adaptation, is a relatively late development (Bulliet, 1975). It came about only after the domestication of the camel, the animal that made possible the exploitation of marginal desert lands, and the invention of the North Arabian camel saddle, which permitted the most efficient use of the animal. Similarly, the advent of the horse, after Spanish colonization of America, made possible the development of the house-mounted, buffalo-hunting Plains Indian society that many Americans think of as the archetypal Indian way of life. Without the horse, the Indians would never have been able to exploit the vast resources of bison available on the Plains.

Changes in the relationship between technology and environment ultimately affect social organization, as well. The development of a new technology is one way of effecting a change. A change in natural resources would also affect social organization. Pastner (1975), for example, has documented the influence of prolonged drought on the Baluchi tribesmen of the Makran district of Pakistan. When pasture became too sparse to support the many ranging groups formerly found among this people, many of the smaller herders banded together to pool their labor. By changing their social organization this way, they were able to maximize opportunities for wage labor among settled populations while still assuring that their herds were adequately supervised.

As with other animal species, man's major task is getting food. It is easy

The camel is highly adapted to desert travel. (courtesy of Claudia Crawford)

to forget the primacy of this need when one lives in a land of 24-hour grocery stores and omnipresent fast-food shops, a land where less than 10 percent of the population has anything whatsoever to do with growing the food supply. An industrial food production system and elaborate transportation facilities have removed most Americans from any direct connection with food production. We only remember our extreme dependency when an occasional strike or disaster cuts normal supply lines. Manhattan Island, for example, where only the rare resident grows so much as a tomato for his own table, could be totally cut off from vital supplies within a week, or less, of a trucking strike.

We Americans view the food-getting activities of most of humanity as if they were taking place on another planet. Many city-bred American children think that food comes packaged in the natural state. "They taste like they're made of peanut butter," a little boy said when he tasted his first peanuts. Euell Gibbons became nationally known for his books suggesting the revolutionary idea that good, nourishing food may be found growing wild in forests and fields. The closest that most Americans ever get to foraging is to trek up and down the aisles of a supermarket.

FOOD COLLECTING

Yet, for 99 percent of the time that man has lived on the earth, people have lived off the land, hunting wild animals or gathering uncultivated plants. Put another way, of all of the estimated 80 billion people who ever lived, 90 percent have lived by hunting and gathering, 6 percent as active food producers, and only 4 percent as denizens of industrial societies like our own (Ember and Ember 1973:87).

Early in man's career, hunters and gatherers exploited much larger areas than they do now. The fertile regions currently devoted to agriculture and industry must have provided relatively abundant livelihoods to the peoples who once foraged and hunted in them. Today, however, hunters and gatherers inhabit only the most barren and marginal areas of the world, areas too inhospitable to interest farmers or herders. Among the fewer than 30,000 remaining food collectors are the Bushmen and Aborigines, who exploit desert environments in southern Africa and Australia, respectively; the Mbuti Pgymies, who exploit a central African tropical forest; and the Copper Eskimos, who live in the polar wastes of North America. They all inhabit areas into which competing ways of life had not previously spread because of the extreme rigor of the environment, but even these remote groups are being pushed off their lands.

The term food collecting includes those food-getting technologies that depend on naturally occurring resources of wild plants, animals, and fish. People using this type of technology make few attempts to control the occurrence of foods: generally, they perfect the skills of locating and taking food, whether animal or vegetable. There have been reports of some collecting peoples burning over forest land in order to prevent its evolution into stages that produce less desirable food resources and, of course, many hunters use domesticated dogs as allies in tracking. Beyond these small modifications, however, food collecting peoples exercise no control over nature's production.

Because a culture is much more than a technology, we can expect other aspects of the cultural systems of food collectors to reflect their subsistence practices. Using the Pygmies and Bushmen as examples, we find that certain uniformities do mark food collecting societies. In general, the people live in small bands and are nomadic, moving from place to place with the seasons and with other changes affecting food resources because no one place provides sufficient food, either animal or vegetable, to sustain life permanently. Constant movement naturally restricts the amount of baggage people wish to lug around with them. Like seasoned travellers everywhere, hunters and gatherers travel light. Food collectors have few personal possessions, and those they do have are often ingeniously designed to provide maximum utility for minimum weight and bulk; this gives rise to much of the technological ingenuity we mentioned earlier. Many of their material items, like housing structures, are small ones that can be left behind and easily manufactured at the new camp.

With only a small number of basic necessities to call his or her own, a food collector cannot endow possessions with important social overtones; no differentiation of possessions along lines of social prestige exists in these societies. Indeed, very little social differentiation exists at all, except by age and sex. Hunting and gathering societies are generally *egalitarian.* This is true, in part, because everyone of a given sex does the same sort of work and because products are widely shared within the group. In addition, the factors that tend to affect the success of one individual, mainly weather and quantities of game and plants, tend to affect everyone about equally. And finally, each individual must exercise a high degree of independence and individuality to carry out his or her work successfully.

Both sexes contribute vitally to group survival. The women, burdened with young children, generally remain relatively close to camp. Their search for roots, berries, nuts, and other vegetable food produces a fairly dependable and predictable supply of foods that is the basic, everyday subsistence of the group. The men range farther, often leaving camp for days at a time while on the hunt. The unpredictable luck of the hunt means there are sudden gluts of food alternating with periods of scarcity; thus, although meat supplements the vegetable fare provided by the women it is generally too irregular to serve as the bulk of subsistence (Lee, 1968).

The sudden catch of a large animal provides the hunter with far more meat than he and his family can eat before spoilage occurs, while many other men hunting that same day will have no luck at all. Hunters and gatherers therefore "bank" available meat by distributing it widely within the group. Often a certain share belongs to the hunter, and other specific shares by right belong to his relatives; they in turn give some to their relatives, until all members of the band share in the feast. In return, when another man has a good day, the first hunter (and all others in the band) will share his meat. In societies practicing group hunting, meat is likewise distributed to all, regardless of actual participation in the hunt. Food collecting societies emphasize relations based on sharing and reciprocity: people give and take freely without immediate expectation of return.

This de-emphasis of individual property extends to land as well, which is held communally by kin groups rather than privately by individuals. Constant movement renders personal ownership of specific plots of land useless, in any case. Groups therefore hold a communal right to exploit certain territories. They try to remain on good terms with as many neighboring groups as possible in case extreme scarcity in their own territory forces them to search farther afield. Through marriage ties, food collecting groups form kinship alliances over a wide geographic area. In addition, bands have flexible membership and, up to the limit of the band's territorial resources, generally accept new members who have some tie of kinship or friendship.

We can see that food collecting societies are built around resources that are finite, even severely limited. The land can only support small numbers of people distributed at low density. Bands based on food collecting therefore tend to be relatively sparsely spread across the land and to contain no more than 20 to 50 persons. It is unlikely that this was true when hunters and gatherers dominated the earth and exploited more fertile territories.

Plant and animal domestication

About 10,000 years ago, when the population of the entire world was two-thirds that of modern-day New York City, people began to take food production out of the exclusive control of nature. They began to domesticate plants and animals and to manipulate their reproduction and growth. Exactly how and where this monumental change came about is a matter of some dispute, but it is likely that plants and animals were independently domesticated at several times and in several places. All over the world, food producers, because of larger population densities, were gradually able to edge food collectors off the more desirable land.

Food-producing technologies take a number of forms, depending on the available soil and water and on the presence of easily domesticated plant or animal species. In some cases, such as that of Old World grain farming, native plant and animal species provided the raw material for domestication. In others, such as the cultivation of breadfruit in the Caribbean, or potatoes in Europe, imported species proved adaptable to new conditions in foreign lands. Anthropologists have divided food producing technologies into three major types: horticulture, or farming with simple tools; advanced agriculture, which uses more sophisticated tools than does horticulture; and pastoralism, an outgrowth of agriculture that depends on large numbers of domesticated animals.

HORTICULTURE

The first form of food cultivation is technically called horticulture, which means "growing in gardens." This name gives some picture of the method of production, which is to employ hand tools, such as the dibble, or digging stick, to cultivate small plots. Many modern-day horticulturalists live in tropical or semi-tropical regions, where the leached jungle soil loses its fertility after a few years. Horticulturalists solve this problem with a method known as slash-and-burn, or swidden, farming. Every few years a cultivated plot is abandoned to the forest and allowed to become overgrown. The gardeners move on, clearing other jungle plots of brush and trees and burning the vegetation over, leaving the ashes to lie on the land as fertilizer. These new gardens are then used for a few years before they too must be abandoned. The repeated fallow periods, however, allow relatively infertile soil to provide intermittent harvests. With a sufficient base of land, a horticultural group can earn a living entirely, or nearly so, from cultivation.

Horticulturalists remain in one place for at least a couple of years, and therefore can store food in some quantity. Their food supply permits more densely populated communities to be formed and more material possessions to be acquired than does the skimpier food supply of hunters and gatherers. It also allows some social differentiation, thus permitting a few persons to spend at least part of their time at pursuits other than food-getting. Typical of such groups are the Yanomamö of Brazil, who cultivate small slash-and-burn gardens deep in the jungle. The Yanomamö live in semi-permanent, fortified villages which sometimes contain up to several hundred persons. The Yanomamö also have part-time village chieftains and a higher elaboration of ritual and etiquette than do many food collecting groups.

It is not clear that horticulture is more efficient—that is, that a given quantity of human energy expended produces a larger return of calories—than food collecting. It is clear, however, that horticulture permits the development of more highly organized, larger, and thus more dominant socie-

Using fire to clear land for coffee planting in Mexico, an example of slash and burn cultivation. (courtesy of Daniel Early)

ties. A food collector band would be hard put to defend its territory against the onslaught of a horticultural group.

AGRICULTURE

The addition of some elements missing in horticulture—the plow, draft animals, irrigation, and other water control technologies—produces advanced agriculture, which literally means "field-growing." Agriculture permits the growth of large, densely populated, permanent settlements. Agricultural societies occupy most of the earth's prime growing land and a good deal of the marginal growing land as well. Agriculture tends to produce larger surpluses than does horticulture, and therefore can support large numbers of individuals and whole towns that do not work directly in food production. Agricultural societies thus contain full-time specialists in arts and crafts, religion, government, or warfare. The complexity of the division of labor implies a greater complexity of social organization. Not only does differentiation of social levels, or stratification, exist, but a market-oriented economic system typically develops and state-level political systems evolve. Agriculture is a necessary prelude to urbanization and the complex societies known as civilizations.

Plow agriculture on the Bolivian Altiplano. (courtesy of Arthur B. Hayes, III)

PASTORALISM

Pastoralists, as a result of their method of food production, share some of the characteristics of both horticulturalists and agriculturalists. Pastoralism tends to exist as part of a more complex society, but herders generally are not fully self-sufficient in producing the necessities of daily life. They often trade with agricultural peoples to obtain certain foods and goods they cannot produce themselves. Pastoralists generally exploit marginal environments unsuited for agriculture or horticulture, such as desert and mountain regions. This ecological adaptation permits the support of specialized pastoral groups and brings their products of marginal environments into the region's general economy.

Like collectors and horticulturalists, pastoralists must contend with an environment that cannot provide them permanent subsistence in one place. They therefore move according to the seasonal availability of pasturage and water, either between higher and lower elevations, as in Iran, Switzerland, and the Himalayas, or between permanent wells and pastures deep in the desert, as among the Arabian Bedouin. Nomadic and semi-nomadic herders are far from aimless in their travels, however. Rather than risk their valuable animals, and indeed their own lives, on unplanned wanderings, nomadic herders keenly study climate and geography and carefully plan their movements, generally to well-known places visited at certain times each year. Only a rare condition of extreme scarcity will force pastoralists from their accustomed course and into unfamiliar territory. The dangers of such excursions are numerous. Not only would the herders not know the locations of various resources and the best routes between them, but the pasture and water supply probably belong to some other group, whose hospitality depends both on their own circumstances and the social relations prevailing between the two groups.

As with other technologies, nomadic pastoralism makes certain demands on the lives of the people who practice it. As we might expect, their material possessions, except for their herds, are not numerous, nor do they occupy an important place in the people's lives. Although animals may be owned by individual families, pastures and wells tend to belong to an entire group, with kinship status determining rights of access. Herders thus exploit territories either by right of ownership by their own tribe or by permission of the owners. Although pastoral societies tend to emphasize organization around kinship segments that expand or contract according to need, the planning of cyclical movements requires a social system emphasizing clear assignment of authority and strong in-group loyalty and obedience.

INDUSTRIAL SOCIETY

The fifth major technological and ecological adaptation may be defined, in part, as the system in which human society attempts to transcend the limits of environment rather than developing a dynamic equilibrium within them. This is the industrial system, based on the harnessing of new forms of power, especially those obtained from burning fossil fuels. The replacement of human and animal labor and other power sources, such as wind, with the products of combustion and nuclear power, so vastly increases the energy available per capita that feats of production impossible under simpler systems become commonplace. Industrial societies are technically a subset of advanced agricultural societies, but they have developed such extreme characteristics that they appear to rate a separate category. In the most extreme cases, fewer than 10 percent of the population are involved in food getting, while the rest perform a huge variety of other tasks. Social differentiation in industrial societies is even greater than it is in simpler agricultural societies; the need for organization and control also expands, so large numbers of people specialize in administering the work of others.

The vast production possibilities and high degree of social differentiation increase the social significance of material possessions. Specialization tends to fragment the industrial culture into a number of subcultures that communicate with one another only imperfectly. Wide areas become tied into an expanding web of transportation and market relationships. Technological advance breeds technological advance in an accelerating body of technical knowledge. Techniques of circumventing, and even subverting, the natural environment abound; there are simple ones like air conditioning and complex ones like weather control. Deserts are made to bloom. The entire paraphenalia of industrial society is transfered to the North Slope of Alaska. Men even bring their capsulized environment to the surface of the moon.

The physical environment appears to exert a limiting, rather than a determining, influence on the technologies we have been discussing. Thus, it is technically possible for someone living on the Kansas plains to be either a hunter and gatherer or an agriculturalist. No one, however, practices pastoralism in a dense jungle. Given a particular technological level, the physical environment does not determine which food-getting technique a group will use, but it does provide some limits of feasibility. About 75 percent of intensive agricultural societies occur in environments that are not in the tropics; about 80 percent of horticultural societies occur in environments that are.

In industrial societies, the environment becomes less a matrix for society and more a source of raw materials. And this, as Americans are coming to realize, is the great weakness of industrial society. Other technologies depend on renewable resources of land, air, and water. Industrial society gobbles up nonrenewable resources of energy, minerals, and land as it seeks to produce more for an ever-larger population. Industrial society has developed the densest settlements in the history of mankind, and has permitted a drastic transformation in the scale of human population.

Authorities estimate that the human population of the whole world numbered under 10 million at the time of the widespread adoption of agriculture. By 1650, it had increased to 500 million. The next increment of 500 million occurred by 1800. World population then began to accelerate ominously: the 2 billion mark was reached in 1930, and humanity doubled again, reaching 4 billion by 1975. In three years during the middle of the 1970s, the net growth of human population equalled the total population of the United States.

Despite industrial man's cavalier attitude toward the limited resources of the planet, and despite his ability to reshape his immediate environment to his own purposes, man remains, at bottom, a physical animal. Our species must retain a balance with the possibilities of our physical environment if we are to survive. No evidence exists from our past evolution that we as a species are immortal. Other species that fell out of balance with their environment paid the price in distress and extinction. We have freed ourselves from many of the constraints suffered by our less technologically advanced ancestors, but not from this basic relationship.

CONCLUSIONS

What do these brief sketches of the various major technological ecological adaptations tell us about the relationship of man to his environment? A first conclusion might be that the concept of environment is rather more complex for man than for other species. On the one hand, we may discuss the physical environment, those features of climate, flora, fauna, and topography that form the physical character of a geographic locality. Man does not function solely in terms of these features, however. He lives in a cultural environment, which we may define as his physical environment modified by technology and by the other human groups occupying it.

FIELD PROJECT: ECOLOGICAL SYSTEMS

PHYSICAL ENVIRONMENT
  A. Describe the climate, geography, and terrain of the territory of the group that you are studying. Tell how these aspects of the physical environment structure the behavior of the group by answering the following questions:
  1. Do changes in the physical environment produce changes in the group?
  2. In what way does the group utilize the energy (including food) resources available in its environment?
  3. Does the group's technology limit the kinds of resources that it can utilize?
  B. If the group that you are studying interacts mostly within the confines of a building, describe the decor in the same way that an interior decorator might. In other words, take a representative space and describe the surfaces (wall, ceiling, and floor) by material, covering, color, and so on. Describe what it is like to be there: is it noisy or quiet (or do they play Muzak), bright or dim? Is the air smoky, scented, or clean? Now tell how those aspects of decor affect the behavior of the members of the cultural system.

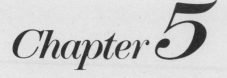

Chapter 5

Economic Systems

"Are you going back to work soon?" a man asked a woman who had left her job to care for her three children and a large house. "What do you think I'm *doing?*" the woman demanded.

The realm of phenomena included in the term "economics" has traditionally been one of the most difficult to understand. The difficulty arises not so much from the intractability of the material itself as from the awkwardness of the category. Westerners, and especially Americans, are profoundly ethnocentric about the parts of their lives touched by money; it is easier for most American students, for example, to grasp the validity, or at least the potential validity, of other religions, than to admit the validity of economic systems that differ profoundly from their own. The money nexus is the truly central institution of our lives, probably the dominant shaper of our values.

The confusion in the example of the woman leaving her job arises because we tend to confound economics with money. That is what the discipline of economics studies in Western societies: the things money will buy (which turns out to be just about everything). Money dominates our thinking even when we don't know it. Many observers have suggested, for example, that both the submerged position of women in American society and the women's liberation movement arise in part because traditional women's work—housework and child care—usually receives no monetary compensation. The labor of housewives does not count as work in the national income figures the government reports; all the food and clothing prepared by wives and mothers, all the miles driven, rooms painted, children taught, and illnesses tended do not count as "production" in the gross national product. Nor do women doing this work count as members of the labor market.

The woman in the story was right in saying that she worked in the sense that her days were filled with continuous chores, some requiring a fair degree of skill, physical strength, organization, and concentration. But the man was right too. In the terms of the money nexus that controls our lives, "working" means engaging in some activity that brings a monetary return.

If we take this little incident and generalize it to other cultural systems, we can begin to grasp the problems Americans encounter when they consider economic systems different from their own. Many societies use money for markedly fewer transactions than we do; some societies make no use of it at all. How, then, can we study their economic systems? From the standpoint of Western beliefs, we obviously cannot. But, as the housewife would point out, work does go on: goods are produced and products exchanged, despite the absence of money. Obviously, something is wrong with our categorization.

Our mistake has been to ethnocentrically view economics as money and the behavior revolving around it, instead of taking an overall view of the functions of economic institutions. An underlying feeling tells us that something corresponding to economics must exist in all societies; empirical data tell us that money does not. The concepts behind the word "economics" existed long before our present economic system; they survive in the somewhat redundant term, "home economics." *Economics* comes from a Greek root meaning "home management"; this has to do with getting the products needed for daily life, organizing the contributions of the various family members, and budgeting supplies in light of projected needs. In this sense, surely, economics exists in every society. And if this sense of the word can be expanded to cover the whole society, rather than just the household, it comes close to what is really meant by "economics."

FUNCTIONS OF ECONOMIC SYSTEMS

Economists, it turns out, only incidentally study money. If you ask them, they will tell you that their true interest is the allocation of scarce goods. Desirable commodities, they explain, fall into two categories. A few, like air, are so plentiful that there is enough to go around. People take all the air they need and still leave enough for everybody else. So there is no problem allocating air to the various members of the population (except in cases in which pollution threatens the supply of everyone). Economists call commodities of this type *free goods.* Most commodities, however, do not exist in sufficient quantities to satisfy everyone who might like to have them. There are not enough diamond rings or World Series tickets to go around. There are not even enough hot dogs or parking places. So, to prevent social chaos, each society must devise methods to decide who wears real diamonds and who wears paste; who sits over the dugout and who stands on the street outside. This is what the economic system does. It decides how, when, where, and by whom goods are to be produced (production), allocates rights to resources and products (ownership), and determines how rights may be acquired in goods one did not start out with (distribution). Money serves these functions in our society, and serves them so nearly exclusively of other methods that we tend to ignore the fact that other methods of allocation are possible. But in this light, it becomes obvious that although money does not exist in all societies, economic systems certainly do.

A logical place to begin a study of how economic systems allocate scarce goods is with a consideration of how goods are produced in the first place. Here we will consider not the technological means used in production, but the organization of the people who apply the technology. How does a society assign individuals to various tasks, and how does it divide the tasks up to begin with? Assuming that several different tasks must be carried out routinely, and assuming that constraints of time, space, or skill do not allow each individual to perform every task himself, a society must devise some method of deciding who does what. This permits different individuals to engage in different tasks at the same time, all individuals to develop skills in their assigned work, and the social unit to benefit from a number of different contributions.

DIVISION OF LABOR

The assignment of tasks to different individuals, or, in social terms, to different sets of individuals, is technically known as the division of labor. Two sets of assumptions underlie a society's division of labor. The first concerns the criteria defining sets of tasks that are believed to go together; the second concerns the criteria defining the sets of people appropriate to each set of tasks. Thus, for example, our society recognizes performing surgery, making diagnoses, prescribing drugs, and reading x-rays as a single set. Another set, in American society, consists of collecting fares, driving a bus, and issuing transfer tickets. In Britain, however, collecting fares and driving a bus belong to two separate sets. One is performed by the driver, the other by the conductor. In our society knitting goes into a single set with sewing and washing clothes. In Arabian Bedouin society, however, knitting goes along with camel herding, while sewing goes into a set along with erecting tents.

Work sets

The range and number of sets varies markedly within societies. Among technologically simple peoples, there tend to be a few large sets consisting of many different tasks. Technologically more complex societies tend to have a very large number of sets, each of which contains a relatively small number of carefully circumscribed tasks. Food collectors, for example, typically divide work into two major sets. One consists of collection of plant foods, cooking of all types of food, preparation of clothing, care of children, and possibly construction of shelters. The other includes hunting, manufacture and repair of weapons and implements, and defense of the group. Our highly industrialized society, on the other hand, recognizes hundreds of discrete work sets. The United States government publishes a book of several hundred pages describing the more common jobs held by Americans; the classification of work sets is in fact a specialty in the field of personnel work. Thus, for example, work is so minutely subdivided in our society that your college may well have a special person who does nothing but teach anthropology, or perhaps even several persons, each of whom teaches a specific portion of anthropology.

Obviously, the nature of the work sets recognized by a society is crucial to both the character of the society and to the quality of work achieved within it. If all or most of the people in a group do the same work, they tend to share with each other a body of meanings, values, and ideas that mark them as a group. The daily experience of each individual is usually relatively varied as he or she carries out a number of different tasks at different times of the day or at different times of the year. In the social sphere, individuals are tied to one another through several different role relationships; that is, roles are *multiplex*. In a technologically complex society, on the other hand, a group consists of individuals doing different kinds of jobs. Most people in complex societies therefore lack a first-hand grasp of the work done by others; consequently there are fewer widely-shared bodies of values and meanings. Instead, the society will contain many small groups who share the knowledge, values, and attitudes that go with a particular type of work. It is likely, furthermore, that each individual will carry out a smaller variety of tasks and that there will be more repetition of these same specialized tasks. In the social arena, roles are *simplex;* that is, individuals tend to relate to one another through one role relationship only, thus leading to a greater number of, but more formal and less affective, relationships.

The interdependence among the members of these two types of societies has a different texture as well. If nearly everybody does the same kind of work, they can help one another in times of misfortune but have the possibility of maintaining a relatively high degree of self-reliance. This type of

interdependence is usually referred to as *mechanical solidarity* because
the cohesion of the group derives from the fact that all individuals perform
the same work and share the same beliefs and values. If many different
work categories exist, however, each individual depends on others for many
functions he cannot possibly carry out himself. An anthropology teacher,
for example, depends on a number of persons, most of them strangers, for
food, shelter, clothing, transportation, and other luxuries and necessities of
life. All those producers of goods and services, conversely, depend on the
anthropologist when they want to learn what he or she can teach them.
Each has developed a high degree of skill in a particular activity, but none
can survive without the others. This interdependence is usually termed
organic solidarity since each specialist can be compared to a particular
body organ like the heart or liver, and the continued existence and functioning of the body is dependent on all the specialists doing their separate jobs.

Labor sets

In addition to dividing tasks into categories, a society must also divide its
members into sets deemed appropriate to the tasks. The criteria used in this
division vary widely from culture to culture, although certain common
themes appear to be close to universal. The simplest and most common
criterion is sex: some tasks are deemed appropriate to men and others to
women. Among food collectors, for example, the collecting–cooking–child
care set belongs to women, and the hunting–weapons-making–defense set
to the men. To a large extent, this assignment appears to follow logically
from the different physiology of the two sexes. Childbearing and lactation
render women considerably less mobile than men and make them naturally
more suited to the care of small children. Men, on the other hand, have both
the larger size and greater mobility required for hunting.

Although nearly every society recognizes a division of labor by sex,
many assignments lack this clear-cut physiological basis. Beyond the facts
that no man can bear or nurse a baby and that the average man is larger
and stronger than the average woman, there is little that is "natural" about
assignment of tasks to the sexes. Most horticultural societies consider cultivation of plants to be women's work, or at least work appropriate to women.
Most agriculturalists, on the other hand, believe that cultivation of plants
is suited only to men. Some authors ascribe this difference to the presence
or absence of draft animals; in many cases, however, the care of dairy
animals is assigned to women.

As we mentioned earlier, knitting carries strong overtones of femininity
in our society; it is even mythically tied to childbearing. The thought of a
man knitting is at least jocular and possibly embarrassing. Among the

Buying and selling in the market is a male work set in Arabia.
(courtesy of Claudia Crawford)

Arabian Bedouin, however, nomadic herdsmen whose male members pride themselves on their manhood and bravery, men pass the time with their flocks knitting uddercovers for their lactating camels. The uddercovers keep the young camels from taking all their mother's milk. To the Bedouin, knitting goes "naturally" with herding as men's work. Women's work consists of such "obviously" feminine tasks as erecting tents and weaving rugs.

Industrialized societies, as well as preindustrial ones, divide work according to sex. Typing and other subordinate office tasks have for generations been archetypical women's jobs in America. Although the post of secretary had, until the late nineteenth century, been an honorable, even prestigious, position for an educated young man, by the early twentieth century secretarial work had become firmly entrenched as women's work. Some countries, however, retain office jobs as a male domain even today. In Pakistan and other countries that observe the ritual segregation of the sexes known as *purdah,* men and women who do not belong to the same family may not associate with one another. Women, in fact, may not even be seen by men outside their own families. Women, therefore, cannot properly work as secretaries to male executives; these jobs go to men, as do all the jobs involving public contact that in the West are routinely filled by women: receptionists, store clerks, waitresses. Those women who hold jobs generally do so in totally feminine establishments such as girls' schools and maternity hospitals. Women staff these female institutions at all levels, instead of filling the subordinate positions in sexually mixed institutions as in our culture. Because women can only consult female doctors, some purdah countries have a far higher percentage of women physicians than the United States.

Although it is the most common one for assigning work, sex is far from the only criterion used. Throughout the world, age divides people into work categories. The United States Constitution, for example, specifies the minimum ages of congressmen, senators, and the president. We also use age to remove workers from the labor force and lessen competition for jobs by arbitrarily declaring that persons of 65 or 70 are too old to continue working, even though their physical prowess may have no bearing whatsoever on their work. We also specify the minimum age at which workers may enter the labor force, and restrict some jobs to people who have reached their legal majority.

Many other personal attributes may figure in the assignment of work. Skill and ability, of course, are prominent criteria all over the world; the method of determining skill may vary, however. In some situations, merely demonstrating an aptitude by doing the work well may suffice; in others a would-be worker needs accreditation by a person or group socially recognized as authoritative. We are likely to permit someone to work as a housepainter, for example, merely because he or she shows a knowledge of the work. But we are unlikely to permit people to perform brain surgery or offer Mass simply because they claim a knowledge of the procedure. In

Buying and selling in the market is a work set appropriate to both men and women in Latin America. (courtesy of Daniel Early)

many societies, religious practitioners need authorization either from a religious body or from a recognized teacher.

In addition to credentials, personal traits such as race, descent, or social class may figure in work assignments. Until recently, in the United States, for example, many kinds of work were unavailable to blacks for the simple reason of their race. Under the Indian caste system, birth is a major determinant of one's lifework. Many caste members enter the trade traditional to their group and learn the work from their parents. Although some caste members may enter other types of work, they are careful not to take up trades that are the preserve of some other caste. Other social considerations may enter into the assignment of work in some societies; in many cases, a class belief that a certain job is "above" or "beneath" a certain individual influences decisions.

OWNERSHIP

Working often entails using raw materials to produce goods and services. That is, the scarce resources of a society are consumed, or at least monopolized, to produce a certain finite amount of output. The facts of consumption and production raise the question of ownership. To prevent social chaos, each society must devise criteria determining access to scarce resources and rights to dispose of scarce products. Who, for example, has the right to plow the richest land? Who may graze his flocks in the best pasture and water them at the best waterhole, and who must make do with the worst? Who has the right to use the water in a river? How much land may each household clear to make its gardens? Who has the right to collect the fruits, berries, nuts, and roots? Who has the right to mine the gold or silver?

American society has devised one answer to these questions: private property, or the theory that a particular individual has exclusive and unlimited (or almost unlimited) access to and rights over any given object (or idea). This notion so permeates our thinking that we tend to refer to land as property, as in "He bought half an acre of property."

But private property is not the only reasonable solution to the problem of access to goods. In some situations, in fact, it is totally unreasonable. Imagine a band of food collectors roaming over a territory. They move from place to place according to the availability of game and plant materials. Now imagine how cumbersome life would be if they held to our views of private property. Collectors would find life impossible if they viewed their world as divided into small plots with individual people's names on them. No one person would come close to controlling sufficient resources to support himself, and everybody would be constantly embroiled in problems concerning permission, access, and fair exchange. Collectors, therefore, don't live in a world of individually-owned plots, but in a world of large territories identified with kinship groups. Individuals exploit particular resources by virtue of their membership in a group rather than of their exclusive ownership. For similar reasons, herders also tend to hold pasture and water resources in common.

Shifting horticulturalists take a slightly different view of the problem. No one plot of land will support a household permanently; the farmer clears a plot, works it for several years, and moves on. During the years he cultivates a plot, however, he invests considerable time and labor in it. Groups following this system tend to favor a combination of private and communal landholding. The social group as a whole formally owns the land. The individual who works it has rights to the use and produce of a plot as long as he keeps it under cultivation. After the plot is abandoned, however, it reverts to the group as a whole, to be given to some other cultivator at a later date. Tenure of this type is called *usufruct,* from the Latin term meaning "use of the fruits." Although very common among semi-sedentary peoples, it also occurs among sedentary groups. The Mexican *ejido* system, for example, permits the periodic reapportioning of land according to need.

One of the most important distinctions between usufruct tenure and private property is that the individual merely occupies the land and has no right to alienate it; that is, to turn it over permanently to someone outside of his group. In fact, he has no right to turn it over permanently to anybody. It ultimately belongs only to the group. A good deal of the bitterness and bloodshed in the settling of the American West resulted from a misunderstanding of this distinction. The Americans, accustomed only to private property, thought the Indian treaties represented the tribes' agreement to give up their lands totally and forever. The Indians, on the other hand, believing the land belonged to the tribes and ultimately to the gods, had no intention of alienating their land and banishing themselves; rather, they thought they were only permitting the whites to use their land, just as they used it. Misunderstanding of usufruct tenure brought grief to Africa as well. European colonizers gave tribesmen title to the land they happened to be working at the time, in total ignorance of the ecological and economic importance of their reserve land, which the Europeans viewed as unused, and therefore free for the taking.

Even in societies that recognize private property, some limitations exist. In the United States it is common to buy property without mineral rights. In Britain, the landed property of certain noble families has traditionally been entailed: a particular property belongs to the holder of a certain title and must be passed on intact to all future holders of the title. Any particular holder enjoys, as it were, usufruct during his lifetime, but can not alienate the property or any part of it. Muslim law, which recognizes private ownership of land, generally requires all property to be divided among heirs in shares set according to sex and degree of relationship. Properties in Muslim countries therefore tend to become fractionalized with the passing generations. A certain category of property, however, is exempt from division. Land left as a charitable foundation or *waqf* may not be divided. Rather, it is administered by a trustee for the benefit of a charitable cause. In mountain villages in Switzerland and Nepal, fields are owned privately but pastures communally. Even among ourselves, the government retains the power to seize private property by right of eminent domain.

Many possible forms of ownership and access exist between fully private and fully communal title. The Cuna Indians of San Blas Islands in Panama, for example, divide plants into a number of categories according to the type of access permitted. Plants growing wild, even on private land, are God's, and therefore free for the taking. Those that were planted belong to certain individuals. The rules of access to non-owners vary, however. A certain category of crops, such as mangoes, may be taken freely by anyone, without an obligation even to inform the owners. Some crops, such as pineapple or sugar cane, may be taken in small quantities without permission and consumed on the spot as refreshment. Others, such as limes, may be taken in small quantities without permission and used elsewhere. For crops such as cacao, which must be picked with care, the owner must be asked, and must generally accompany the recipient to do the picking. Rice may not be taken and must not even be asked for; the owner must offer it. In this complex ownership system, the definition of theft and the social sanction applied vary with the type of crop in question.

DISTRIBUTION OF GOODS AND SERVICES

Production of goods is really a preface to economics: only when goods change hands does economics truly begin. This insight—that the central economic issues have to do with distribution rather than production—was the beginning of both the modern science of economics and of the cross-cultural study of economic systems. In order to play this double role, the principle had to be discovered twice. Throughout the nineteenth century, scholars studying economic phenomena assumed that production, the expenditure of resources and labor, was the key both to Western capitalist economies and to the arcane practices of primitive peoples. Western economists grappled unsatisfactorily with the workings of the market, and anthropologists grouped people into categories such as those we used in the last chapter.

The break came in Western economics when Karl Menger and Alfred Marshall independently discovered the law of supply and demand: the principle that the value of an object derives not from the resources and labor that went into it, but from the fact that someone wants it badly enough to pay for it. If the price it will bring meets or exceeds what it cost to produce, the owner will sell it and the item will change hands. Value arises in exchange; goods are worth only what they will bring. The central fact of the Western economy is that goods change hands in the market; that is, according to the law of supply and demand. The central means of Western exchange is money. This discovery opened a broad highway for those studying Western economies, but it barred the way for those studying non-Western economies. If economics is the study of the market, then it cannot apply to primitive societies in which the market does not exist.

The break came in economic anthropology when Karl Polanyi (1944) discovered that, despite its overwhelming importance in Western society, the market is just one of several principles of distribution found in the world. Economic systems exist, he discovered, that totally ignore supply and demand and yet distribute goods according to principles just as systematic, predictable, and legitimate. Polanyi enumerated two major principles apart from the market, *reciprocity* and *redistribution,* although he recognized the possibility that others may exist. Polanyi went on to propose that the major difference between economies lies in the methods of allocation or distribution they emphasize—although one type dominates, others may be present as well.

Reciprocity

We can take advantage of Polanyi's proposal to gain some understanding of reciprocity and redistribution, because both exist in our society to a limited extent. Reciprocity consists of exchanges that grow out of personal relationships between people of equal or nearly equal social standing. The relationship exists apart from the exchange; indeed, the exchange is merely a facet of the relationship. Reciprocity can be defined as the giving and taking without the use of money. There are three different types of reciprocity. The first is called *generalized reciprocity,* which refers to gift giving without expectation of immediate or necessarily equal return. The second type is called *balanced reciprocity,* which is an exchange of goods and services whose values are roughly calculated as equal. Balanced reciprocity, as exemplified by barter, is much more explicit and short term than is generalized reciprocity, and the exchange of the goods and services is often more important than the friendship bond developed by the exchange. The third type of reciprocity is called *negative reciprocity,* and it is an attempt to take advantage of another for one's own self-interest.

Marshall Sahlins (1965) theorizes that the three kinds of reciprocity make up a continuum of exchange that is associated with kinship distance. Generalized reciprocity, he finds, is the rule for family and close kin. Balanced reciprocity is found among social equals who are not closely related, and negative reciprocity is usually only practiced with strangers or enemies. Generalized reciprocity is most commonly seen among hunters and gatherers who, as detailed in the last chapter, live in harsh environments and are highly dependent on one another for survival. In America, generalized reciprocity is most often found in the nuclear family. Parents and offspring give and take freely, with no accounts or records being kept.

Although balanced reciprocity occupies only a small place in American economic life, it shows itself in such magnitude that whole bureaucracies must organize major logistical efforts around it. Once a year, as if at a given signal, Americans engage in reciprocal exchange of Christmas cards. Several billion cards deluge the mails within the space of a few weeks. Forests of trees and oceans of ink are consumed in this annual ritual. Senders and recipients keep careful accounts of greetings sent and those received; the overtones of initiating the exchange by sending a card to someone new or of breaking off the exchange by not replying to one received reverberate throughout the relationship.

The rules of the exchange are precise and widely known. The missive must carry one or more of a repertory of symbols that identify it as a Christmas card: an ordinary letter or a card bearing an inappropriate symbol, such as a turkey or a rabbit, will not do. It must arrive during the month of December: cards knowingly sent to arrive later must carry the message "Happy New Year" in order to count. It must affect a note of relative informality and personal warmth: a Christmas card may not begin with "Dear Sir" or end "Sincerely Yours." And, most importantly, it must be reciprocated. That is, the sender must receive a card of similar correctness (although not of the same design) within the permissible time limit. If factors such as distance or ill health make timely reciprocation impossible, then an explanation and apology must be offered as soon as possible.

The most important aspect of the Christmas card exchange is that only a Christmas card will serve as a counter. One cannot, for example, send each of one's friends 25¢ and a note saying, "I didn't have time to buy a card, but here's the quarter it would have cost me." Such a letter might break off not only the Christmas card exchange, but the underlying friendship as well.

Redistribution

Redistribution is a form of exchange in which goods are collected by a central authority and then reallocated to members of the group. This system depends on the unequal relationship between the group member who contributes goods and the central authority who collects and then redistributes them. Once again, the relationship itself and the obligations it entails motivate the exchange. Redistribution is not often found in hunting and gathering or horticultural societies, but rather is found in societies with political hierarchies that have the specialized officials or agencies to coordinate the collection and subsequent redistribution. Most societies with redistributive economies are chiefdoms. The system of redistribution and the ranked social hierarchy that together characterize a chiefdom seem to reinforce each other. Most chiefdoms get their subsistence from relatively diverse environments, thus avoiding over-exploitation of resources and gaining some security from local food shortages. Thus, chiefdoms are capable of supporting larger and denser populations than are bands and tribes. Redistributive systems range from those in which goods are distributed equally to systems of gross inequality.

Redistribution exerts considerably more influence over the American economy than does reciprocity, and it also annually clogs the mails. Once a year, at a clearly given signal, Americans redistribute wealth in a great, complex ritual culminating in mid-April. Virtually every adult citizen files a declaration with the Internal Revenue Service, which gathers in the wealth for the federal government. In fact, the gathering goes on all year long, as does the redistribution. Throughout the spring, however, Americans spend millions of hours determining and justifying the size of their obligation.

Another modern form of redistribution occurs in religious groups that still practice tithing, or the contribution of one-tenth of one's income to the church. In this case, the member makes the contribution as a token of his or her membership; the church redistributes the wealth to clerical personnel, the poor, and others. The tithe is not a freewill gift, but a positive obligation. A teen-aged member of one particular church, for example, was criticized for not contributing a tenth of her baby-sitting money to the church.

Non-market economies

Economies dominated by methods of exchange other than the market naturally have a very different texture than our own. Personal relationships, whether with an equal trading partner or with a central authority, dominate, rather than the impersonal, short-term contract on which market exchange depends.

Probably the most famous example of reciprocity is brilliantly described by Bronislaw Malinowski in his classic study of the Trobriand Islands,

Argonauts of the Western Pacific (1922). The book describes a number of different economic institutions but concentrates on the Kula ring. Ironically, most American readers find the Kula strange and inexplicable, although its elements should be familiar to them. It contains, after all, the same social compulsion, rigid etiquette, and apparent irrationality as the Christmas card exchange.

In the Kula, male islanders exchange pieces of treasure, specifically, red shell necklaces and white shell arm bracelets, instead of folded pieces of paper. The exchange is far more complicated than a mere handing over of tributes, however. In the first place, these particular valuables may be used only in Kula exchange. In the second place, one may only exchange them with particular long-term partners. In the third place, all the people participating in the exchange live in a ring of islands, and each type of valuable moves in only one direction around the ring. Each member of the ring both gives and receives both types of valuables, but he gives or receives each type in only one direction. If, for example, he gives necklaces to his partners to the east, then he receives arm bands from them in exchange. He then gives arm bands to his partners to the west and receives necklaces from them in exchange. White shell armbands always travel counterclockwise; red shell necklaces travel in a clockwise direction.

The Kula exchange is a great event in Trobriand life. Lengthy preparations precede the exchange, and great pomp accompanies it. To reach their partners, men undertake long voyages in their ocean-going canoes. The object of the Kula exchange is not to accumulate pieces of treasure, but to hold them for a while and then pass them on. The goal, more particularly, is to possess and pass on fine and famous pieces of treasure. Like great diamonds, the finest necklaces and arm bands have names and histories, and great prestige accrues to a man who can attract important pieces and then bestow them on his partners.

Some anthropologists have seen in these trips and the more mundane commerce that they generate, an etic "reason" for the Kula ring. It is true, of course, that Kula traders often engage in ordinary barter with residents of their partners' communities and thus have a means of disposing of their island's specialized surplus goods. But this trade is an explanation for the Kula exchange only to the extent that the "reason" for the Christmas card exchange is to provide seasonal employment in the post office and a livelihood to card manufacturers. Although we do not know the origin of the Kula, we can clearly understand the central position of reciprocity in Trobriand life.

An example of redistribution is the traditional exchange system of the villages of India, the *jajmani*. A village community consisted of a number of families belonging to various castes, each of which followed a traditional trade such as farming, barbering, carpentry, clothes washing, or street sweeping. Relationships stretching over generations bound various families together in this system of trade exchange. The *jajman,* or farmer, was the center of the nexus, and he could use the services of a barber or carpenter, within the recognized limits of the reasonable, at no immediate cost. The artisan received no pay for each individual service. Rather, at harvest time each artisan family had a right to a traditional share of the produce of the farmers it routinely served. In this way, the farmer served as collector and redistributor in a system of continuing relationships that allocated both the goods and the services produced by the community in shares traditionally considered proper. Under the ideal jajmani system, the workers enjoyed great security in bad years, and in good years prosperity spread throughout the village. As the system actually functioned, however, the lower caste workers usually lived in great poverty and the jajman was the one who reaped the profit from the good harvest.

The market

The third type of distributive system is market exchange. In a market system, all material livelihood is derived from buying and selling through the market. Goods and services are exchanged on the basis of negotiation, and money, a general purpose medium of exchange, is used to make the transactions. Markets are usually associated with large, dense populations that regularly produce surplus food and that contain many specialists who need the products of others.

The market occurs in primitive as well as advanced economies, although in the former it occupies a far less dominant position than among ourselves. In many cases, the market handles only a limited number of commodities, or totally separate markets exist for different categories of commodities. Among the Tiv of Nigeria, for example, three wholly separate exchange spheres existed (Bohannon, 1960). In the first, subsistence goods and household articles changed hands by barter. The second dealt only with certain prestige goods including cattle, slaves, a special type of white cloth, and metal rods. Within this economic sphere, brass rods served as a measure of value, a medium of exchange, a method of payment, and a repository of wealth; in other words, they were as all-purpose as is money, but *only* within this sphere. These goods could be exchanged only for one another, never in exchange for subsistence goods. The third sphere of exchange involved a supreme and unique commodity: rights to women. Within this sphere, men contracted marriages by exchanging sisters or other close relatives with another man.

It was right and proper to exchange items *within* a category, but wrong

An Otomi bank account. These turkeys serve as both a respository of wealth and a standard of value in rural Mexico. (courtesy of John Young)

to exchange them between spheres. The Tiv regarded the transactions within these three spheres of exchange as different in moral character. Strong emotions safeguarded the distinction and came into play, particularly when circumstance forced an individual to exchange goods from a "higher" sphere for those of a "lower." Occasionally, for example, a person in distress would pay for subsistence goods with brass rods. It was also possible to use brass rods to gain a wife. If a given group or individual found it impossible to offer a woman in exchange for a wife received, they could offer brass rods or cattle, not in payment, but as an indication of their debt, which could only be discharged by providing a woman in exchange. This marriage by unequal exchange gave the husband rights over the woman, but not the right to claim her children as members of his family: they remained members of their mother's, rather than their father's, kin group. To acquire rights to the children, the father made additional payments of brass rods to the woman's group after each birth. But brass rods did not in any sense "buy" the wife and children, whose true "price" was another woman and only another woman.

The marriage by property exchange, the *kem* marriage, was a distinctly inferior type of union among the Tiv. It indicated that the new husband had made a fine deal and that the family of the wife had made a bad one. Despite the moral distinctions separating the three spheres of exchange, or perhaps because of them, much prestige accrued to the man who was able to turn "lower" commodities into "higher" ones. Thus, a sharp trader could transform subsistence goods into brass rods and brass rods into wives. He did so

113

Producing a cash crop, coffee, for the world market. (courtesy of Daniel Early)

at the expense of the good will of those he traded with, however, and therefore simultaneously gained the respect and the dislike and fear of his fellows.

You probably have been struck by the complexity of the financial machinations among the Nigerian Tiv. Conversion of one type of commodity into another is both daring and cumbersome. Strategy centers not so much on the accumulation of goods as on their transformation into some other type of goods. The tripartite nature of the market arises out of the absence of a *general purpose money*.

General purpose money

General purpose money is the kind of money we know best. It is defined technically as currency that can be used for all exchanges: as the dollar bill itself states, it is "legal tender for all debts public and private." General purpose money functions as more than a means of payment or medium of exchange. It also serves as a universal standard of value in societies dominated by a single market.

This fact may appear obvious on the surface, but its ramifications are so broad that it deserves further attention. To say that money serves as a universal standard of value means that the values of a large number of commodities can be expressed in money. And because this is true, money and values are implicitly expressed in terms of each other. You will remember that Tiv economics does not permit commodities from different spheres of exchange to be valued in terms of one another. Although, for example, food may be exchanged for brass rods, it is not morally "worth" brass rods. And though brass rods may be given for wives, they are not morally "worth" wives. Our market economy, however, dissolves such differences. Anything that can be valued in money is morally equal to anything else that can be valued in money. Anything with a money value can ultimately be exchanged for anything else.

Thus, for example, a worker's time may bring $7.50 an hour. A car may cost $7,500. A house may be worth $75,000. A lawsuit may result in an award of $150,000 for "pain and suffering." That is to say, the car equals 1,000 hours of the worker's time, the house is equivalent to 10 cars, and the pain and suffering is equal to two houses. A general purpose currency like our own provides a way of adding apples and oranges: everything is first reduced to dollars. This greatly facilitates exchange because it permits anything to be traded for anything else. Moreover, it permits exchange to take place among strangers, and even anonymously. It allows purchasing power to be accumulated and stored for later use. It does many things that the Tiv tripartite economy cannot.

But it cannot do one thing that the Tiv economy can. It cannot protect any part of the economy from any other. The Tiv economy makes it very difficult for anyone to sacrifice his or anyone else's subsistence for prestige goods; it makes it very difficult for anyone to monopolize necessities by the expenditure of luxuries. It segregates the exchange of subsistence and prestige goods and therefore protects them from one another. This is not possible in a market-dominated economy.

The market knows no moral scruple other than the law of supply and demand. By its nature, uniform and anonymous, money cannot distinguish between frivolous and socially necessary purposes, nor between subsistence and luxury goods. The market responds not to human needs, but to effective demand, which is cash on the barrelhead. It does not distinguish between alternative uses of resources according to validity of the need, but only according to the ability to pay. Thus, for example, a rich country such as the United States is able to use a high proportion of the world's scarce fertilizer supply on lawns and flowerbeds, while the material is desperately needed to produce food in poor countries such as Bangladesh. Or, in the nineteenth century the American market was able to attract a large proportion of the buffalo meat and hides "produced" by the wholesale slaughter of the animals; the market took no notice of the fact that the destruction of the buffalo herds meant the destruction of the Plains Indian culture that depended on them.

The method of allocation a society uses influences far more than the distribution of goods: it is a major determinant of the types of relationships that prevail within the society. A market-dominated economy such as our own operates through single-purpose contracts between those wh sell commodities, be they goods, land, ideas, labor, or even "good will," and those who buy them. The anonymity and interchangeability of money guarantees that the salient part of a market transaction is the goods that are exchanged, rather than the relationship. An economy based on reciprocity allows a much more constricted flow of goods and much less leeway in the number of exchange partnerships. But, in contrast to the market economy, it emphasizes the personal relationship between individuals rather than the exchange of goods. A redistributive economy also depends heavily on social relationships in determining allocation. In redistributive systems, a person contributes and receives goods according to his social position or status. This is not the case in market systems.

Because of the social ramifications of allocation, the clash of changing systems does considerable violence to the people caught in the middle. The change represents not only a new system of allocation, but a new set of values and personal relationships. The vast social misery of early capitalism in England, for example, resulted in large measure from the only dimly understood shift in the nature of relationships. Villagers who had lived for centuries in an economy anchored in personal status, reciprocal exchanges, and paternalistic redistribution suddenly found themselves adrift in a sea of monetized relationships as land, labor, produce, and other commodities that had previously been facets of a social relationship became commodities for sale on the open market.

A similar phenomenon has been observed in parts of India since the introduction of "green revolution" crops that vastly increased the yield of certain high quality farmlands. As their harvests rose, the value of the fields owned by landlords rose with it. To achieve a maximum return, many landlords began to pay their workers a fixed cash sum equivalent to their traditional share, rather than a true share of the new, higher yields. Money payments have tended to dissolve the personal nature of the landlord-laborer relationship; landlords feel that they are free of any obligation beyond the payment of wages. Torn from the traditional relationships that protected them and receiving a smaller share of the crop than ever before, the workers appear to be the green revolution's victims rather than its beneficiaries.

FIELD PROJECT: ECONOMIC SYSTEMS

I. DIVISION OF LABOR

A. Make a list of the various tasks carried out by members of your group. Try to list the tasks as specifically as possible. That is, don't count "keeping house" or "running the church" as single tasks. Instead, analyze them further until you arrive at something like: "buying food, putting food in storage compartments in house, planning meals, cooking meals, serving meals, clearing the table, washing dishes, putting dishes away" or "planning service, selecting hymns, choosing sermon topic, doing research for sermon, writing sermon, delivering sermon, leading congregational prayers, leading congregational singing, leading choir, and so on." List as many tasks as you can think of, but at least 25.

B. Group these tasks into work sets. Determine which tasks your group considers to go together into the same job or type of work.

C. List the criteria that define each work set. Why does each task belong in the set it does?

D. List the categories of people who may carry out each work set. What are the criteria of these categories? Does age or sex determine membership in any of these categories? Which ones?

II. OWNERSHIP

A. How are rights to the use of scarce goods, labor, ideas, or other resources assigned in your group? To what entities do they belong?

B. Are there several categories of property or of ownership? What are they?

C. What rights does an owner have in various types of his property? Can he, for example, alienate or destroy property?

III. DISTRIBUTION

A. Which scarce goods change hands within your group? These may include material objects, non-material property of various kinds, and labor.

B. By what systems do transfers take place? Does reciprocity, redistribution, or market exchange dominate within your group? To what extent are the other systems present as well? How is the dominant exchange system reflected in the quality of personal relationships in the group?

C. How do members determine the appropriate quantity or quality of property to hand over in a given transfer? Are these standards formal (for example, an hourly wage or fixed rate of exchange) or are they informal?

Chapter *6*

Social Systems

A random collection of individuals is not a social group. Fifty people who happen to find themselves on the same bus, or 30 people eating by chance in the same restaurant, or even a dozen people cast adrift in the same lifeboat, do not constitute a social or cultural unit. When people relate to one another through a system of recognized ties and habits, when their interaction is patterned, they may be said to form a social group or, on a larger scale, a society.

Collections of people gathered by chance can, of course, come to constitute a group. From Hart Crane's classic story "The Open Boat" to the movie *Lifeboat,* the evolution of bands of random survivors into tight social units has provided a theme for writers. Gradually, painfully, these people devise systematic ways of dealing with one another and with their common problems. By the time they reach safety they know who they are in relation to one another and how they should act: the two pieces of information required to change a random bunch of individuals into a society. In an important sense, they are sides of the same coin; who an individual is in relation to others determines how he will act; how he acts is, to a large extent, related to who he is.

SOCIAL STRUCTURE: STATUS AND ROLE

Social scientists customarily use the terms *status* and *role* for these two ideas. *Status* is a recognized social position within a social group; *role* is the behavior appropriate to a status. Despite the common slang use of the word "status" to imply high prestige and position, the correct usage does not connote any sort of relative ranking. The term "status" simply refers to any socially defined position. Statuses are the components that, combined into sets or groups, form the patterns of social life. For example, within a lifeboat there might be statuses such as commander, navigator, and oarsman. Within a classroom there are the statuses student and teacher. A status has meaning only as a member of a particular set; it derives its meaning from its relationship to the others in its set. The status of student, for example, belongs in a set with teacher, dean, and so on. None makes much sense without the others. The status *son* goes together with father, mother, and daughter, while the status *private* goes with others such as corporal, sergeant, and lieutenant. In any social situation, individuals must select statuses and roles from the same set.

The larger pattern of the arrangement of all statuses within a group constitutes its *social structure*. Social structure organizes the statuses into relevant groups and assigns individuals to various statuses, thereby sorting out the appropriate position of each individual. Thus, to a very large extent it governs behavior. Human beings spend nearly all their lives within one social structure or another. Even such scenes of apparent social chaos as natural disasters and refugee camps quickly sort themselves out in social terms. From the standpoint of the individual, the social structure represents a structured means to achieve his ends. Within it he must fashion the strategies of social life and derive whatever satisfactions his existence might offer. The individual's success in gaining his objectives depends on the luck and skill with which he manipulates the opportunities and rewards available to his status and role, and his ability to move to better-situated statuses.

Each status carries with it a body of appropriate behavior, called a *role*. G. Morris Carstairs (1961) quotes an Indian villager as saying, "It's a man's way of life that shows his caste." When appropriate statuses are agreed upon; that is, chosen from the same set, the accompanying roles will complement one another and smooth interaction is more or less assured. The responsibility of an occupant of a status is to perform his role or, in other words, to carry out the actions expected of him. If the person with the status of leader of the lifeboat does not lead, the group, in danger of perishing, may decide to toss him overboard. If the teacher of a course does not hold classes in her announced subject at the agreed-upon time and place, the students have justified recourse to the dean. If any member of a group violates the conventions of his role and does not meet its minimum requirements, he can expect to be sanctioned and possibly lose his status.

The recognized role is in an important sense inherent to a status. By

Cooking for the family is a common female role. (courtesy of Daniel Early)

acting appropriately, the individual validates his right to occupy his social position. We have all heard admonitions to "act your age" or "be a lady (or gentleman)". If people refuse to perform their roles, they lose the social approval that gives them the right to occupy their statuses. This connection is made explicit in the highly formalized status system of India; members of given castes are said to deserve their positions because they fulfill the requirements of their roles in such matters as personal hygiene and food consumption. Anyone who refuses to abide by his designated role can be formally excluded from his caste group, and this exclusion deprives him of the means of social life. Furthermore, in some situations social position may depend not only on actual conformity, but on the appearance of conformity as well. In Muslim countries the status of virgin, and therefore of marriageable young woman, depends not only on physical virginity, but on an unblemished reputation of virginity. Thus, society's estimation of an individual's behavior is often as important as the behavior itself.

Role equipment

Roles generally demand more than behavior; personal characteristics called *role equipment* come into play as well. These may include the things,

In many cultures the role of child includes helping to earn the family's livelihood. Here Guatemalan children help dry coffee beans. (courtesy of Daniel Early)

knowledge, skills, or other people playing complementary roles that permit a person to perform a role. Knowing the proper etiquette and speaking with the proper accent are examples of role equipment in America and England. In Western society, the unfailing ability to use the right fork can generally help establish a claim to a particular high status, or at least, ignorance of the subtleties of cutlery may foreclose certain claims of status. In England, the proper accent remains an inflexible requirement of high social position. In the United States, the mere possession of a college degree is a significant social demarcator, quite apart from any knowledge a person may or may not have acquired on campus. Specific ideas or outlooks may also be role equipment. While he was first lord of the Admiralty, for example, Winston Churchill wrote a report justifying an increase in his agency's budget. Soon afterward he became Prime Minister and his new perspective on the budget as a whole convinced him to *reject* the recommendations for the increase that he himself submitted when he was Lord of the Admiralty Churchill.

For many roles, other people form a vital part of the role equipment. Some American men discover that to advance further in business they need a wife. A living husband is the main difference between the social roles of wife and widow. Role equipment may also include physical objects or modifications of the human body. Clothing, ornaments, tools, decorations, and uniforms not only advertise a person's status but may help him carry out his role. Particular types of hairdos, scarifications, and cosmetics may fulfill the same function. Among the Hopi, for example, unmarried and married women wore different hairdos. Many items of personal property Americans call "status symbols" also serve to help carry out a role. The individual, wishing to perform a particular role and thereby claim the concomitant status, attempts to equip himself with the accoutrements that will both grant him the social recognition required and facilitate his performance.

The status of policeman requires several types of role equipment.
(courtesy of Henry Stern)

Even temporary statuses may require special role equipment. A Muslim performing the *haj,* or pilgrimage to Mecca, for example, undergoes a ritual when he passes into the special status of pilgrim. At the border of the sacred area surrounding the holy city, the pilgrim performs special ablutions and recites special prayers indicating his desire to carry out God's command- ments; he also dons a special garment, the *ihram,* which he wears contin- uously until the most sacred portion of the pilgrimage is complete. As long as he wears the ihram, the pilgrim is in a special state of purity that permits him to undertake the rites of the haj and forbids him from taking part in violent activities and in sexual relations. At the conclusion of the pilgrim- age, each successful pilgrim enters the new status of one who has fulfilled the commandment to perform haj; he adopts the honorific *hajji* before his name. He also reverts to a more normal pattern of behavior, a change symbolized by the removal of the ihram.

Role conflict

During their lifetimes, individuals occupy a variety of statuses and perform a variety of roles. Even within a given day, a person finds himself involved in several groups and in several statuses and roles. You, for example, in addition to your present role as student, may within the next few hours perform the role of child, spouse, sibling, employee, neighbor, parent, friend, or customer. Furthermore, you will attempt to balance the demands of these various roles. Sometimes, however, you may find some of your roles incompatible; that of student may compete for time with that of parent or spouse. When the demands of your different roles pull you in opposite directions, you experience *role conflict.* For reasons we will discuss shortly, this condition is far more common in complex, advanced societies than in simple ones.

RITES OF PASSAGE

As an individual progresses through his or her lifetime, he or she occupies a number of statuses, often mutually exclusive, in sequence. First an individual is a child, then, in our society, a teenager or adolescent, then an adult. An individual will first be single and then, perhaps, married. Later, he or she may be divorced or widowed. He may be a high school graduate, then a college graduate, and then a doctor of philosophy; a raw private, then a brigadier general; a pledge, then a full fraternity brother. All of these statuses are stages in various temporal progressions, and movement between them requires a discreet and formal break in the individual's life. It is difficult to enter any of these statuses or pass from one to another in the same series without participating in some sort of ceremony that serves to set the status apart. As we have seen, not all statuses are marked by such ceremonies, but in nearly all societies the important ones are.

The rituals that serve as thresholds between statuses are called *rites of passage.* The most important of these occur at the times of crucial transition known as *life crises,* when the individual passes from one major status to another, discarding one major role to assume a different one. The literature on the social and psychological functions of rites of passage is voluminous. Two of the rites' major functions are to announce to society at large the nature and justification of the individual's change in status and to teach him how to act in the new status. The irrevocability of the new role, and the importance of performing it whole-heartedly, is impressed on the individual undergoing the ritual. All rites are composed of three distinct stages. During the first stage, *separation,* the individual is physically removed from his or her former situation and separated from society at large. The period of separation often includes elements of awe or reverence that impress the initiate with his new responsibilities and with his ability to carry them out. Second is the phase of *transition,* during which a leader may offer the initiate actual instruction in the mechanics of the new role or merely attempt to instill the values surrounding it. The third step is *incorporation,* the establishment of the individual in his or her new status (Van Gennep, 1960).

The American wedding ceremony illustrates many of the elements of the typical rite of passage. The wedding is invalid unless witnessed by approved members of society; it thus is public in the sense of including the presence of someone other than the principals, even though not all states require the presence of a clergyman or judge. The ceremony takes place at some distance from the witnesses; throughout the ceremony, the bride and groom stand alone, with the clergyman, their backs to the guests. Their role equipment consists mainly of stylized clothing that sets them apart from everyone else present. Traditionally, of the women present, the bride alone wears white, signifying virginity, and the bridegroom wears a flower different from those worn by the other men. The bride comes down the aisle on the arm of her father, as a symbol of her role as dependent daughter. The father formally relinquishes her to her husband-to-be, and withdraws. Then the two of them, alone, face the clergyman. In Jewish weddings, the bride and groom are further segregated under a special canopy of cloth or flowers.

The wedding ceremony consists of a recitation of the idealized role of husband and wife, with an exhortation to the bride and groom to live up to these ideals. With their promises to do so, the bride and groom acquire new pieces of role equipment—their wedding rings. Then the leader declares the marriage valid, and the newlyweds, in their new roles of husband and wife, turn to face the congregation. To music that was not played earlier in the ceremony, they walk arm in arm down the aisle to rejoin society. Wedding ceremonies in societies throughout the world include some elements of separation from society at large, accomplished either by the distinctive clothing worn by the bride and groom or by the requirement that they sit or stand in special places. Exhortation, often informal, on the proper behavior and dedication appropriate to their new roles is a part of the transition phase of every wedding ceremony. Some element of travel, whether it is down the aisle of a church or to the village or house of one's intended, comprises the reintegration of the newlyweds. To announce the change of status to society at large, there is always a witness at the ceremony itself.

The marriage ceremony fulfills the psychological and social functions of the classic rite of passage. It convinces the newlyweds that their change in status cannot be reversed without serious inconvenience and embarrassment. It instructs them in the rules of their new roles and in the importance of carrying them out acceptably. It states clearly what society may expect from the individuals in their new statuses, and offers powerful social sanction of the change.

The prominence of a given rite of passage appears to some extent to be related to the significance of the actual social change. Those societies in which marriage represents a drastic discontinuity in the individual's life and relationships customarily have the most elaborate and awesome ceremonies. In traditional Muslim societies, for example, the festivities may last a week or more. In the United States, the marriage of a young girl living with her parents is generally a far greater occasion than the marriage of a widow or divorcee living on her own. Among rural Sinhalese in Sri Lanka, however, the beginning of marital cohabitation may be nothing more than a long-expected stage of the relationship between cousins; because this development may change little in the statuses of either the spouses or their relatives, the ceremony may be omitted altogether.

Initiation rites

Although the wedding is one of the last rites of passage observed nearly universally in the United States, many other societies mark other life crises with equal gravity. Initiation rites, or formal induction into adulthood, are very widespread, especially in smaller societies. A period of instruction in secret knowledge, generally concerning ancestry or manipulation of the supernatural, often precedes formal initiation. The initiates are generally secluded from members of their former status group during indoctrination. In a typical example, boys are taken to a special camp where they are taught by older men, and then reenter society after a public ceremony that invests them with their new status.

Male initiation may take place because male groups are significant within the society. In many cases, such as the Hopi and the Dogon, the men possess secret religious knowledge that women are supposedly forbidden to know. Initiation of boys into this knowledge binds them irrevocably with the adult males and separates them from the females. A Hopi chief, for example, has poignantly described his emotions on being initiated into adult knowledge. Learning that the *kachinas,* sacred figures of the Hopi, were the village men in disguise rather than true spirit beings, was one of the great disappointments of his life and permanently demarcated his innocent childhood from his young manhood (Simmons, 1963).

Even without a formal ceremony of initiation into adulthood, the transition can be formally recognized. In Arab countries, full adulthood comes only with parenthood. At the birth of a first child, preferably of a son, the parents adopt new names indicative of their new status. The father of Ahmad becomes, for example, Abu Ahmad, and the boy's mother, Umm Ahmad. In the absence of a son, the name of the firstborn daughter is used. This aspect of full adulthood is so important that childless people are sometimes given names relating to fictitious children.

On the other hand, in American culture there is no clean break between full adulthood and the stages of immaturity preceding it. Rather, there are several minor steps—a person is considered an adult for driving at 16, for voting and being drafted at 18, and for drinking at 21. There is no set age at which an American is recognized as an adult. Some observers, such as Margaret Mead, attribute much of the difficulty and stress young people experience during their teenage years to the absence of a formal break with childhood. In fact, American society is one of the few that recognizes the status of teenager or adolescent, a status unknown to many groups. Moreover, this transitional status appears to be a product of the twentieth century. Historical evidence indicates that earlier generations of Americans did not pass through a special status of adolescence. The fact that the industrial and post-industrial economy has difficulty absorbing unskilled youths probably accounts for the expansion of dependency long past childhood, into years that in other societies constitute adulthood. The relative newness of the status of teenager probably accounts for the lack of ritualized recognition of it.

Initiation rituals are considered severe when they involve prolonged seclusion, beatings, circumcision, or other forms of mutilation. In a 1964 study, John Whiting attempted to show that there is a statistical association between severe male initiation rites and several other factors, including: (1) low protein diets; (2) prolonged nursing of children; (3) a post-partum sex taboo of at least one year; (4) polygyny; (5) prolonged mother-infant sleeping arrangements that exclude the husband; and (6) patrilocality. Whiting explained that low protein availability and the risk of Kwashiorkor make adaptive an extended post-partum sex taboo allowing the mother time to nurse the child through the early critical stages before she becomes pregnant again. The institution of polygyny provides the male with alternative sexual outlets during the taboo period, and most often the child sleeps in the mother's bed for the duration of the taboo. Whiting believes that these sleeping arrangements promote extreme dependence of boys on their mothers and hostility and resentment between father and son. Severe male initiation rites are then needed to break the boy's cross-sex identity and allow the father to express his hostility to his son. Moreover, patrilocal residence demands that boys develop strong masculine identification to promote solidarity and cooperation with the other males. To this end, Whiting believes, societies establish severe male initiation rituals.

TYPES OF STATUS: ACHIEVED AND ASCRIBED

Although many mechanisms exist for acquiring them, statuses can be usefully distinguished into those that are obtained by effort on the part of the individuals concerned and those that are not. If a status can be achieved by the individual's efforts, it is called an *achieved status;* examples might

These young boys are Buddhist monks. They will occupy this status for a short period during adolescence. (courtesy of Geoffrey Hurwitz)

include the statuses of bachelor of arts, husband, quarterback, president of the United States, or 32nd degree mason. If society attributes the status to a person for reasons other than his or her own achievements, it is called an *ascribed status;* examples are the statuses of brother, female, untouchable, or British peer of the realm. Some statuses, for example, Daughter of the American Revolution, depend on both ascription (being of a certain ancestry) and achievement (application to and acceptance into an organization).

Distributing statuses primarily by ascription or primarily by achievement has a crucial effect upon a social structure. Societies in which ascription predominates tend to emphasize the differences between the various statuses and to sharply differentiate their roles and role equipment. Societies in which achievement predominates tend to emphasize training in the means of status acquisition and to downplay the importance of status differences. Significant civil rights and liberation movements in the United States and elsewhere have attempted and to some extent succeeded in abolishing certain ascribed statuses in favor of achieved ones. The traditional American ascription of social and professional superiority to whites and inferiority to blacks has lost its legal justification, permitting the distribution of favored statuses more nearly according to criteria of personal achievement.

Every individual occupies a number of statuses simultaneously: as we have mentioned, the same person is at once spouse, child, parent, employee, and neighbor, among other things. But societies differ in the number and kinds of statuses they call on their members to occupy at once and in the degree to which these statuses are interrelated. Compared to the situation in a complex society such as ours, the statuses of many members of simple societies are more closely related, or clustered. In the United States, such features of a person's status as residence, occupation, relationship to property, political power, and potential spouses may have no relationship to one another. Furthermore, to carry out each of the roles one may have to deal with different sets of people.

In simpler societies, statuses tend to be far more concentrated. Where one lives, what occupation one follows, what property one owns, what political group one belongs to, and whom one may marry may well be defined by birth or family position. In many cases it is possible to predict any of these factors from any of the others. Thus, for example, a member of lineage A must necessarily marry a member of lineage B; lineage A people also enjoy the right to hunt in certain lineage-owned territories. Or, to take another example, all the members of family C live in a certain quarter of the village and belong to a certain political faction. The correlation between statuses in these societies is very high; consequently, the social characteristics of any individual are relatively predictable. Ascribed rather than achieved statuses dominate social interactions and personal identity.

As a result of such clustering of statuses and roles in simple societies, the same individuals tend to interact in many or even most dimensions of life. In a Muslim village, for example, two adult brothers might well live in the same household, farm the same piece of land in conjunction with their father, stand to inherit parts of the same estate, arrange the marriage of their children, one to the other, and belong to the same political faction. In such a situation, the status of brother includes elements of the American statuses of neighbor, business partner, in-law, and fellow political party member. Relationships tend to be intensive rather than extensive. *Integral contacts,* or intense interaction with a limited number of individuals, are the rule in simpler societies, whereas in complex societies, *segmental contacts,* or more superficial interactions with a larger number of individuals, predominate.

Several factors combine to produce such differences in intensity of relationship. In a small, isolated group, there are fewer people with whom to interact than there are in a large, complex settlement. A highly specialized economy requires interaction with a larger number of persons than does a small, simple economy. And a society built around tightly bounded social groups encourages relationships with fellow members rather than with outsiders.

The extremes in intensity of relationship may even be said to constitute differences in kind. The experience of dealing with a person on many levels over a long period of time transforms the relationship into something quite different from the experience of dealing with a person on one level only. The richness and intimacy of a long-term, multi-faceted relationship emphasizes ties between individuals as individuals; the impersonality of short-term, single purpose relationships emphasize the roles that momentarily bring people together. Social scientists call relationships that involve people acting in a large number of different statuses over a long period of time *primary* relationships; those that involve more superficial contact, *secondary* relationships.

The predominance of primary or secondary relationships is one of the major factors differentiating simple and complex societies. In small-scale societies, whether tribes, bands, or villages, the vast majority of relationships are of the primary type; members of such a society may deal only rarely with individuals they have not known intimately in many roles for most of their lives. In a complex society, on the other hand, the vast majority of relationships are secondary. People rarely know one another in more than a few of their many roles.

The ethic of fairness and evenhandedness so prevalent in American society derives in large part from the predominance of secondary relationships. Bureaucratic and legal procedures require that individuals be treated solely in terms of the single role or small cluster of roles salient at the moment. Judges, admissions officers, and bureaucrats, for example, are required to disqualify themselves from cases involving persons they know in other roles. To act otherwise constitutes conflict of interest or "pulling strings." In many developing countries, on the other hand, traditions of the primacy of primary relationships clash with the new bureaucratic procedures recently adopted in order to be "modern." Westerners having to deal with such bureaucracies often complain of corruption, when in fact people are merely continuing their life-long practice of placing primary relationships first.

A social status does not exist in a vacuum, but as part of a system of reciprocal statuses. Various organizing principles arrange statuses and the individuals occupying them into sets, and the sets into patterns. By this process, individuals are gathered into groups and even into whole societies. You may have noticed that in this chapter we have used the words group and society as if they were to some extent synonymous. Although the differences between them are great, the concepts do have important features in common, at least as regards the matters we have discussed so far. For clarity we must now distinguish them, however. By *society,* we mean a body of people that carries a total culture: examples might be American society, Dogon society, or Yanomamö society. By *group,* we mean a body of people that exists within a larger society and carries a less than complete culture. Examples include the Knights of Columbus, an Indian sub-caste, or a Yanomamö village.

GROUPS

As we have seen, social groups have the characteristic of internal organization; that is, their members relate to one another according to a particular pattern of statuses and roles. Two other characteristics are necessary to a true group: interaction among the members, and self-recognition of their common group membership. Although it is unlikely that all members of a large group such as a labor union, a church congregation, or a tribe interact with one another, all members interact with at least some other members in the context of the group.

Many of the collections of people commonly thought of as groups are therefore not really groups in any useful or technical sense: they are categories. A *category* is a set of people that share a culturally relevant attribute. Thus, a body of people such as "the working class" is a category rather than a group. Some of the collections of people generally called "ethnic groups" in the United States are also in reality only categories. Italian-Americans, for example, may strongly identify themselves as such, but there exists no internal organization based solely on this identity that provides distinctive group statuses, and there is no likelihood that all or even most Italian-Americans interact with one another. Nevertheless, some Italian-Americans do belong to true groups, such as Sons of Italy, composed of persons of the same ethnic heritage who are dedicated to advancing the interests of people of that heritage. These groups draw their membership from people belonging to the category "Italian-American," but they, rather than the category, fulfill the requirements of social groups.

Because groups play such an important part in assigning social status and roles, it is important to speak of them precisely. To discern groups rather than categories or accidental clusters, we must analyze individual cases with care. For example, some geographically-bounded residential communities have the characteristics of groups. And in general, although there are groups composed of members of a particular class, the class itself does not constitute a group. It generally lacks group identity or consciousness, internal organization, and widespread interaction. In certain American communities, however, especially in small and traditional towns, the *upper* class may form a true social group. All members may be listed in a special book, such as the *Social Register* or the *Green Book,* or they may all belong to a certain country club. At any rate, all the "right" people of the "good" families know who they are. Furthermore, the class may be internally organized into divisions like debutantes, post-debutantes, members of the Bachelor's Club, and so forth. And finally, members of the class may interact as a group at such gatherings as cotillions, hunt balls, and debuts. Although such closed class groups are increasingly rare in the United States, they retain their currency and vitality in Britain and some other countries.

Although they all must share the three characteristics mentioned, groups nevertheless vary widely along other lines. They may be voluntary or involuntary, they may be mutually exclusive or not, and they may be formal or informal. Groups that you may choose to join are called *voluntary* groups; those that give you no choice are *involuntary.* The college drama club, the Democratic Party, and the Ku Klux Klan are voluntary groups. There is no social necessity to belong; those who join such groups share an interest and base their group membership on that interest. It is not possible, however, to decide not to join the family of your parents (at least until you are of age) or the citizenry of the United States (or any other country you happen to have been born in). Similar involuntary groups in other societies include tribes, castes, lineages, and political factions. Some groups monopolize their members' loyalty within their own field of interest, and are therefore *exclusive.* If you belong to the Catholic church, for example, you may not belong to any other religious denomination. You may, however, belong to several literary societies, professional organizations, or country clubs. Finally, some groups have overt and official procedures and membership; that is, they are *formal* bodies. These include various types of clubs, societies, religious bodies, and, in some societies, family and tribal bodies. Viable and authentic groups can often be totally informal, however. The men who hang out at a certain street corner or the body of "regulars" at a particular bar may well develop the feeling of identification, the degree of interaction, and the organization necessary for a true social group.

The type of groups that compose a society are important because they heavily influence its character. Societies that tend to emphasize voluntary associations also tend to emphasize achieved status; those that emphasize involuntary groups generally emphasize ascribed status. A prevalence of mutually exclusive groups tends to heighten group conflict as a dynamic of interaction. Societies dominated by formal groups tend to value the trappings of office and position. As societies become more complex, they differ markedly in the number of groups to which an individual may belong. An

Arabian Bedouin, for example, may view himself as belonging only to his family, his tribe, and the community of Islam. An American business executive listed in *Who's Who* may belong to literally dozens of religious, political, social, fraternal, professional, and athletic organizations.

SOCIAL NETWORKS

So far we have discussed social structure as organized statuses, roles, and groups. Anthropologists studying social structure have traditionally concerned themselves with social groups. In recent years, however, they have also increasingly studied the actual social contacts of given individuals in order to gain insight into the workings of societies.

We have stated that to be defined as a group, members must interact with one another. But, as you know from your own experience in groups, people rarely interact with all members equally. Usually everybody has his own favorites among fellow members, or his own special friends outside the established group. Societies may be viewed from a structural standpoint as being composed of groups, but the experience of daily life is composed of the people that individuals know, like, and deal with. Generally, different individuals have their own networks of contacts. Even people with identical or nearly identical group memberships maintain somewhat different networks. A *network* is set of social relationships that flow from one individual; it is *ego-centered*. A person's network serves many important functions. "It provides him with a surrounding field of friends and relatives who help give his life meaning, establish and maintain the norms by which he regulates his behavior, and protect him from the impersonal world beyond" (Bott 1957:200).

Network Analysis. Anthropologists have recently turned their attention to these personal networks and have begun to explore how the concrete contacts of individuals influence social behavior. They have found that networks vary along certain dimensions, and different societies foster different types of networks. Some of the dimensions of networks are *size,* or the number of contacts a person has; *concentration,* the number of interests served by individual relationships (for example, a priest may also be somebody's brother); and *density,* the closeness that occurs if one individual's contacts are also linked to one another through other ties. In some simple segmentary societies, for example, the number of persons each individual interacts with may be small but the interaction may be very concentrated. In some others, such as complex post-industrial societies, individuals may have relatively large networks of contacts but the contacts are not linked to each other except through ego (the term *ego* refers to the hypothetical individual whose relationships with others are being investigated). The degree to which the networks of different individuals resemble one another, and the way a particular network is limited to a certain sector of the society, also tell something of the society's degree of group differentiation. In American society, for example, the networks of most people tend to emphasize members of their own ethnic, sex, and class categories. Some Americans have no contact with those of other categories outside of formal economic situations. In some Muslim countries, people have no social contact with members of the opposite sex outside their own families.

Personal networks can also serve important functions for societies. Middle Eastern Arab villages, for example, are built of compact and mutually exclusive kinship groups constructed around relationships among men. All significant property and personal statuses derive from membership in a group of kinsmen related through their fathers. Many individuals, however, maintain informal contact with their mother's kin and other relatives through women. Analyses of village life have shown that these ties through women are of crucial importance in resolving conflict. When a dispute arises between men of different kin groups, men line up to support their paternal relatives. Conflict often escalates to high levels of bitterness. Since they are free from the necessity of choosing sides, men who are related to the disputants through women, instead of through men, are frequently able to mediate disputes through informal contacts. Thus, personal contacts, the network of relationships outside the "official" kinship system, function to help keep the society on an even keel (Lutfiyya, 1966).

The study of the networks of contacts exploited by particular individuals is particularly useful in illuminating complex societies, in which social groups tend to be relatively diffuse and role relationships are segmental. Every American who has looked for a job or an apartment knows the utility of the network of "friends of friends." Even in simpler societies, however, network analysis can lay bare the mechanics of social interaction.

SOCIAL STRATIFICATION

Groups do not combine randomly to form societies any more than individuals combine randomly to form groups. Relationships among groups, and between groups and individuals, constitute what is known as the *social structure* of the society. As in all other aspects of culture, societies differ markedly in the ways they organize their social life. They divide their people into different types of sets and consequently organize them into different types of patterns. A society that distinguishes, for example, hereditary nobility from commoners, must be different from one that makes no such distinction. A profitable way to compare social structures, therefore, is to compare the criteria they use to establish their major sets and thus their major patterns of organization.

A very common type of social distinction divides people into higher and lower categories and assigns roles and privileges according to position in the hierarchy. Social scientists have generally pictured such societies as consisting of social strata, or layers; the social processes by which the layers are formed is technically called *stratification* (literally, layer-making). Social strata segregate people into groups that have differential access to desirable features of life, particularly prestige and wealth, or economic resources.

Stratification takes a variety of forms and manifests itself in many different ways. Generally, however, there is an emotional aspect to the system, often tied to an ideology or symbolism justifying it. People in a stratified system feel strongly about their place in it and the places of members of other strata. Perhaps the most extreme example of such emotion is found in the Indian caste system: members of the lower strata are viewed as polluting to members of the upper strata. The top strata of some Polynesian societies are believed to have a spiritual power, *mana,* that is so dangerous to members of lower strata that it renders objects touched by the elite *tapu* (from this word, Westerners have derived *taboo*).

Egalitarian societies

Although extremely widespread, social stratification is far from universal, though this, as in most things, depends upon one's definition. Many societies lack important hierarchial distinctions and emphasize the social and material equality of all members. Prominent among these are African Bushmen bands. Nomadic hunters and gatherers, the Bushmen lack both the means and the desire to accumulate personal wealth. Nor does their way of life lend itself to accumulations of power or prestige. Those who lead do so solely because of personal characteristics and can claim no social superiority to their fellows.

The fact that egalitarian societies recognize no structured social inequality should not lead you to believe that they do not recognize differences among individuals. One person may be an outstanding hunter, another a superb dancer, a third an excellent raconteur. An individual may gain prestige through his personal accomplishments, but this prestige affects neither his economic standing nor the prospects of other members of the group who hope to gain similiar prestige. Thus, any number of people may be recognized as excellent hunters if their abilities warrant it. The number of prestige positions is not fixed: it matches the number of persons available to fill them. This prestige is not hereditary and can even disappear if the person's talents wane.

In egalitarian societies, those who produce more economic resources than their fellows do not enrich themselves. Meat, for example, cannot be hoarded, as there is no means of storing it for long periods. The animals killed in the hunt are distributed among the band according to prescribed rules, generally based on kinship. Many people share in the hunter's kill. Although he may gain their gratitude and admiration, a successful hunter does not gain an economic advantage over his fellows. In fact, egalitarian social organization seems related to hunting and gathering economies. These modes of life require a high degree of personal independence, show a low level of specialization, allow equal access to the basic means of production, and do not permit large accumulations of wealth. Stratification appears in societies with characteristics opposite to these. The need for coordination and control, a high degree of specialization, unequal access to the means of production, or the opportunity to amass substantial wealth encourages social differentiation of a hierarchical nature.

Rank societies

Anthropologists have divided stratified societies into two general types: those based on rank and those based on caste or class. In a rank society, members have equal access to economic resources but unequal access to prestige. North Arabian Bedouins live in a rank society. All tribe members follow a similar nomadic way of life, sharing in wells and pastures owned communally by lineages. The severity of the environment and the continual movement do not permit marked distinctions of wealth; indeed, cultural mechanisms exist to redistribute wealth if an imbalance occurs. The tribal value system strongly emphasizes the essential equality of all tribesmen. Nevertheless, special prestige adheres to certain lineages that produce the tribal leaders. Although leadership among the Bedouins is not inherited automatically, but is based on individual ability, only members of certain lineages receive consideration when a vacancy arises. Among the Bedouin, leadership depends on persuasion rather than command; the leader is always the first among equals. He validates his position through personal qualities such as wise judgment, bravery, and especially hospitality. The *shaykh* or *amir* is expected to offer open-handed hospitality to all his tribal brothers. Thus, rather than accumulating wealth, he redistributes it throughout the society.

Although rank societies generally arise among pastoralists and agriculturalists, the Kwakiutl Indians of the Northwest Coast are an intriguing exception. These sedentary fishermen traditionally harvested such a bounty of salmon from their rivers that they were able to live in sturdy wooden villages with sidewalks and devote much of their time to carving and other crafts. A sizeable proportion of the goods thus produced were destined for *potlatch,* a ceremony at which a man raised himself to a higher rank by lavishly giving away or destroying sizeable quantities of wealth. The material goods thus circulated through the society rather than accumulating in the possession of one or a few wealthy men; the value of wealth was the prestige gained by giving it away rather than the prestige gained by having it.

Caste and class societies

Societies stratified according to class and caste are characterized by both unequal access to wealth and unequal access to prestige. Social scientists are not in total agreement about the causes of these more complex forms of stratification, but they appear to be related to complexity of organization and large-scale accumulations of economic surplus. The United States is a good example of a class society. Americans are born into one of a number of categories that roughly determine their chance of achieving wealth and prestige. Although the American class system is fairly open in that it permits some movement between classes, most Americans nevertheless live and die in the class into which they were born. Some class societies, such as Great Britain, have traditionally had much more closed classes than the United States. In such societies, the membership of the various classes has been stable enough over a period of generations to permit the development of distinctive role equipment such as class-related accents.

If a social organization ascribes immutable statuses to members at birth, it is called a *caste* society. The classic example is the mosaic-like society of India, composed of tens of thousands of specialized occupational groups in which people are born, live, marry, and die. No movement between castes is possible. In addition, the emotional content of the Indian caste system is very high: from the Brahman priests, who may be polluted by contact with objects or people (or even shadows) of less spiritual purity, to the lowest of the untouchables, who perform the least desirable jobs and are considered so polluting that higher castes shun them, the castes form a hierarchy of spiritual purity.

The strictly stratified racial groups of South Africa form another caste system. Here, the spiritual explanation is missing, but differential access to wealth and prestige is ascribed at birth and carries the force of law. Pay scales, residential patterns, and even legal rights follow racial identity; the entire force of the state backs the system of structured inequality. Although less stringent in practice and less pernicious in effect, racial discrimination in the United States has constituted a similar caste system. Structured racial inequality, the law of the land a generation ago, is now a major target of legislative action. The social effects of ascribing status by race have not disappeared as quickly, however; racial identity remains a major determinant of access to wealth and prestige.

Social mobility, or movement to a different status, necessarily takes a different form in class societies than it does in caste societies. A single individual may, in a class society, move up to a class higher than that of his birth or at least assure that his children will. College education has traditionally served this function in the United States, permitting young people of modest social origin to master the ways of the higher class they wish to enter. In caste societies, however, there is no leeway for individual movement. Two basic strategies, aside from destroying the caste system entirely, are possible, however: to rise to the top of one's own caste or to maneuver an entire caste into a higher position.

Age-grading

Another widespread system of stratification apportions social status and economic opportunity by age. In such societies, many of which are found in Africa, a system of age grades divides the men and boys into a series of sets that advance as groups through the various stages of life. Possibly the most extreme example of age grading occurs among the Nyakyusa, an agricultural people of East Africa (Wilson, 1963). Beginning at age 10 or 11, boys move out of their parents' home to live in a separate village with their contemporaries. When the eldest boys in the village reach 18 or so, the group closes membership; all younger boys must then join a new group. The members of an age village live together all their lives, bringing their wives to their village and maintaining family homes from which their own sons depart upon reaching the proper age. Leadership of the people at large rests with the senior generation until, at an elaborate ceremony known as the "coming out," they relinquish it and pass it on to the rising younger men of a different village. In some groups, the passage of age sets through a system of predetermined grades regulates access to both ritual and political power. But elements of age grading are found in many societies that carry the principle to less extreme ends than the Nyakyusa. American society, for example, appears increasingly age-graded; the "youth culture" of the late 1960s indicated the strength of social identification based solely on age.

FIELD PROJECT: SOCIAL SYSTEMS

I. STATUS, ROLE, ROLE EQUIPMENT

A. Make a list of statuses found in the group that you have chosen to study. If this is a formal group like a business or church, you may be able to collect an "organization chart" that shows the relationship between statuses, based on power. If your group is an informal group such as a group of friends, the statuses may be related to group activity; that is, in some situations the group may have a leader, subordinates, "police," and so on, whereas in other situations the statuses may change to driver, musician, or others. If the group is an informal one, make up titles for the statuses, basing them on activity. Remember, statuses are not the same as people—a person may occupy many different statuses. Status means *a position* within a group and has no high/low implications.

B. Select three statuses and describe the role of each. If your group is a formal one, these roles may be the same as the job descriptions found in an employee handbook. In informal groups, roles are much less well defined and are equivalent to sets of behavior.

C. For the three statuses that you have chosen, list the role equipment. In this case, the role equipment corresponds to components and may be divided into three types: (1) special knowledge that enables the member to perform his or her role congruently; (2) material items, such as a policeman's badge or gun, or a carpenter's hammer; and (3) other members who complement the member in question and without whom it would be impossible for the member to perform his or her role. A mother must have children, a policeman needs lawbreakers, and a sales clerk needs customers.

D. Empty your pockets, purse, or wallet and list the material role equipment that you find. To which statuses does the role equipment belong and to which groups (sets) do these indicate membership?

II. RITES OF PASSAGE

A. Observe a rite of passage that occurs in your group. This may be a wedding, graduation, or initiation ceremony; a promotion or retirement; or even a court trial. Assume that this piece of behavior is a pattern. Divide it immediately into its three major sets: separation, transition, and incorporation (it may be possible to subdivide these further into subsets) and make a list of the components (role equipment) for each set or subset. Your list might look something like this:

Pattern: A Protestant Wedding.
    Set #2: Transition (the marriage ceremony)
    Components:

Material	*Member*	*Knowledge* (idea)
a brooch (old)	bride	symbolic of
shoes (new)		new relation-
a friend's necklace		ships (refer
(borrowed)		to description
bridal bouquet (tied		in chapter).
with blue ribbon)		

B. Major rites of passage are easy to isolate for observation; after all, the behavior of a bridal party is very different from the ordinary day to day behavior in which we are all participants. Yet, in a sense, we go through numerous changes in status, role, and role equipment during any representative period. As you leave your home in the morning (separation) you leave behind the status of son or daughter, husband or wife, and become a student. In between, you may occupy the status of automobile driver (transition), which requires you to use a different set of ideas, material, and people (role equipment). Upon arriving at school and entering the classroom, you become a student by acquiring books, concepts, and other students and teachers (incorporation). Select one of these minor rites of passage and describe it the same way you described the previous, major one.

Chapter 7

Kinship Systems

Kinship concerns the realm of social relations among kinsmen, those people who stand in special relationships to one another because of recognized ties of descent or marriage. Although kinship systems are many and varied, all are ultimately based on the fact that certain people are descendants of the same ancestors (formally called the *principle of descent*) or that certain people have married one another (the *principle of affinity*).

"You can choose your friends," the old saying goes, "but you can't choose your relatives." You acquire relatives through a variety of means, practically none of which are voluntary. Once acquired, they generally remain your relatives for life. Even if, as in American society, the selection of a spouse may be an act of free choice, the selection of in-laws is not. Your spouse's relatives come as a package: you may not accept Cousin Bernie but reject Aunt Jane. Your only choice is which set of nonreturnable in-laws you will get.

As to your own kin, there is no way, short of a major break, to divest yourself of your relatives, and you have essentially no choice who they will be. You cannot choose your parents, your brothers and sisters, your uncles and cousins. You may be able to choose how many children you will have, but you cannot choose who they will be. In American society, except for marriage, adoption is the only way to make a particular individual your relative.

You have probably concluded by now, and quite correctly, that family membership is the very model of ascribed status. You occupy your family status as son, sister, niece, uncle, brother-in-law, regardless of any wish on your own part. The only statuses over which you have the slightest control are parent and spouse; even grandparent is out of your hands.

These observations about relatives apply, in many cases with even greater force, to practically everybody on earth. Kinship relationships are one of the universals of human culture. Regardless of which society they belong to, the vast majority of all people on earth spend their entire lives as members of families. Families are the first, often the last, and in many cases the only, group anyone belongs to. Family membership creates the most durable ties in the life of the individual, the only ones that routinely survive separation, ill will, and even death. "Home," the poet Robert Frost said (although he might as well have been talking about family), "is where, when you go there, they have to take you in."

The irrevocable nature of family ties gives an important insight into their function, which is to lock people into the statuses and roles necessary to the maintenance of the domestic arrangements of their society. Family ties thus ensure that the most crucial and intimate needs of survival, both of the individual and of the culture, are met. Family patterns, or in anthropological terms, *kinship*, are means of assigning critical permanent or quasi-permanent kinds of statuses.

In most societies, kinship is, next to sex, the most important determinant of social status. It is also the most important principle in the organization of social groups. That is, the majority of people in the world derive their most important statuses from the kinship system and live in a society dominated by kinship groups. It is essential to remember that cultural systems divide the phenomena of the world into sets and organize the sets into patterns; that the sets recognized by different cultures are different, so that the patterns are therefore different too. Note that we defined kinship as having to do with *recognized* ties of descent and marriage. This should warn us that not all cultures recognize the same ties, or organize them in the same way.

It's often hard for Americans, for whom the role of kinship has shrunk until it is only one of a number of status-assigning and group-forming mechanisms, to grasp the importance of kinship in simple societies. In many societies, however, kinship figures crucially in such elements of status as place of residence, acquisition of property, choice of livelihood, political loyalty, religious belief, selection of marriage partner, and social rank. One might protest that family membership plays a role in these elements of our lives as well, but modern Americans have far greater leeway to ignore the demands of their kinsmen, or to live differently from them, than many other peoples do. The following statements don't make much sense in the context of American culture: "John can't get married because his father's brother used up all the cattle"; "Susie's mother-in-law makes her do all the laundry"; or "Fred can't marry Anne because their mothers are sisters, but he should marry Hazel because her mother is his father's sister."

Kinship systems do much more than determine the guest list for Thanksgiving dinner. Although in American society kinship serves a relatively small number of functions, in many simpler societies it is the single most important system of social relationships. Kinship often completely overwhelms any competing institutions, sometimes incorporating them and their functions. Just as the functions of kinship systems vary, so do the forms. People may trace their kinsmen through a variety of different systems emphasizing links either through men or women, or through relatives of both sexes. Based on the principles of the different systems, kinsmen may form either tight, self-conscious groups with rigid criteria of membership or loose clusters of people tied only by their relationship to a particular individual. Kinship ties range all the way from those of the single American adult who lives alone in a city and flies to a faraway place once a year for a Christmas reunion, to those of an Arabian Bedouin tribesman who rarely has dealings of any kind with a nonrelative and even marries a member of his own kinship group.

Like other systems for assigning statuses, kinship systems function both to form groups and to organize behavior by sorting out roles. Perhaps the simplest way to begin is to consider the sorts of groups kinship systems form: families.

THE FAMILY AND HOUSEHOLD

When Americans think of families, they generally think of what social scientists call the nuclear family, the group composed of husband, wife, and unmarried children. Americans tend to add a further assumption about the family: that this group ideally lives apart from other such groups. In adding the second element, we have confounded two concepts that must be kept separate in order to permit clear analysis: family and household. Because the nuclear family is the most significant grouping in American culture, as well as the ideal set of occupants of a separate home, Americans tend to assume that living together in a group composed of parents and minor children is almost the same thing as belonging to a family. Americans even refer to having children as "starting a family." We must carefully distinguish family from household, however, because, as we shall see, they are not necessarily the same thing.

Because the nuclear family so dominates the European and North

American cultures in which anthropology arose, it has occupied a place of inordinate importance in anthropological theory. The nuclear family is the basic unit of American and Western European culture; its functions include some of the most significant in the society. It channels sexual drive, providing each spouse with a socially acceptable sexual partner. It nurtures and socializes the young. It is the basic unit of consumption, and used to be an important unit of production as well. It provides an individual with his or her most intimate and significant personal relationships. Anthropologists rightly perceived that these processes are necessary to the proper functioning of all societies. Blinded by their ethnocentrism, however, they wrongly assumed that the nuclear family was essential to *all* societies.

Most students of kinship through the 1950s assumed with George Peter Murdock, whose work influenced several generations of anthropologists, that the nuclear family was universal. The reproductive combination of man, woman, and minor child is a universal biological fact. The functions this combination fulfills in Western society are universal social requirements. That the particular social institution of the nuclear family can alone fulfill these functions, however, is an assumed conclusion not borne out by investigation. The assumption that the nuclear family is both universal and universally basic led to serious misinterpretations of family and household structures that function according to other patterns.

Although it is the basic unit of kinship and household structure in Western industrial societies, the nuclear family is the dominant institution in only a minority of societies elsewhere. Among other cultural groups, some other set of kinsmen, generally larger than a nuclear family, is the desired household unit. In many parts of the world, an *extended family* household is the most desired arrangement. A common variant is the *joint family* household, which consists of a man, his wife, their unmarried children, their married sons, the sons' wives, and the sons' children. Although nuclear units consisting of the sons and their wives and children may be discerned within the joint family, in very few cases do these nuclear groups constitute the basic unit on which the family is built; people conceive the household, rather than the nuclear groups within it, as the basic unit. In many cases, the "nuclearness" of the nuclear family is recognized only in the sexual intimacy of the married couple, which takes place in a private room.

In this arrangement, domestic work, economic property, social status, and childrearing are organized around the household rather than around the nuclear family. Men contribute financially to the household at large rather than to their particular wives and children. In much of India, for example, all male members of a household own the family home, land, and other property in common. The father acts as chief executive. No man may show affection for his wife or children in the presence of his father. The senior generation handles the money and assigns the work even *after* the children have reached adulthood. In many cases, a nuclear family living alone, far from their relatives, for work or some other reason, is not considered to be an independent, complete household, but a fragment of a household living away from home, much as an American student might be "away at school."

Another common household form is the *polygynous* family, which is found in large parts of Africa and the Middle East. "Polygynous" comes from a Greek root meaning "many women," and describes the form of marriage in which a man takes more than one wife at a time. Although not numerically dominant, this household arrangement is often the preferred form of organization and, as such, of great cultural importance. A man's various wives and children may live in the same or different households, but in either case are aware of the existence of the others. Children of different wives may occupy different statuses within the family, but from the standpoint of the society at large, all the full and half-siblings are equally legitimate children of their father. Only by distortion of true relationships can this type of household be construed as consisting of nuclear units; the true constituent parts are groupings composed of each wife and her children.

The *polyandrous* (meaning "many men") household, though far less common than the polygynous, is even more intriguing from a structural standpoint. In this case, a single woman marries a number of men, who are usually brothers. This form of organization has been reported in only a few societies, such as the Toda of South India and the Sinhalese of Sri Lanka. It has also been reported in some areas of Tibet. Because of the biology of reproduction, the polyandrous household cannot be a mirror image of the polygynous. A woman with several sexual partners is unlikely to bear any more children than she would if she had only one sexual partner, and there is no biologically obvious method of assigning a child to a particular father. In such cases, social means are used to give the children a social identity. Nevertheless, all the husbands share sexual access to the woman, contribute to her and the children's support, and consider themselves full members of the marriage.

In some societies, the Manankabau of Sumatra and the Ashanti of Africa, for example, married couples do not live together at all. Each spouse lives with his or her own natal family; one parent cares for the the children. Ashanti women cook for their husbands, however, and mealtimes see a substantial traffic of children carrying food from their mother's home to their father's home.

A polygynous family in Tanzania. Note that the two wives have identical dresses, indicating the husband's attempt to treat his wives equally. (courtesy of Leonard J. Gallagher)

Functions of the family

In all the household types we have described, certain necessary functions of society are carried out. Adults know who their approved sexual partners are, children receive love and nurturance in a stable home, and on-going economic activities support the household. The fact that none of these households is based on the nuclear family does not detract from their ability to fulfill the needs of the individual and the society. Today, some people are saying that the nuclear family is going out of existence in American society. With more than a third of all marriages ending in divorce; growing numbers of children living in one-parent homes (or shuttling between parents' homes); sexual relations loosened from its ties to marriage; procreation coming under increasing technological control; and television, day care, and schools providing a major portion of children's training, one may well question whether the nuclear family is indeed as essential to American society as traditional social science analysts have suggested.

In evaluating the many household forms we have mentioned, one might argue that they all can be found in American society as well. Not everyone lives in a nuclear family household; after all, many people live in three-generation households, with their brothers or sisters, or apart from their

In many cultures, looking after younger children is the task of older children. (courtesy of John Young)

spouse. Various kinds of unorthodox group arrangements have come into being lately as well. The point is, however, that in American society these households are recognized as deviations from the accepted norm. People generally expect a newly married couple to establish their own home rather than to move in with relatives. Any deviation from this pattern requires an explanation. For example, the popular television program "All in the Family," which depends for much of its comic tension on the friction between Archie and his son-in-law Michael, chronicles a joint family household. The presence of the daughter and son-in-law in the parents' home required elaborate explanation. (Michael was unable to support an independent household while attending college.) Archie's attitude—presumably shared by the viewer—was that Michael's dependence on his father-in-law demonstrated one of his many serious character flaws. At the earliest opportunity, Michael and his wife moved into their own home; significantly, this occurred just before they became parents and thus "started their own family."

RESIDENCE PATTERNS

In many societies, however, various other residence patterns are not only acceptable, but preferred. A society's social structure and its architecture encourage people to adopt their society's preferred mode of residence. American domestic architecture, for example, makes it difficult for more than a nuclear unit to occupy a "single family" house or apartment.

In anthropological terms, Americans are *neolocal* (literally, "new place") in their residence patterns. That is, after marriage they establish a new household. If the newly married couple moves in with the husband's family or establishes a household nearby, they are termed *patrilocal* (father's place) or *virilocal* (man's place). Those who live with the wife's family are *matrilocal* (mother's place) or *uxorilocal* (wife's place). In some cases, a newly married couple establishes residence with the husband's mother's brother (for reasons we will shortly explore); this pattern is known as *avunculocal* (uncle's place). In some cases, the couple lives first with one family and then with the other. For example, the woman may remain with her own family until the birth of her first child or until the child reaches a certain age; or her husband may owe his father-in-law a term of bride-service, or labor in return for the hand of his bride. This is *bilocal* residence.

Although these rules of residence appear clear-cut, we must always

guard against the mistake made by early anthropologists, who applied their categories to someone else's emic reality. The important thing is not what *we* think people are doing, but what *they* actually are doing. In a famous case of analytical confusion, two excellent fieldworkers, John Fischer of Harvard and Ward Goodenough, then of Yale, both studied the same group on the island of Truk. Fischer reported that the Trukese were bilocal. Three years later, Goodenough reported that the Trukese were matrilocal. A check of census data indicated that the difference could not be explained by changes in Trukese residence patterns. The problem lay in the fact that two anthropologists had seen the same situation and called it by two different names.

Finally Goodenough suggested a solution. The problem was not whether the Trukese were matrilocal or bilocal; the problem was that they were neither. Trukese newlyweds did not select their place of residence on the basis of living with the family of one or another of the spouses. They had no ideology that prescribed residence with particular kinsmen. Rather, Trukese newlyweds chose among various large kinship land-owning groups with which they might affiliate, generally following the dictates of available resources. No set rule of live-with-this-particular-relative existed (Goodenough, 1956). The anthropologists had applied their own sets to Trukese social behavior, totally obscuring the reality of the case and ignoring the fact that their sets are not appropriate to all cases.

MARRIAGE

Central to the concept of the universality of the family group is the concept of the universality of the institution of marriage. Because marriage is the central relationship of the nuclear family, early anthropologists often assumed that it was central to society as well. Many argued that marriage was both necessary and universal in human society. In rebuttal, however, Kathleen Gough (1959) reported the provocative case of the Nayar of India, a caste group that had nothing resembling marriage in the generally understood sense of a long-standing, socially approved relationship between a man and a woman. Nayar households consisted of several women, their brothers, the women's sons and daughters, and the daughters' children. Shortly after puberty, a girl underwent what might be termed a wedding ceremony with a young man. This ritual, however, did not create any relationship between the girl and the man: most commonly, he disappeared from her life forever.

The ceremony, however, changed the girl's status to that of a mature woman. She was then entitled to receive lovers of specified castes. Some of her liaisons might last only one night; others might endure for years, with the man bestowing occasional gifts on the woman. Children born to the woman lived in her household, where they grew up as fully accepted members of her descent group and of society.

The Nayar proved to be the exception that proved (that is, tested) the rule about the universality of marriage and found it lacking. Marriage, as it had traditionally been understood, clearly did not fit the Nayar case, but Gough suggested a reformulation of the definition that did. She proposed that marriage be more broadly defined as a relationship between a woman and one or more other persons that legitimates the woman's offspring. This definition clearly fits the Nayar: the marriage ceremony undergone by the

Marriage is a family affair in Borneo. Here family heads negotiate a brideprice. (courtesy of John Landgraf)

girl socially qualifies her to bear children. Those born after their mother's ceremony are considered fully legitimate members of society. The utility of the revised definition is made clear by another case as well. In parts of Africa, a rich woman is permitted to marry a female slave. The slave is then permitted to conceive children by an authorized lover. The children, however, belong to their social father, the noble woman.

If a female father seems an impossibility, the fault lies with the English word, which in general usage covers three distinct functions, some or all of which are recognized in most societies. The *physiological father* is the male who actually impregnates the woman. Recognition of this function is not universal: some societies have no accurate understanding of the physiology of conception, believing, among other things, that a child grows from repeated infusions of semen that may even come from different men. Trobriand islanders believe that a child grows from a spirit that lives in the water but enters the mother after sexual intercourse has opened her vaginal canal; the male's contribution is only to widen the passageway for the spirit child to climb in.

The *genitor* is the person socially recognized as fathering the child, if such a concept exists. He may or may not be the same person as the physio-logical father. The person responsible for the child's social identity is the *pater;* this man may or may not be the same as the genitor or the physiologi-cal father. This is the role Americans refer to when they speak of a child "born without a father." Even those who use this expression acknowledge, however, that some genitor "fathered" the child. In a similar way we may also divide the woman's role into *genitrix* and *mater*. Motherhood, being a fact, as Bernard Shaw observed, while fatherhood ("genitorhood," in our terms) being nothing more than a strong supposition, it is, logically, more difficult to separate genetrix from physiological mother.

The institution of adoption, which gives a child a pater and mater differ-ent from his genitor and genitrix, demonstrates the purely social nature of the former roles. American culture tends to combine the various aspects of parenthood into one indissoluble role. American adoption procedures, for example, include changing the child's birth records to indicate that his adoptive pater and mater are his genitor and genitrix, which in fact they are not: if they were, the adoption itself would not be neces-sary.

The incest taboo

Regardless of whether they recognize marriage in our sense, all societies regulate sexual relations among their adult members. Some individuals are forbidden as sexual partners and others are permitted. An apparently uni-versal regulator of sexual relations operates through the kinship system. This is the incest taboo, which prohibits sexual relations between certain relatives. All known human societies forbid sexual relations between at least some categories of kinsmen, but, as we might expect, the forbidden categories of kinsmen vary from society to society.

The strength and universality of incest prohibitions have long fas-cinated scientists, and many different explanations have been offered. None, however, is completely satisfactory. It has been suggested, for exam-ple, that incest prohibitions exist in order to prevent excessive inbreeding, which can cause deterioration in a genetic stock as harmful recessive traits become manifest. This theory, first of all, assumes that people with no knowledge of genetics, or even the physiology of reproduction, understand the potential harmful effects of inbreeding well enough to establish elabo-rate safeguards against it and to hedge them round with significant mystical and emotional values. Second, it is not entirely clear that close inbreeding necessarily produces visible genetic deterioration. In fact, in a small population living close to the environment, it might have the oppo-site effect. Cleopatra, renowned as the greatest beauty of her age, was the

product of 11 generations of brother-sister marriage, a type of union practiced not only among the royal families of ancient Egypt, but also among
the Incas, the Hawaiians, and some other Polynesians in order to avoid di-
lution of the sacredness of the ruling line. Incest prohibitions, moreover, do
not necessarily prevent marriage of close relatives. They might, for example, taboo sexual relations with one type of cousin, but permit marriage
with another that is equally close genetically. For all these reasons, the biological explanation of the incest taboo does not seem very satisfactory.

Another theory advanced to explain incest taboos is that men and
women raised in the same household feel no sexual attraction for one another, and therefore, do not make desirable marriage partners (the prox-
imity-breeds-contempt hypothesis). Studies have shown, for example, that
children raised communally on Israeli kibbutzim rarely show any sexual
interest in one another after early childhood and most often marry outsiders. Additionally, A. Wolf's (1968) study of the Chinese custom of "adopt a
daughter-in-law, marry-a-sister" showed that men's marriages to their
adopted sisters were not as successful as other arranged marriages that
united individuals reared in separate households. On the other hand, there
is also evidence to dispute this hypothesis: the ethnographic record shows
that marriages between first cousins raised in the same household are relatively common and relatively successful among Arab Muslims. In any case,
if the theory were true that people raised together felt no sexual attraction
for one another, then there would be no need to construct an explicit, elaborate taboo against such matings.

Some theorists, particularly Bronislaw Malinowski (1931), hold that incest taboos serve to prevent sexual passions from disrupting the internal
structure of the family. According to this theory, rivalries and jealousies
would inevitably arise if intrafamilial sex were permitted, thus causing a
disruption of the proper functioning of the family, the core social unit of
the society. Sexual relations, however, are a time-proven method of achieving intimacy, and there is no reason why sexual relations within the immediate family, particularly between brothers and sisters, should prove
disruptive if rules were formulated to regulate them. Polyandrous marriages, in which a group of brothers marry the same woman, imply the
possibility of avoiding or overcoming jealousies generated by brother-sister
marriage in people socialized to accept it. Moreover, there is nothing more
disruptive to families and households than removing a long-established
member and replacing her (or, less frequently, him) with a relative stranger.

Another explanation for the incest taboo emphasizes the favorable effects of *exogamy,* or marrying outside one's own group, over *endogamy,* or
marrying within one's group. Contracting marriage with another group,

according to anthropologists from Tylor (1888) to Harris (1975), has the advantage of widening the circle of people on whom one can rely and the potential resources to which one may have access. In some cases, two groups routinely exchange women, reinforcing their ties over a number of generations.

As this brief survey indicates, the reason for the incest taboo remains a significant but unresolved theoretical problem in anthropology. It might prove more fruitful, therefore, to bypass for now the cause of the incest taboo and concentrate instead on its effects. Regardless of the particular form it takes, the incest prohibition forms an integral element of the marriage system, which, in turn, is a crucial element of any society's kinship structure.

KINSHIP BONDS

Kinship, in all societies, encompasses more than the immediate household. People recognize ties of kinship to a larger group of relatives, sometimes numbering into hundreds or even thousands of individuals. In general, kin relations depend on: (1) ties of marriage, technically called affinity; (2) ties of descent; or (3) a combination of both. That is, your relatives are people from whom you are descended, who are descended from you, and with whom you share a common ancestor or descendant, and the people these relatives have married and their relatives.

No social group recognizes bonds of kinship with *all* the individuals to whom biological or affinal relationships could possibly be traced. The numbers would become too cumbersome and the obligations too burdensome. As we might expect from what we have learned about culture, these exclusions and inclusions in recognizing kin are systematic and operate according to certain principles. Anthropologists recognize two main classes of descent rules: *cognatic rules,* which use both male and female lines to establish the duties, rights, and privileges of social life; and *unilineal rules,* which use either the male line or the female line exclusively.

Cognatic kinship systems: bilateral descent rules

The pattern of kinship most familiar to Americans recognizes kinship ties equally through both the father and the mother, and through both sons and daughters. Because this system gives equal weight to both sides of one's descent, it is called *bilateral.* The kin group formed by this system extends equally on both sides of ego in concentric rings, including all those related to ego by blood to as many degrees as are deemed suitable. This group, called ego's *kindred,* includes all the relatives of both ego's father and his mother.

If you consider the kindred of your son or daughter, however, you will note an interesting feature of bilateral descent. Your child's kindred includes your kindred (although some of the more distant relatives will probably drop off) and the kindred of your husband or wife, too. Thus, your child's kindred is not identical to your own. In the same way, the kindred of neither of your parents is identical to yours. Your father's excludes all of those relatives you reckon through your mother, and your mother's, conversely, excludes all those on your father's side. Only you and your full brothers and sisters share a similar kindred at birth.

The kindred is thus called an *ego-centered group,* although it is actually not really a group at all, according to the definition we used in the preceding chapter. A kindred acts in common only in reference to a given individual; that is, a person's entire kindred to the third degree of relationship may gather for his wedding or his funeral. But relatives on different "sides" of a given person's kindred are not necessarily related to each other, and thus concerted action of any kind by a bilateral kindred is not at all likely. One of the few kindred organizations known to undertake any sort of concerted action was the Anglo-Saxon *sib.* In Anglo-Saxon society, the sib was the body responsible for revenge when one of its members was murdered, or for blood money when one of its members committed murder. Calculated on a bilateral basis from a particular individual, it included all relatives to the fifth degree of relationship. The sibs of even the members of one's own sib therefore differed slightly. Except for the blood feuds of the Appalachian mountains, which are based on the Anglo-Saxon system, the bilateral kindred has lost any semblance of concerted action in the United States.

Cognatic kinship systems: ambilineal descent rules

A type of kinship organization somewhat less familiar to Americans, but still based on tracing ties through both men and women, is the *ambilineal* (two lines) lineage. In this case, all descendants of a given founding ancestor, whether traced through men or women, form the lineage. Unlike bilateral systems, which give equal weight to all lines of descent, the ambilineal only considers those lines leading to the founding ancestor; like the bilateral systems, it ignores the sex of the intervening relatives. Unlike the bilateral kindred, with its ambiguous membership, the ambilineal lineage has a potential for unambiguous boundaries. The clans of Scotland also represent a variant of ambilineal descent. This descent rule became known relatively recently and is still subject to some confusion. A unilineal form also exists and is discussed below.

Characteristics of cognatic systems

Both bilaterial and ambilineal descent recognize both parental lines in reckoning group membership and thus belong to the first of the two major types of kinship systems: the cognatic and the unilineal. Cognatic systems (from the root meaning "born together") contrast with unilineal systems (from "one line"), which recognize only a single line of descent, either the father's or the mother's (but not both simultaneously), in reckoning group membership.

As we noted in discussion of the bilateral kindred, a serious structural problem of cognatic kin groups is that they generally have ambiguous membership. There may not be a generally agreed upon rule stating at which degree of relationship people stop being considered relatives. Are your sixth cousins, for example, whom you probably have never met and whose identities you probably don't even know, your relatives? What about your third cousins, people about whom you may have heard but have never seen? What about your brother's great-grandchild or your father's great-aunt? Although this problem is most obvious in bilateral systems, ambilineal systems may have similar flaws.

Unilineal descent systems: patrilineal, matrilineal, and ambilineal

Under a unilineal rule of descent, however, such ambiguity is not possible. If the system is patrilineal, you belong to the same group as your father and his brothers and sisters, and his father and also his father's father. Other members would include your father's brothers' children (both sons and daughters) and your father's father's brothers and their children. Women born into the group are considered members but their children are not, because children always belong to the kin group of their fathers. Because everyone has only one father, everyone can belong to only one group. In a similar manner, a matrilineal system affiliates an individual with kinsmen of both sexes, related through women only. In an ambilineal system of the unilineal variety, descent is traced through men *or* women, but only through one in each generation. Therefore, an element of choice exists in affiliating with an ambilineage. In Samoa, ambilineal groups control the farming land; individuals affiliate with either of their parents' groups, depending upon which presents the more favorable situation.

Power and matrilineal systems. As we observed when comparing polygyny to polyandry, man-centered and woman-centered organizations are not mirror images of one another. Social structure accomodates the different roles of men and women. The patrilineal group concentrates power in the hands of men, who pass it to their sons. In the matrilineal group,

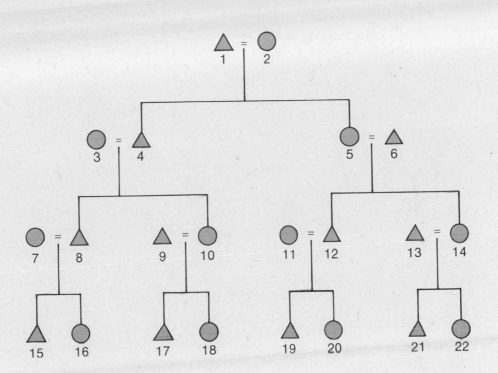

Patrilineal descent system — includes individuals 1, 4, 5, 8, 10, 15, 16

Matrilineal descent system — includes individuals 2, 4, 5, 12, 14, 21, 22

Ambilineal descent system — might include individuals 2, 4, 5, 8, 10, 17, 18

Bilateral descent system — includes everyone

Figure 7–1. Descent systems.

power also lies in the hands of men. Contrary to legend, no true matriarchy (society dominated by women) has ever been reported, nor is any believed to have existed. Although the matrilineal descent system recognizes only ties between women, that does not mean that women hold the power in matrilineal societies.

In a matrilineage or matriclan, the powerholders are the men of the group; that is, the brothers and sons of the women members. Authority, and in many cases, possessions, pass to a man from his mother's brother and from a man to his sister's son. If the society combines matrilocality with matrilineality, the household consists of a core of women, their children, and their husbands. The husband, however, is neither property-holder nor power-holder in his wife's household; these roles belong to her brother. A husband, meanwhile, has important economic, social, and often ritual interests in his sister's household, which is also his own natal home. Marriage tends to be a more fragile institution in matrilineal, matrilocal groups than it is in patrilineal, patrilocal ones where power and property are concentrated in the hands of husbands instead of brothers.

Unilineal descent groups

Their unambiguous membership gives unilineal descent groups a capacity for concerted action and a permanence that ego-centered cognatic groups lack. For this reason, unilineal groups may develop features that make them, in technical terms, corporate groups. Like the modern business corporation, they have an existence apart from the individuals that compose them. Such corporations function as true groups: members are aware that they belong to the group, and they organize themselves for interaction in terms of this membership. Such corporate kin groups often have officials analogous to the officers of a business corporation, who act in the name of the corporate group and administer internal affairs and external relations. And also like the modern corporation, corporate kin groups can own property. In many societies the most important economic resources are the property of unilineal kin groups rather than of individuals. Among the patrilineal Arabian Bedouins, for example, wells, waterholes, and oases belong to corporate kin groups, as does agricultural land among the matrilineal Trukese.

Like cognatic relationships, unilineal relationships can be traced to any degree of relationship. In many unilineal societies, different degrees of relationship represent different levels of social organization. Among the Bedouin, for example, if we were to trace descent from an ancestor in the oldest living generation, we might well find that the descendants are now all members of the same household. Tracing descent from a common ancestor known to have lived four or five generations in the past (one who was, for example, an old person during the childhood of the present-day old people), we find that the descendants form a group composed of related households all descended from this man. Such a group, which traces actual links to an historically known ancestor, is called a *lineage*. If descent is traced even further back, one eventually enters the realm of quasi-mythical ancestors to whom people cannot trace their relationship by secure or historically proveable links. The lack of such proof, however, does not lessen the importance of the social bonds tying the various lineages into a higher level of social organization known as a *clan*. Members of a clan claim common descent from a quasi-mythical ancestor. Often a clan is named for a plant or animal. A number of clans may in the same manner be bound together into a tribe (*phratry*) by descent from a yet more distant ancestor.

Many groups, like the Bedouin, use unilineal descent as a ideological charter to establish present day groups at several levels. In other words, they justify their various political and military alliances on the basis of purported kinship ties. Beyond the four or five generations available to living, or recently living, memory, Bedouin geneaologies tend to consist only of those ancestors who provide foci for existing groups. Conveniently, the names of ancestors who have no bearing on the formation or ratification of existing political groups often tend to be forgotten after five generations. The advantage of ancestry as an ideological charter, and the resultant formation of a segmentary lineage, is illustrated by the Bedouin. The Bedouin call their clans, lineages, and tribes *Beni* (sons of) or *Al* (people of) of the founding ancestor. At each level of organization, some ancestors become founders and others are forgotten. Thus, for example, the Al Murrah tribe consists of the Al Shoraim and Al Jabar lineages. At a higher level of organization, all the tribes of Arabia can theoretically group themselves into two great federations based on descent from ancestors who predate the Biblical patriarch Abraham.

When put to political or military use, this type of organization, the *segmentary lineage,* permits extraordinary flexibility. At every level of organization, as represented by a level of descent, roughly comparable groups mass according to the principle E. E. Evans-Pritchard (1940) called "complementary opposition." Thus, for example, brothers mass together in a dispute with their cousins, but grandsons of the same grandfather mass together in a dispute with the grandsons of their grandfather's brother. All these men would mass together in a dispute with the descendants of a yet more distant ancestor. Thus, disputes tend to escalate to the maximum appropriate level of complementary opposition. In times of danger, however, such a kinship segment has extraordinary resources of aid. Marshall Sahlins (1961) has ascribed to this feature of the segmentary lineage the tremendous success of certain groups in what he calls "predatory expansion" at the expense of groups organized in other, less flexible ways. By allowing kinship to ramify into tribal structure, this system of organization makes the tribe nothing more than a very large family.

The segmentary lineage system gains its strength by giving equal (or nearly equal) geneaological weight to all unilineal lines of descent. To accomplish different purposes, however, unilineal groups can be organized along other lines. In some systems the various subsidiary lineages radiate out from a central "spinal chord" lineage. A kin group of this type usually owns a valuable office, often a monarchy, or a piece of property. The office is inherited from the present incumbent by his (or her) eldest child of the appropriate sex. The subsidiary lineages take precedence according to their closeness to the primary line of descent. An example of such a lineage is a European royal family.

Kinship and ecology: determinants of descent systems

Much anthropological theory has attempted to determine the causes of the various kinship systems, and to explain their incidence in different societies. Although correlations are far from exact, it appears that family structure is related to ecological adaptation. Cognatic kinship, especially the bilateral variety, appears to be related to the nuclear family household, which is usually found at the two extreme ends of the technological scale, among hunting and gathering and industrial societies. In both kinds of societies, the subsistence system encourages, and even requires, relatively high mobility of small units. Hunters and gatherers must move in small groups through sparsely endowed countryside, always ready to join with or separate from other groups. Members of industrial society are highly mobile as well, and must be ready to move to distant places to exploit job opportunities. The nuclear family is, therefore, the only viable household in these societies.

Unilineal systems, on the other hand, tend to be correlated with societies in the middle range of cultural complexity; that is, among pastoralists, horticulturalists, or agriculturalists. Wherever important immovable economic resources, such as gardens, agricultural land, pastures, or waterholes exist, the unilineal descent group acts as a corporate landowner, ensuring cooperation in such activities as clearing land, sponsoring feasts, and providing aid to the sick and the elderly. In addition to its basic economic functions, the unilineal descent group generally has important social functions (regulating marriages), political functions (settling disputes and organizing fighting), and religious functions (holding its own rituals and ceremonies). Not all societies in the mid-range have unilineal descent groups. Generally, societies with unilocal residence that also engage in warfare are most likely to have unilineal descent groups.

Patrilineal systems dominate in societies in which the solidarity and continuity of the male group has survival value, either for subsistence, as in nomadic herding and many types of agriculture, or for warfare. Men of the lineage learn to work together and, since they remain on lineage territory, they have a thorough knowledge of the area and its resources. Patrilineal systems are markedly more common than matrilineal ones. Some conditions appear to favor matrilineality, such as subsistence patterns that require the men to be frequently away from home, tending flocks of sheep

In American society, the nuclear family pattern tends to isolate the elderly. (courtesy of Henry Stern)

or engaging in industrial wage labor while the women keep gardens. In these systems the women provide essential food, which the men supplement. The family's basic economic resource is thus in the hands of women.

KINSHIP TERMS

As we noted early in this chapter, kinship systems do more than provide the structure for social groups. They also assign statuses and roles to individuals. The tremendous variety we have seen in household and kin groups suggests that equal variety exists in the possible kinship statuses people may occupy or the roles they may be called upon to perform. At this point, it is extremely important to be aware that actual genetic or biological relationships have no bearing on kinship status and role. A clear example is the treatment accorded by various societies to the relatives who are the sons and daughters of our parents' siblings. In the American system, the sons and daughters of both the brothers and sisters of our parents occupy similar statuses, play roughly similar roles, and are referred to by the same term: cousins. This is a result of our bilateral descent system.

Under a unilineal system of descent, however, most of the people Americans call cousins do not belong to ego's own kin group. In a patrilineal system, for example, only the children of ego's father's brother are necessarily in the same lineage as ego. The children of father's sister and mother's sister belong to the lineages of their fathers, while the children of ego's mother's brother belong to the same lineage as ego's mother. In a matrilineal system, the situation is reversed. The children of ego's mother's sister share lineage membership with ego. The children of ego's father's sister belong to the same lineage as ego's father. The children of ego's mother's brother and ego's father's brother belong to the lineages of their mothers.

The kin relationships that we cluster under the term "cousin" may thus be construed quite differently in other societies. Anthropological terminology recognizes this fact by making distinctions between cousins according to the sex of the intervening relatives. Parallel cousins are linked to one another by parents who are siblings of the same sex; that is, ego's parallel cousins are children of either father's brother or mother's sister. Under a unilineal system, one of these belongs by necessity to ego's own descent group. Cross cousins are linked to one another by parents who are siblings of opposite sex; that is, ego's cross cousins are children of either mother's brother or father's sister. In unilineal systems, neither of these ordinarily belongs to ego's lineage. In many societies the cross cousin is the preferred marriage partner while the parallel cousin falls under the incest taboo. The difference in social roles could not be greater!

Descriptive and classificatory systems

The example of the cousin underlines the importance of looking at kinship systems through the eyes of those within them and of taking care to apply the criteria relevant to the actors themselves. For many years kinship studies foundered because early students ignored this proviso. The first major student of kinship, Lewis Henry Morgan (1870), distinguished two types of kinship terms, those he called descriptive and those he called classificatory. A descriptive term is one that names a single genetic relationship; in Morgan's terms, it described a relationship. Examples are father and brother. A classificatory term is one that groups together several genetic relationships; in Morgan's terms, it classifies them. An example of this might be the South Indian term that includes our idea of both father and father's brother.

Morgan then lost much of the value of his insight by making two mistakes. He went on to distinguish systems of terminology as descriptive (based on descriptive terms) or classificatory (based on classificatory terms), with the implication that descriptive systems of terminology—of which ours was the leading example—were more "advanced" than the

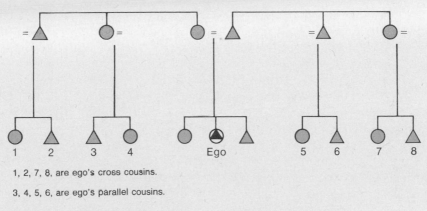

1, 2, 7, 8, are ego's cross cousins.

3, 4, 5, 6, are ego's parallel cousins.

Figure 7–2. Cross and parallel cousins.

"primitive" classificatory systems. But, as we have seen, "cousin" is a classificatory term that other systems analyze and therefore "describe" more closely than ours. Our system contains other classificatory terms as well: uncle, which is father's brother, mother's brother, or the husband of father's sister or mother's sister; grandmother, which is father's or mother's mother, and so forth.

Morgan's second error was to confound the term applied to a person with the perception of that person. Morgan assumed that because a person referred to his mother and her sister by the same term he could not distinguish between them. This is obviously no more true than the assumption that an American does not know which of his uncles is his father's brother and which is his mother's brother. An important contributory factor in this crucial mistake was the use of English translations for foreign kin terms rather than the terms themselves. Thus, for example, if a term referred to both mother and mother's sisters, translators often rendered it as "mother," giving the impression that an individual calls his mother's sister by a term meaning what the English term "mother" means. In fact, to the native speaker of the language in question, the term means no such thing. It probably means something to the effect of "woman of the senior generation of my own matrilineage." If the term is rendered in this fashion, it clearly applies equally to mother and her sister, and it clearly is no more "primitive" or inexact than our "cousin."

Principles of kinship

Little real progress occurred until anthropologists realized that only emic criteria yield the proper meaning of kinship terms. An analysis of the

American kinship system uncovers our assumptions and the emic criteria implicit in the terms. On the most obvious level, for example, American kinship recognizes sex: every term except cousin has a masculine and a feminine form. Secondly, it recognizes differences in generation, such as the difference between father and grandfather or daughter and grand-daughter. Every term (except perhaps the somewhat vague "cousin") indicates the generation of the person in question, relative to the speaker's generation. In addition, American kinship distinguishes between kinsmen by descent and kinsmen by marriage. This criterion, known as *affinity* (your relatives by marriage are your *affines*), recognizes the distinction between mother and mother-in-law, or brother and brother-in-law. Finally, American kinship recognizes line of descent. It separates those individuals in ego's direct line of descent from those in related but different lines; that is, it distinguishes lineal and *collateral* (on the side) kin.

To understand the difference between lineal and collateral kin, let us study a pair of terms. Father and uncle are alike in sex (both masculine) and in generation (one above ego). The difference between them is that father is an ancestor of ego, while uncle is not. The word father may therefore be translated as "male of the first ascending generation of my direct line." Uncle, on the other hand, means "male of the first ascending generation of a close collateral line." We may observe the same distinction between daughter and niece: they match in sex and generation, but differ in lineality or collaterality. Daughter is ego's descendant, therefore a member of his own line; niece is a descendant of a collateral line, that of one's brother or sister.

In addition to these four criteria—sex, generation, affinity, and collaterality—anthropologists have isolated four other criteria commonly used in the hundreds of kinship terminologies they have analyzed. These criteria require some explanation because they do not generally appear in American terminology. The first makes a distinction between the uncle who is father's brother and the uncle who is sister's brother. It divides relatives, including those we call aunt and cousin, according to the parent through whom the relationship is traced. It means more or less what we mean by an "aunt on my father's side." Called *bifurcation,* this distinction produces different terms for "uncle through my father" and "uncle through my mother." The second criterion makes a distinction (already noted) between parallel and cross cousins. It divides those relatives linked through two siblings of the same sex (a mother and her sister, for example) from those linked through relatives of opposite sex (a mother and her brother). The third criterion recognizes the *relative age* of the individuals within a category. In such systems, ego distinguishes his older siblings from his younger ones by using different terms for them. He also uses different terms for the older and younger siblings of both his parents. And finally, the fourth criterion is the *sex of ego*. Sometimes there are two sets of terms used for kinsmen; which is used depends upon whether the speaker is a man or a woman.

Kinship terminological systems

In addition to isolating a relatively small number of criteria operative in kinship systems all over the world, anthropologists have isolated a relatively small number of terminological systems that, in different languages, appear in many different societies. By convention, anthropologists describe each system by giving an abbreviated version of it, showing the terminology used for ego's generation and the generation directly above. Each system is called by the name of a society in which it was reported.

Eskimo terminology. Americans and most, if not all, Europeans use the Eskimo terminological system, which is found not only in industrial and commercial societies, but also in many hunting and gathering societies. There are three interesting features of the Eskimo terminology:

1) The terms used for the nuclear family members are not used for anyone outside the nuclear family;
2) The system distinguishes lineal from collateral relatives; and
3) No distinction of any kind is made between relatives on the mother's side and those on the father's side.

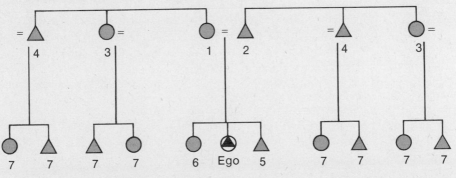

Figure 7–3. Eskimo terminology.

The prominence of lineal descent in the Eskimo system is probably related to the importance of the nuclear family in the neolocal household system that prevails in these societies. Both hunting and gathering and industrial societies emphasize mobility and the independence of the nuclear family as a productive unit. Societies using the Eskimo system generally lack corporate descent groups and rely instead on the bilateral kindred, whose vastness is particularly advantageous for the hunting and gathering family in times of need.

Hawaiian terminology. The Hawaiian system is similar to the Eskimo, but it lacks the criterion of collaterality. It groups all relatives of the same sex and generation, whether lineal or collateral, paternal or maternal, under one term. This system appears to be associated with extended households in which the nuclear family is relatively insignificant and descent is ambilineal.

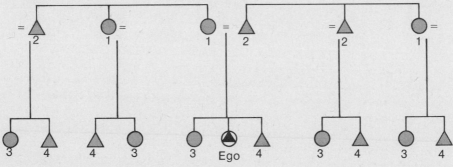

Figure 7–4. Hawaiian terminology.

Iroquois terminology. Although it plays little part in cognatic societies, the criterion of bifurcation comes into play in unilineal societies. In the Iroquois system, the same term is used for father and father's brother; likewise, mother and mother's sister. But father's sister and mother's brother each have their own terms. Parallel cousins on both sides form one category and are distinguished from cross cousins on both sides. In ego's

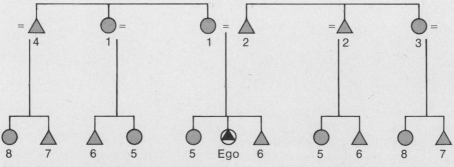

Figure 7–5. Iroquois terminology.

own generation, male parallel cousins are classed with brothers and female parallel cousins with sisters. All male cross cousins are called by a particular term and all female cross cousins by another. This system clearly indicates unilineality, and 70 percent of the societies that use it have unilineal descent groups. The reason for equating the parallel cousins who belong to ego's descent group (father's brothers' sons, if patrilineal) with those who do not (mother's sisters' sons) is not definitely known, but the system is often associated with marriage alliances based on cross cousin marriage.

Omaha terminology. Omaha terminology, which is associated with exogamous unilineal descent groups, distinguishes father's kin from mother's. In fact, it applies different naming criteria to members of father's patrilineage than to members of mother's. On the mother's side, it groups all members of her patrilineage by sex only. On the father's side, however, it groups all members of the father's patrilineage by generation as well as by sex. This system groups all parallel cousins with siblings and distinguishes the two types of cross cousins from each other and from all others of their generation. The grouping of the patrilateral parallel cousins with siblings obviously indicates membership in the same patrilineage. The inclusion of matrilateral parallel cousins in the same category, however, may appear puzzling. If, however, we remember the requirement of group exogamy, a solution suggests itself. Father's brother probably married a woman of the same patrilineage as did father, possibly even mother's sister. In that case, mother's sister's child is also father's brother's child and a member of the same patrilineage.

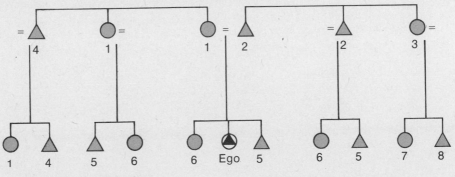

Figure 7–6. Omaha terminology.

Crow terminology. Crow terminology describes a matrilineal system and is, if only two generations are considered, the mirror image of Omaha terminology. If however, the generation of ego's children is represented, then the criterion of sex of the speaker comes into play and the systems are no longer perfectly reversed. This is so because the children of a male ego in a patrilineal system belong to ego's lineage, as do the children of a female ego in a matrilineal system. The Crow and Omaha terminological systems appear to be the product of unilineal descent, since 90 percent of the societies with Crow or Omaha systems are based on unilineal descent groups.

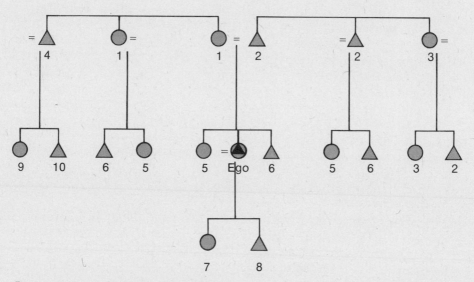

Figure 7–7. Crow terminology (female ego).

Sudanese terminology. The final terminological system, the Sudanese, is relatively scarce and quite complex. It differentiates each status in both

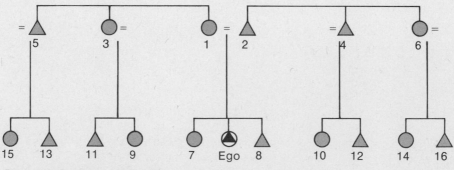

Figure 7–8. Sudanese terminology.

generations; that is, it is a completely descriptive system. Found throughout the Middle East, this system is often associated with *endogamous* patrilineages. That is, a man's preferred marriage partner is father's brother's daughter. Thus, one type of parallel cousin is a potential wife and the other is a member of an entirely different lineage. The two cross cousins also belong to different lineages. Father's brother may become father-in-law, which is something father could never become. This may account for the large number of distinctions.

FIELD PROJECT: KINSHIP SYSTEMS

I. CHART

Because nonfamilial groups and voluntary associations figure so prominently in American society, it may be that kinship has no bearing on the group that you are studying. In this case you may carry out the following study on your own family or on one you know well.

A. Using the standard anthropological symbols,* chart your personal kindred to G+2 (include all your grandparents and their siblings, but not the siblings' children) and C² (include all your first cousins). Extend it to as many generations as you have.

B. Label your kin with their personal names.

C. Underneath the personal names, label yourself ego and label the others by the appropriate kin term.

II. PAPER

A. List all the principles of kinship used in the family under study.

B. Using the chart with yourself as ego, indicate an example of each principle. The examples should be stated in the terms "I call (*personal name*) (*kin label*), but I call (*personal name*) (*kin label*)."

Example: Generation is the principle of kinship that sorts kin according to levels of descent. I call John Jones "father," but I call Tony Jones "grandfather," indicating a different generational level in our kinship system.

* STANDARD ANTHROPOLOGICAL SYMBOLS

△ male	⊓ sibling line
○ female	≠ divorce
= marriage	∅ death
∣ descent line	

It is possible to chart adoptions, children out of wedlock, divorces, remarriages, and other skeletons from the family closet. If there are skeletons you wish to remain hidden, you need not include them. If there is some reason for preferring anonymity, you may give the family fictive names.

Chapter 8

Control Systems

We now have the people arranged in their statuses, and well trained in their appropriate roles. We can therefore expect social life to flow along smoothly and effortlessly, right? Wrong! Social life, as everyone who has ever lived in a society knows, consists in part of correct, expected, harmonious behavior. And, in part, of mischief, dissension, arguments, injuries, and worse. The norms of the culture may be deeply embedded in peoples' minds and actions, but people do not always agree on what they ought to do and even if they do agree, they don't always do it. No society ever works like a machine, and not even a machine works perfectly all the time.

Well-designed machines, however, have special mechanisms to determine their proper course and to protect them from malfunctions. They have steering, guidance, or control systems to determine what they ought to do, when, at what speed, in what direction, or whatever is relevant. And they have built-in safeguards that keep the works from being destroyed when something goes haywire. Even more than machines, societies need systems of control and safeguard. They have more "moving parts," more delicate "works," more possible ways of going on the blink. No social life is possible, after all, unless a minimum level of order prevails.

FUNCTIONS OF CONTROL SYSTEMS

For a society to maintain order, it must be able to fulfill three major functions. First, a society needs an orderly method of making decisions that affect the entire group. Should we, for example, break camp to seek a different waterhole or should we stay to see if more animals will come to drink at this one? Should we move the flocks through the mountain pass or by way of the meadow? Should we treat a rival group's action as an insult or merely as an annoyance? Should we hold the initiation this year or next year? Should we end the oil depletion allowance or let it continue? A number of different opinions may exist on each of these issues, all backed up with valid, even moving, arguments. Each of these decisions vitally affects the interests and future of some or all members of the group. People may care about them passionately enough to resort to blows. But if group life is to continue, then some orderly means of arriving at group decisions must be found.

Secondly, a society needs an orderly way to deal with people who break its norms. What should we do about a person who takes more than his share of the meat from the hunt? One who steals the harvest of his neighbor? One who runs off with her friend's husband? Or one who kills a fellow group member? Should we leave the repair of the damage caused by these acts to the efforts of the individual affected? Should we rally the whole group on one side of one or the other? The injured victims demand retribution. The nature of society demands that norms be enforced; a norm that goes unenforced, after all, shortly ceases to be a norm. Thus, there must be some recognized means of handling people who break the rules.

Finally, a society needs an orderly way to deal with disputes among members. A claims that B has willfully planted on A's land and is ready to tear down B's fences to stop him. B claims that A is mistaken: the land in question was left to B by a relative. C claims that D promised to sell an animal for a certain price; D says that the agreed price was half again as high. E says F hit his car while he, E, was proceeding properly along the highway. F says E pulled unexpectedly out of his lane, forcing F to hit him. A society, in order to survive, must have an established means for settling disputes among its members.

Institutional differences in control systems

These decisions relate to the realms of politics and law. In American society and in Western societies generally, we are used to dealing with policy decisions affecting large numbers of people through the political process, and with those serious disputes and departures from important norms through recourse to the law. We have special roles and institutions to deal with these problems. There are elected and appointed officials of all kinds: presidents, members of Congress, governors, and commissioners. The courts, both civil and criminal, play an important part in handling these problems.

Special roles in the judiciary include those of judge, jury member, and lawyer. The role of policeman is part of our control system, as are the institutions of elections, hearings, trials, lawsuits, and grand jury investigations. Recalls, petition drives, conventions, and the unofficial customs of lobbying, letter writing, demonstrations, and even bribes, are all part of our control system.

Furthermore, our society is large, complicated, and very diverse. Its members represent an enormous number of special interests. We have an enormous number of specifically enforceable norms, and therefore an enormous number of potential and actual violations of norms. Many people, taking part in their normal activities, naturally become embroiled in many disputes. Because of the size and complexity of our society, Americans spend a large amount of time and resources on politics and law. Selecting a president, for example, takes two years and millions of dollars. Buying a house, driving a car, finding a job, any of a hundred ordinary activities may bring an American into contact with the law.

Our system of law and politics, furthermore, represents an evolution that has taken place over thousands of years in many countries on two continents. We view it as embodying the distilled wisdom of the ancient Hebrews, the Greeks of the Golden Age, the Roman Empire, the French Revolution, British history since the Norman conquest, and some particularly momentous periods in the United States. So, in our typical ethnocentric fashion, we see our system of politics and law not only as social mechanisms a good deal swankier than say, a tribal religous leader poring over scorched bones pulled from a fire or two Eskimos composing insulting songs about one another, but also as being different in kind.

In strictly functional terms, however, all societies have mechanisms that serve the purposes that politics and law do among ourselves. Decisions affecting the entire group, or even large sections of it, must be made by means that the people regard as legitimate. Whether this involves taking a vote or throwing darts at a target is immaterial so long as the people accept the result. Likewise, people must feel that those who break the norms important to the group are restrained and the social balance restored. Whether the method used to determine guilt involves a jury of one's peers or a dose of poison is likewise immaterial. And finally, people must feel that their disputes will be settled according to some system of consistent values, whether it involves consulting a law book or chicken entrails.

Because our institutions of politics and law are surrounded with such pomp and reverence and spring from such venerable antecedents, Americans often find it difficult to regard them in a strictly functional light. We ethnocentrically believe, for example, that the Supreme Court, meeting solemnly in its majestic building, in some way embodies a nobler or more real expression of human rightness than does, for example, a meeting of family elders among the Tiv of Africa. Although it is certainly true that the law expounded by the Supreme Court represents a greater intellectual sophistication and draws on a richer background than the decision of the Tiv moot, both serve the same purpose in terms of the functioning of the society: they enunciate the society's considered opinion on issues in dispute.

Even anthropological discussions of law and politics have not entirely escaped ethnocentrism. The very enormity of these institutions in our own society have encouraged anthropologists to seek counterparts in less complex and very different societies. This has led in some cases to a type of confusion we have encountered before. Instead of seeking *those institutions that fulfill, in other societies, the functions that law and politics do in ours,* some anthropologists have sought law and politics in all other societies. While it is true that all viable societies contain mechanisms that facilitate arriving at group decisions, enforcing norms, and settling disputes, it is not true that all societies carry out these functions through special institutions, as we do. Americans tend to think that these three functions are similar to each other because they all fall under the purview of one of our most salient institutions, the government. In the United States, in fact, the government takes responsibility for a much larger range of activities than those associated with maintaining order. Trends stretching over several decades have gradually transferred to the government functions that formerly belonged to the family, the church, and the local community. The United States belongs to that group of societies near the extreme in government involvement in social life. This perhaps hampers our ability to understand the functioning of some other societies that lack such an active government or lack a government altogether. A search for similar institutions results in two kinds of distortions: either politics and, especially, law are so broadly defined as to lose all their specific meaning; or non-Western institutions are forced to conform to the categories of Western thought.

A society that lacks anything we would recognize as a government carries out the three functions of our government through different institutions, such as religious and family organizations and ad hoc gatherings, or through the basic structures of the society itself. An important factor influencing a society's methods of maintaining order is the society's definition of itself. Presumably, every member of a group knows who else belongs to the group and for what reason. We don't mean by this that members can enumerate all other members (although this is sometimes possible), but that they can define the set of "fellow members of my group." Thus, for example, Americans can define their fellow members (called citizens) roughly as "all people born or naturalized in the United States, or born to

American citizens living abroad, who have not given up their citizenship."

For Americans, membership means a tie based on personal affiliation and residence; a "member" of any state, county or city can adopt membership in another merely by calling a moving van. Not all societies define membership this way, however. For an Eskimo, membership entails living and travelling with a group of people; any individual can change membership by joining up with another group. Particular pieces of real estate (a concept quite foreign to Eskimos) have no part in defining membership. For a Berber of North Africa or a Tiv of Nigeria, membership arises out of common descent from a given ancestor. Descent not only places any given individual within the group, but defines the limits of the group as well. In both these groups, however, territory does relate to group membership, as members of the same descent group collectively own the land of their ancestors.

All the group units we have discussed so far are similar (or at least were before the intrusion of Westerners) in that they form the matrix for the functions related to maintaining order. Within these units, people make decisions of common concern, enforce norms, and settle disputes. But the differences are so great that they may appear to obliterate the similarities! In studying systems of social control, anthropologists have grouped societies into four main categories roughly representing levels of complexity, size, and, perhaps not incidentally, technological development. Each ascending category contains societies that integrate larger numbers of people into more intricately organized units according to increasingly impersonal rules. The categories are conventionally known as bands, tribes, chiefdoms, and states.

BANDS

Bands exist at the lowest level of technological development, among hunters and gatherers. As we noted in an earlier discussion, these people exploit their environment through a system that requires a migratory existence and produces very little surplus. They are egalitarian and have little private property beyond a few personal effects; productive resources belong to the group at large, with all members enjoying substantially equal access. Bands consist of small groups of people; each band may contain from a dozen to one or two hundred members.

Within the band, social organization is simple. Ties of friendship or bilateral kinship bind individuals to the band and bands to one another. Except for households, no group intervenes between the individual and the band at large. Each band operates as an independent unit that may dissolve or recombine according to circumstance.

Decisions concerning the group at large are made informally, by consensus. The entire group may discuss the matter, either in a large meeting or in separate conversations. A consensus emerges as people weigh the various arguments proposed as well as the known intelligence, judgment, experience, or eloquence of the proponents. The group is so small that all have an intimate knowledge of the abilities of each member. If the decision requires technical knowledge, the opinion of the leading hunter, tracker, or holy man or woman carries special weight. This individual may even act as group leader for a time. Leadership, however, inheres in the situation rather than in any particular individual. A particular individual functions as leader only as long as his or her special characteristics are required to resolve the issue at hand. He or she enjoys no social or economic superiority, however; the basic egalitarian nature of the group prevails. The !Kung Bushmen of the Kalahari desert have hereditary leaders, but these men function largely as consensus-takers within the group or as spokesmen for the group to outsiders. If a headman is an ineffective leader, he is simply ignored. In no case does he enjoy special privileges or higher rank.

In enforcing norms and settling disputes (which in bands may often be the same thing), personal procedures also dominate. Among the Pygmies, for example, disagreements between individuals are usually settled by verbal confrontation, with each aggrieved individual shouting out the particulars of the dispute to anyone and everyone around (Turnbull, 1961). The other villagers are then free to make comments, chide, or ridicule the person they feel is in the wrong. If the verbal release of hostility does not succeed in clearing the air, eventually the whole village rises to quell the dispute by saying "You're making too much noise." Since the villagers do not judge who is right, village consensus forces the termination of the argument in an informal manner that does not create permanent divisions between members. For serious offenses that threaten the survival of the society, such as non-sharing of meat, violation of the incest taboo, and murder, bands sanction the offender by ostracizing him or her. Since a person cannot survive on his own, banishment from the group means death, and usually the mere threat of ostracism is enough to keep would-be offenders in line. Disputes in bands rarely involve theft or acts against property, since all productive resources belong to the community at large and individuals own only small quantities of portable personal effects. When an offense occurs, the injured party seeks to help himself in two ways. First, he (and most parties to disputes are men) seeks to restore his own standing and injured dignity. Second, he seeks to restore the social balance. Since there is no disinterested party to referee, the outcome depends on the community's view of the equities of the situation and on the relative power of the disputants. Several options present themselves. For example, disputes involving women dominate among the Eskimo. An Eskimo whose wife has been stolen by another man may kill the offender. If the murdered man has relatives, however, an attempt on the killer's life is almost sure to follow, necessitating another killing by the relatives of the now deceased wronged husband. With the proper demography and a bit of bad luck, this situation can rapidly develop into a protracted blood feud, with each side avenging successive killings. If, however, the offender is widely recognized to have transgressed the group's norms so often or so badly that there is no right whatsoever on his side, the wronged party may quietly obtain the prior approval of all members of the group and then kill him with no fear of retaliation. In some cases, however, an avenger is himself killed by his intended victim. Now two unavenged killings have been perpetrated by a single person. In such a case, the group may delegate the execution to one of the offender's own relatives, thereby obviating the possibility of feud, or a leader may act for the group at large.

A nonviolent Eskimo method of settling grievances is by holding a song contest. The victim challenges the offender, and the community gathers at an appointed time and place. Each attempts to compose songs that insult, ridicule, and belittle the other in an attempt to swing public opinion to himself. Eventually, one of the two emerges the winner, based as much on his ability to insult and entertain as on the issues of the case.

TRIBES

Tribal organization prevails among many peoples whose sedentary, food producing way of life permits somewhat larger, more densely settled and complexly organized groups than is possible among hunters and gatherers. Tribal societies resemble bands in their egalitarian social structure, however, as they lack marked stratification or economic differentiation along other than sex and age lines. The principal difference between tribes and bands is that tribes have integrating institutions or associations within the group; that is, individuals may belong to organizations intermediate between the immediate household and the tribe at large. Common examples are age sets and corporate kinship groups such as lineages. These entities integrate a large number of individuals over a wide geographic area into related units and provide each member with a well understood status vis-a-vis all other members.

The tribe generally lacks permanent, full-time leaders. As in the band, leadership often tends to be situational, arising out of particular needs and personal characteristics. Many tribes have a headman who inherits his status at least partially from his position in the kin group, but his role in influencing others is very limited. He cannot issue direct commands, but can only try to influence other members to act in a particular way. The success of a headman depends on his personality and the number of people he can get to support him. In Arabian Bedouin tribes, for example, leadership is generally the prerogative of certain lineages that have produced leaders for generations. The selection of a particular individual from those lineages, however, depends on a consensus of family heads from all the segments of the group. The vagaries of life in the desert make the personal qualities of a leader far more important than any automatic rule of succession.

Another example of an intermediate association in tribal organization is the age set system, which most frequently occurs in East Africa. The age sets of the Karimojong of Uganda typify this organization. Male status and political interaction derive from membership in one of the hierarchies of Karimojong age sets. Before initiation into a set, a young man takes no part in tribal decision-making. As his set advances through the grades, however, he becomes more and more involved in the affairs of both his set and his local community. Upon reaching full manhood, members of the set take the lead at both the tribal and local levels; the close personal ties of set-mates permits communication and consensus-making to occur relatively quickly throughout the tribe. Membership in the senior set also gives individual members authority within their own localities.

Segmentary lineages

In tribal societies, corporate kin groups are the most commonly-occurring example of the intermediate group that functions as a mechanism of social control. The segmentary lineage is one such kin group that has received considerable attention from anthropologists. Segmentary lineages occur among societies in Central and Western Asia, throughout the Middle East, and in North and sub-Saharan Africa. Theoretically, the members of a tribe are all descendants of a common, named ancestor, although, of course, this is not necessarily historically accurate. The group is in fact divided into segments based on descent from intermediate ancestors. Thus, for example, if the tribe contains two main segments, members say that the original ancestor had two sons. Within the main segments, smaller segments also define themselves according to descent from the original ancestor's grandsons, great-grandsons, and so forth.

Segmentary lineages, as discussed in chapter 7, serve as mechanisms of social control by mobilizing support or opposition at all levels of the tribe. Those segment members most closely related to the disputant ally themselves against the kinsmen closest to his opponent. At each level, kinsmen view themselves as a single body that is opposed to all other such groups (see Fig. 8–1). Thus, the grandsons of brothers from two different groups (H and J, for example) are normally in opposition to each other, but they mass together in opposition to the descendants of the brother of their common great-grandfather (L, M, N, and O). This principle can be called into operation on an ascending scale until an entire tribe may mass in opposition to another tribe.

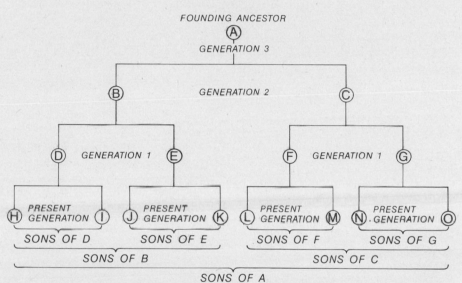

Figure 8–1. Schematic representation of a typical segmentary system.

Segmentary lineage systems operate "automatically" and without permanent leadership. Kinship obligation, rather than any central direction, calls the mechanism into motion. While a given level is active, a leader at that level may emerge, but his power lasts only as long as does the situation. Within a tribe, the segmentary lineage functions to mobilize opinion on issues and to enforce sanctions and settle disputes. Individuals with ambiguous or equal ties to feuding segments often serve as mediators. Mediators have no power to enforce settlements, however, and if the process of mediation breaks down, blood feuds between opposing segments can develop.

When a conflict involves two entire tribes, however, the segmentary lineage system offers no possible mediator because no one stands equidistant between the tribes. In a few parts of the world, however, permanent neutral intermediates do exist. In the Atlas Mountains of Morocco, for example, holy men whom Ernest Gellner (1969) calls "Saints of the Atlas" claim descent from special holy lineages entirely separate from the tribes. This descent gives them both the social standing required to deal with the tribes and the moral authority to declare truce and impose settlements. The Saints are not, however, leaders of the tribes. Rather, they rule special sanctified settlements recognized by the tribes as off-limits to violence.

The ability to mass large numbers of people quickly gives tribes organized by the segmentary lineage system a certain adaptive advantage over tribes organized according to other principles. In a process Marshall Sahlins (1961) calls "predatory expansion," a tribe such as the Nuer, which has segmentary lineages, is able to expand at the expense of a tribe such as the Dinka, which does not, because of the superior manpower the Nuer can bring to bear in any conflict.

CHIEFDOMS

While a tribe uses association to integrate its members into a single entity, a chiefdom uses the authority of a central leader. *Authority* may best be defined as legitimate or recognized power; that is, the group accepts as right and proper that certain individuals exert influence denied to others. The difference between the police and a vigilante mob, for example, is that the police use force under authority granted them by the community, whereas the vigilantes do not.

The chief, who often inherits his position and generally occupies it on a permanent, full-time basis, is differentiated socially from the group at large. The same is usually true of his family and close associates. Thus, chiefdoms exist in societies that can support some full-time specialists and that recognize differences of rank. Group members owe deference to their chiefs, who are often believed to possess extraordinary spiritual powers. Chiefdoms are rank societies, and thus operate on the principle of differential prestige and privilege for individuals, even though they may possess similar abilities. Nonetheless, a prestigious status does not necessarily involve real economic and political power.

The chief's influence extends to a number of areas of life. He may coordinate the cycle of religious observances; he often directs which crops are to be planted and where; he almost always coordinates a system of redistribution of goods; and he certainly acts as mediator in important disputes and as an enforcer of norms. Decision-making generally falls within the chief's authority as well, although the degree of influence other members of society may exert varies from group to group. The chief's power to actually enforce decisions is still limited by the number of people who will support him in a given instance.

A chief is expected to be generous, and, living in a kin-based society he must pay attention to the requests of his relatives. The islands of Polynesia produced many chiefdoms, along with often elaborate systems of redistribution and deference. Chieftainships have also been found in sub-Saharan Africa, among Bantu-speaking peoples.

THE STATE

The state is the form of organization we know from our own experience. It has the most centralized authority and the highest degree of specialization of all forms of political organization. It also has the densest population and the highest degree of social stratification. A state integrates a large population spread over many communities, usually including cities, into a single unit bound by a central administration. Stateless governments are based on the principles of kinship and association, whereas states are based on the principle of territoriality; that is, membership is defined by birthplace and residence.

According to Morton Fried (1967), the state political organization has two major functions: (1) to preserve the stratified order of the society, and (2) to maintain the entire social order for the state's population. The first means that the rules of the state are concerned with preserving property relations, the idea of hierarchy, and the power of the law. The second means that the state maintains internal domestic order and protects itself from external forces. Furthermore, in order to carry out these two major functions, states have evolved four secondary functions. Broadly, these are: (1) population control, which includes census taking, boundary maintenance, and definition of categories of citizenship; (2) judicial control, which includes codified bodies of law, courts, and judges; (3) enforcement control, which includes policemen, jails, and various state officials, and (4) fiscal control, which includes taxation and forced labor.

In states, we can speak of "the government" as opposed to "the society," whereas in simpler forms of organization the functions of government are merely functions of society. States monopolize legitimate force within their territories. Only the government, therefore, has the authority to settle disputes and enforce norms. The machinery of the state is the machinery of decision-making, and decisions made by the central authorities are binding on the people. State organization, by removing from the hands of individuals the means of settling many disputes or enforcing many sanctions, takes over the means and responsibility for social order. Disapproved behavior thus becomes a matter between the offender and the state rather than between the offender and the injured party. Among the first requirements of the establishment of state organization in tribal areas is ending the blood

The late King Faisal of Saudi Arabia at a public gathering. In many state societies, especially monarchies, the leader is separated from the common people, as indicated by the empty chairs. (courtesy of Claudia Crawford)

feud and the legitimacy of vengeance. Because the state monopolizes force, it monopolizes legitimate retribution. Thus, for example, when a national state was established in the Arabian desert in the early twentieth century, King Abd al Aziz al Saud, the founder of Saudi Arabia, carefully reserved for the state the right to punish wrongdoers; vengeance became a responsibility of the central government rather than of the tribal *Khamsàh,* or vengeance unit, that operated in the past. Injured parties ideally now had to turn to the law courts rather than to their own devices.

A particularly poignant example of the difference between state and tribal organization, reported by Turnbull (1968), comes from Africa. An elderly man killed a younger man for what appeared, to him and others, good cause. The young man's kin group, recognizing that the victim deserved to die, renounced vengeance and agreed to accept bloodwealth, rather than a life, from the old man's group, in order to restore the social balance. The old man, to forestall any possibility of a feud developing, openly admitted his act and the reasons for it and eagerly offered a bloodwealth payment.

The British colonial authorities, however, entered the case and took the old man to trial. Viewing the killing as an offense against the state authority rather than against the young man's kin group, the British accused him of murder. The judge therefore advised the old man of his rights under British law and cautioned him to keep silent, admit nothing, and prepare his defense. The old man, however, took the trial for a tribal council, interested, as any tribal council would be, in restoring the social balance while avoiding feud. In this context, a denial of his act, which he viewed as justified and even meritorious, was senseless; it would only heighten the danger of feud. He therefore insisted on explaining to the judge in detail what he had done and why he had done it. Because the reason given did not fit the British notion of proper justifications for homicide, the judge was forced, under British law, to find the old man guilty. And because the killing was obviously premeditated, he was forced to condemn the old man to death.

The relatives of the young man, much to the judge's chagrin, pleaded with the judge not to carry out this sentence. Frightened and surprised,

State societies often impose the trappings of democracy on pre-state groups. Here an American official observes an election in Ponape, Micronesia, Trust Territory of the Pacific. (courtesy of Marjorie Grant Whiting)

State societies have special functionaries whose job it is to maintain order. (courtesy of Henry Stern)

they insisted that executing the old man would only make matters worse. If they did not accept the bloodwealth openly offered, and furthermore exacted the life of the old man, the social balance would tip so badly against them that only the killing of several of their members would restore equilibrium. The judge, however, rejected their pleas. According to his system of laws, the crime against the authority of the state had to be punished; the execution of the old man was required to give the victim's family the justice they desired. (After the execution, events took the course the young man's relatives had foreseen, and a long, bloody feud took the lives of several more from each side.) In a tribal system, offenses are against individuals and kin groups. In a state system, they are against the state.

AGGRESSION AND WARFARE

It may be that societies erect such complicated barriers against disorder because disorder is so disruptive of essential social relations. Despite all our defenses against it, violence is a commonplace of human life. Rage, anger, aggression, and revenge live in our dream life, our symbolic and artistic life, and sometimes explode into our lives of action as well. People, both as individuals and as groups, fight to maim and kill, either with the sanction of their culture or without it. Any theory that would explain the political lives of people in groups is incomplete without a discussion of the realities of individual aggression and warfare.

Is aggression a human instinct?

In recent years, theorists such as Konrad Lorenz (1966) and Robert Ardrey (1961) have attempted to explain human violence as a result of what they believe is a human instinct toward aggression and war. Ralph Holloway (1968) and others counter this argument by pointing out that an instinct is a specific response pattern that does not vary in its development and that occurs in response to a specific cluster of stimuli. Like the rooting response of all primate babies, an instinct is not learned, but rather comes from an innate genetic pattern. It can be easily noticed, however, that human aggression occurs in response to an incredibly large and variable group of stimuli. Incidents that would bring a member of one culture to murderous rage might cause a member of another only mild irritation or even amusement. The distinguishing aspect of human violence is the joining of the old biological mechanisms of aggressive behavior, shared by most animal species, with man's cognitive symbolic systems. Culture can displace, channel, or diffuse aggressive feelings, or aim or discharge them symbolically, instead of physically. Neurology, genetics, and universal human nature cannot explain the difference between the gentle Pygmies and the fiercely aggressive Yanomamö. We must seek explanations in culture, rather than in biology.

Definitions

Before we can discuss aggression and warfare, we must be certain that we are all referring to the same things. By *aggression* we mean an individual act of violence presupposing some emotional basis; by *warfare* we mean collective hostile action, by members of one territorial group against another, that is regarded as a legitimate policy of the group. Warfare is a cultural and technological phenomenon; it is organized violence used as an extension of group policy but carried out on a different plane of action from simple aggression. To the question of whether all human groups experience warfare, our definition requires us to answer no. However, small-scale societies that do not have war do have feuds and homicides, so the lack of war does not reflect the absence of violence but rather the scale of the action and the strictness of our definition.

Interpersonal and intergroup violence exist throughout the world and

Aggression is culturally patterned, as this scene from American society shows. (courtesy of Henry Stern)

take widely varying forms. Understanding the place of violence in human
life requires that we sort out these forms. As with several other aspects of
culture we have examined, this task becomes simpler if we approach societies in terms of levels of scale, technology, and complexity.

Warfare among hunters and gatherers

War, as we have defined it, rarely exists among band societies of food collectors. Bands, as we have seen, lack tight organization and permanent memberships. People drift in and out, visiting relatives briefly or staying for
years. Bands merge or separate depending on ecological conditions. Marriage alliances tie widespread bands into a network of kinsmen. Band
society thus lacks the rigid division of people into "us" and "them" that
facilitates communal violence by one group against another.

This is not to say that band societies lack violence—only that they lack
the organized violence we have defined as warfare. Despite the stereotype
of gentle, pacific hunters and gatherers, research shows that some band-
level groups such as the Murngin of Australia have traditionally ex-

perienced a high level of aggression. Yet combat at the band level generally involves personal or, at most, family grievances; it is usually sporadic, relatively unplanned, individualistic, and fairly disorganized. It is carried on without elaborate weaponry and tactics.

Warfare among horticulturalists and pastoralists

In food-producing societies organized either as tribes or chiefdoms, we begin to approach conflicts recognizable as war. The nucleation and permanence of settlements, the higher population densities, and the capital investments represented by villages lead to an intensification of the warfare pattern, if not to its origin. Herdsmen, although nomadic, share many of the features of villagers in this regard. Both have the intense and unambiguous identification with their groups that can turn whole communities into enemies. Warfare at this level of organization is often vicious and deadly, with neighboring groups living in constant danger. Chagnon, for example, has vividly described the atmosphere of relentless hostility that surrounds the slash-and-burn farming Yanomamö. In food-producing societies, the settlement of private scores through homicides and feuds, as well as group-oriented violence, continues.

Conflict shows two faces among horticulturalists—that of an elaborate pageant and that of a bloody campaign of annihilation. In some groups, ritualized forms of combat follow well-known rules. Among the Dugum Dani of New Guinea, for example, warfare closely resembles the pomp and pageantry of a Sunday afternoon football game, the main difference being that a Dani "player" occasionally dies. The rules of warfare are strictly followed: fighting is stopped at the death or serious wounding of one person and each side is allowed one day of cease-fire for celebrating the death of an enemy. Dani warriors may even call a "time-out" for bad weather in order to keep their best feathers from being ruined by rain. Similarly, the Arabian Bedouin practice the *razzia,* or *ghazu,* which is a stylized raid to steal another group's camels. A well-executed raid follows strict standards of procedure: only a group of equivalent standing is attacked, and no blood is spilled. Etiquette, however, does not reduce the economic impact of the raid on the group whose camels are plundered.

On the other side of the coin, some food-producers have full-scale campaigns of conquest and killing that differ from modern warfare only in scale, effectiveness of weaponry, and degree of organization of military exploits. The Tsembaga Maring of New Guinea, for example, fight in deadly earnest to wipe out their enemies and take their lands. Tactics such as surprise attacks on sleeping hamlets or on women working in the fields are practiced by some of these warring groups. Although our general view of horticultural societies is one of balance, a more accurate representation of the situation in many societies is that of a constantly shifting scene of people being driven out, killed, or scattered, and of tribal territories expanding or contracting.

Causes of warfare

To explain the incidence of warfare among primitive agriculturalists, some anthropologists have turned to population pressure on resources as a cause. One of the most sophisticated versions of this argument is Harris' discussion of the constantly warring Yanomamö. Harris (1975) argues that the Yanomamö began to depend heavily on bananas and plantains for their food only in the last two centuries. This new food source permitted an increase in population and caused the land to be denuded of animals needed for the protein that bananas and plantains lack. The results of his ecological analysis lead Harris to conclude that warfare is an extremely subtle mechanism of population control.

Real population control in a society lacking contraception does not, Harris points out, depend on limiting the number of men: it is the number of women that is critical. Although about a quarter of Yanomamö male deaths result from warfare, according to Chagnon, realistically this need have little influence on the size of the next generation. Warfare does *not* lead to the deaths of a sufficient number of women to control the number of births. Rather, warfare controls population size by encouraging the development, over a period of time, of a set of values that favors males over females, because it is men and not women who become the warriors necessary to defend the group during warring periods. A strong bias in favor of boy babies leads inevitably to a bias against girl babies, to neglect of female infants, and occasionally even to female infanticide. Evidence from around the world suggests that societies that strongly favor men give girl babies inferior care and consequently suffer higher female infant mortality. Throughout the Arab Middle East for instance, male infants are nursed nearly twice as long as females. Harris claims that the ratio of boys to girls is often as high as 3 to 2 in warring groups.

A high death rate among female babies leads to an imbalance among adult men and women and, among the Yanomamö, to raiding for females. The constant stealing of one group's wives by another group merely continues the prevalent warfare and strengthens the preference for fierce male warriors, which in turn reinforces the low value placed on female babies. Because warfare inverts the relative value of women (who are biologically more valuable because they produce offspring) and men (who are more valuable only in situations of warfare), it is an effective mechanism of population control, Harris argues, and thus helps keep a society within the carrying capacity of its environment.

Other anthropologists, such as Andrew Vayda (1967), argue for a more generalized relationship between warfare and ecological variables. Taking a systems approach, Vayda claims that war is the response a cultural system makes to counteract a disturbance. Warfare, then, is a regulating mechanism, maintaining such ecological variables as population size, territory, or economic resources within a certain tolerable range. In an incredibly intricate fashion, Roy Rappaport, in his book *Pigs for the Ancestors* (1968), shows how the Tsembaga Maring engage in periodic, ritualized warfare in response to the productivity of their land, their caloric and protein needs, and the population level of both their people and their pigs.

Motives cited by the people who go to war seldom include population pressure, any more than motives cited for war among ourselves include control of oil fields or overseas markets. The Dugum Dani go to war for religious reasons: they must have an enemy death so that their loved one's ghost can rest in peace. The Yanomamö say they go to war over women. Most commonly, people believe they are fighting to avenge themselves of injuries or insults received from others. Anthropologists, however, point out that the incidence of such complaints goes up as the population approaches the carrying capacity of its lands. The commission of offenses likely to provoke anger, hatred, or revenge can conciously or unconsciously express the need for territory. It may seem strange to noncombatants that people who lose their lives don't ask the "real" reasons why. But the masking of the deeper causes of conflict is essential to groups locked into a system of population control that depends on war.

To recognize the general adaptive value of most primitive war does not imply that we must concede that every given instance of war can necessarily be explained by ecological considerations. Nor must we conclude that warfare always best serves its population control function. As Harris points out, warfare is at best a poor solution to a difficult problem. If it comes to dominate a way of life, warfare can cause constant suffering while depressing population levels well below the carrying capacity of the land.

Warfare in state societies

In states with systems of central control, the fragmented group pattern of tribal warfare gives way to a different scale of war: it is an instrument of the state, with conquest, slaves, or tribute as its aims. State systems make warfare more impersonal, both for the warrior and for the leader who calls him to combat. Modern soldiers rarely, if ever, fight to avenge a wrong against themselves, and usually have never even come in contact with the enemy. Furthermore, state stratification systems assure that members of the elite who make the decisions about going to war never risk their own safety in combat. "It is the privilege of the great," the French playwright Jean Gireaudou wrote of war, "to watch disaster from a terrace." Tribal leaders, by contrast, must show personal bravery in battle. No man could lead the Bedouin, for example, who did not enjoy a reputation as an outstanding warrior.

The progression of warfare from band to tribe to state consists of expanding the scale of the "we" and the "they." Large nation-states can marshall hundreds of millions of "we" against hundreds of millions of "they," in an aptly named "balance of terror." The conceptual model of insiders versus outsiders has not changed, but the technology has: devices of war now have the capability to end all human life. A new conceptual model, one that would join people together rather than separate them into "we's" and "they's," is necessary if humans are to adapt to the current ecological situation. Hunters and gatherers, who lived in marginal areas and needed and depended on one another for survival, did not practice warfare. In a different way, modern industrialists, who have the capacity to obliterate the world's population by pressing a button, also need and depend upon one another for their continued survival. It is time to form a new sociopolitical level of organization beyond the nation-state—one that will recognize and be built on this mutual need and dependence.

FIELD PROJECT: CONTROL SYSTEMS

I. Decision-making

Groups reach decisions by methods that range from an informal search for consensus, agreement of all group members, to a formal process of decision-making in which matters affecting everyone are decided on by persons at the top of a hierarchy and handed down to those occupying the lower statuses. For example, in a loosely organized social group of teenage boys, the decision whether to go for a drive or to a concert, to drink or to pick up girls, is generally made in an informal manner. Consensus is achieved by asking Tom and Harry what they want to do, finding out how Billy Joe feels about it, and discussing the desirable and undesirable aspects of the various alternatives until a decision is reached. Members of the group are often not even conscious that a decision-making process has occurred. To take a different example, two female secretaries working in an office decide that they would like to be able to wear pants to work. Two female clerks in the office don't feel pants are suitable, however. The secretaries ask the office manager if they may wear pants. The office manager is aware of the differing views that exist on the topic and the vehemence with which they are held, and feels the matter is important enough to merit the attention of the boss. Two weeks later the boss declares that it is permissable for the women in the office to wear formal pantsuits but not casual slacks. Members of this group are very conscious of the decision-making process.

A. Describe a situation in which a decision was made in your group. What is the general pattern of decision-making? The sets? The components?

   1. Is there a formal process of arriving at group decisions? Is there an informal process instead of, or in addition to, a formal process?

   2. Does your group have a formally recognized leader? What power does the leader have to enforce decisions? How does a member come to be the leader? What are the qualities that he or she must have? Are there different leaders for different tasks?

   3. How does this pattern of decision-making relate to the social structure of the group?

II. Norm Enforcement

   A. Describe what happened when someone in your group overstepped the bounds of acceptable behavior. What was the reaction of the

group? What is the general pattern of norm enforcement in your group?
1. Are there different types of transgressions that evoke different reactions? Can you rank these in terms of seriousness?
2. Does your group have any codified system of laws? If so, are all parts of it enforced equally? If not, how are newcomers (and anthropologists) taught proper behavior?
3. If your group is stratified, are there different norms and different degrees of norm enforcement at the various levels?
4. Groups vary in the amount of deviation they allow. Would you say that your group allows members much or little leeway in conforming to group norms? How does the amount of deviation allowed relate to the social organization of the group? How does it relate to and help to explain the behavior of members of the group?

III. Settling Disputes
A. Describe a quarrel, personal antagonism, or dispute in your group. What is the group's reaction to the dispute? What is the general pattern of settling disputes in your group?
1. Are disputes handled formally (for example, through a judge or mediator) or informally (for example, through peer group pressure)?
2. Are disputes settled by peers or are decisions handed down by higher status members?
3. Do other group members usually decide right and wrong or innocence and guilt for the disputants?
4. What do you think are the long-term effects of handling disputes in this manner? In other words, does this method of handling disputes contribute to the stability and cohesion of the group or does it promote ill-will and factionalism?

IV. Aggression
A. Does any form of violence or aggression occur in your group? If so, describe a particular incident during which violence occurred.
1. What are the beliefs, norms, and values of the group with regard to violence?
2. Is violence directed toward other group members or is it directed against people outside the group? What is its effect on group structure and dynamics?

Chapter *9*

Belief Systems

In 1633 the distinguished Italian astronomer and physicist Galileo Galilei went on trial for acts so dangerous to the established authorities of his time that he was threatened with torture and spent his last years in prison. One of the major criminal trials of Western history, this proceeding seems odd, even quaint, by modern standards. But Galileo was prosecuted in deadly earnest by his accusers. His crime: publishing a book, *Dialogue of the Two World Systems,* that argued that the earth moved around the sun. His judges: the Inquisitors of the Roman Catholic Church.

On the rare occasions that scientists have stood before the bar of justice in our time, their crime has generally been supplying secret information to an enemy state, not publishing a theory with little or no immediate practical advantage. But Galileo's act was thought to be as dangerous to the established order as handing over atomic formulas is today. In fact, it was probably more dangerous, because it threatened not just the strategic advantage of a government, but its authority as well.

How could the publication of the astronomical theory familiar to every school child of today threaten the basic order of society? As Galileo's accusers accurately perceived, his theory could ultimately bring about their overthrow by force of reason. It pulled the keystone from the arch of doctrine that supported the spiritual and temporal power of the Church. For their continued survival, the theory had to be discredited and Galileo silenced.

The specific issue at hand was the literal truth of church teaching. The Christian world at that time, relying on the best authorities and centuries of church doctrine, believed and taught that the earth was the center and goal of creation. The heavens revolved in perfect clockwork around the earth, the planet that claimed the special and continuing interest of God. Heaven occupied a region in the celestial heights clearly demarcated by the moving spheres; hell a dingy recess far below. The entire universe centered on the earth and on the continuing moral drama of the salvation of the human soul that the Church taught was the goal of life.

Galileo's writings knocked the earth rudely from the center of creation. Rather than a unique and enormously important element of the cosmos, earth became one of a number of planets (and an insignificant one at that!) circling an uncaring sun. Worse still, Galileo's solar system provided no handy left-over corners for the heavenly hosts and the demons of hell. Furthermore, his means of justifying this radical scheme (and of building on the work of the earlier astronomer Copernicus) depended not on the venerable authority of religion, faith, and revelation, but rather on the impudent authority of the human mind and the logic of mathematics.

Galileo was prosecuted because he threatened the Church's view of reality, its theory of the universe. Rightly perceiving what would follow if one such threat went unpunished, the church hierarchy called him "more dangerous than Luther and Calvin put together." They tried and convicted Galileo and forced him to repudiate his book because they knew that the institutional system they represented could not rule Galileo's scientific universe as it had ruled the one that derived truth from faith in church teachings. They intuitively grasped a truth that anthropologists have only started analyzing formally in the last 50 years.

What Galileo and his prosecutors disagreed about is called *world view* or, in more technical terms, *cosmology*—that is, a view of the world explaining the way things "actually" are; a theory of the nature of the universe and of man's place in it. The world view is an element of the larger set of *belief systems* found in every culture—the beliefs that stand behind and support the myriad items of thought, behavior, and emotion that comprise the patterns of behavior in any culture. Such a theory of the universe, such beliefs about what is real, natural, and right, are as basic to a cultural system as its means of economic survival or its mode of communication. The belief system binds the culture together at the same time that it anchors the individual firmly inside. It guides actions and molds institutions. It explains to human beings *why* they ought to act in the way that their culture and society make necessary.

BELIEF: A COGNITIVE SYSTEM

Man is a reasoning, inquisitive being, and cannot live adrift in a sea of random phenomena and purposeless activities. He seeks what the anthropologist Clifford Geertz (1965:7) calls "conceptions of a general order of existence" that have "such an aura of factuality" that the "moods and motivations" they inspire in men "seem uniquely realistic." In short, humans cannot exist without order, meaning, and understanding, which are provided for them by the culturally given belief system.

At its most basic level, a belief system is a cognitive system, or a system of perception, shared by the members of a group. It provides the individual with all-important explanations and meaning, thus helping him to understand the eternal "whys" of life: why death and suffering, war, and social injustice, and why does this happen to me? Moreover, it also provides the individual with a means for satisfying his desires for things such as rain, good crops, victory, and sons. If one understands what beings and forces make the world work, it is possible to manipulate these to get what one wants.

Many cultures, for example, provide concrete means for gaining, or attempting to gain, specific desired ends. These usually involve appeal to or control of the personal or impersonal forces that have the power to influence outcomes. Procedures such as rain dances, visits to saints' shrines, cloud seeding, and sacrifices of goods or livestock (or even human beings) are all attempts to bend the forces controlling the world to man's wishes.

ELEMENTS OF BELIEF SYSTEMS

At the cultural level, a belief system gives a cohesive view of the world and serves to integrate the various parts of the culture. At this level it can be analyzed as having four different elements: cosmology, values, myth, and ritual.

Cosmology

Cosmology, or world view, is a theory of the universe and its different parts, the beings that populate it (be they men, animals, spirits, ghosts, or *djins*) and the nature and hierarchy of these beings. The Dogon of Africa, for example, believe that each person consists of several spiritual parts. The *nyama,* inherited from various ancestors and spirits, provides the vital force that makes physical life possible. The *kindu kindu,* (double soul), a pair of twin souls of opposite sex created by the water spirit, permits thought, will, and action. The *kindu bomone* (stupid soul) permits further spiritual ties. Furthermore, each Dogon carries in his clavicles eight millet grains arranged in a pattern that indicates his standing. The complexities of Dogon cosmology preclude a complete explanation here. Nevertheless, it forms a complex and internally consistent body of belief.

A cosmology is a coherent explanation of the way things truly are, not necessarily of how they seem. Thus, because of Galileo's subsequent vindication, we all "know" that the earth revolves around the sun, even though to our uneducated eyes it seems that the sun rises and sets each day as it moves around the earth. A cosmology thus defines what is "real" in nature and explains the nature of reality.

Values

In every cosmology there is an evaluation of the elements composing the universe; that is, a set of beliefs and feelings regarding what is good and what is bad, what is desirable and what is undesirable. These beliefs, known as *values,* help mold behavior and thought. The Church authorities, for example, did not fear only Galileo's theory—it was not original with him and had circulated for some time in scholarly circles—but also feared that his prestige would encourage people to place a positive value on it, to accept it, and possibly to act on it. "Good" situations, in Galileo's view, included free investigation, the authority of science over that of tradition, a generally skeptical attitude toward received truth, and adoption of a more humble opinion of man's place in the cosmos. These contrasted sharply with "good" situations in the Church's view. The Church judged respect for authority, acceptance of the centrality of man in the scheme of creation, and desire to achieve heaven and avoid hell to be "good."

Sometimes values are explicitly stated in maxims like "Do unto others as you would have them do unto you." Other times values are unconscious and unexpressed (implicit), but still just as real and binding. Most Americans, for example, positively value material things more than spiritual endeavors. This inclination motivates a good deal of daily behavior as Americans strive to increase their material comfort. Those who reject this valuation, such as members of monastic religious orders, often follow behavior patterns that set them apart from the bulk of their countrymen. Very few Americans, however, were explicitly taught that material wealth outranks spiritual growth as a goal of action. Much explicit instruction of children, in fact, teaches precisely the opposite view. The pervasive materialism of the culture is nonetheless transmitted to children by example, and they generally learn to behave like their elders.

Like the cosmology, the values of a culture, particularly the implicit values, are difficult to change precisely because they are thought of as "natural" and "real" and so completely taken for granted. For example, people involved in the Women's Liberation Movement feel very strongly that Western society places a *negative* value on women and that they must work hard to convince a skeptical audience that women are in fact equal to men because the opposite is an implicit, not an explicit, value.

Myths

People normally do not learn their cosmology and values by taking astronomy lessons. Rather, they absorb a theory of reality and a set of values slowly, as children of their cultures. They learn them in part from the action of their elders, and in part from the stories and legends that explain the world and its history—the stories that anthropologists call *myths*. Often cast on an epic scale, peopled by heroes embodying the culture's virtues and villains embodying its vices, and filled with fabulous events much grander than those experienced in contemporary days, myths provide the specifics about the origin of the world, where man came from, and how society got to be the way it is.

Myths help shape the mental universe of the culture's members. They provide models for righteous action by showing cultural members how to behave properly in a variety of situations. Thus transmission of myth is an important and formalized pattern of culture, whether the myths are transmitted in written, codified form, as in many technologically advanced cultures (for example, in the Bible and the Quran), or orally. Among Hindus, for example, an important traditional function of Brahmin priests was the memorization of ancient myths, known as the *Vedas,* that glorify the mythic ancestors. In many groups, the time just before or during initiation rites is devoted to a telling of origin myths. American history, as taught in the elementary grades, has many of the ingredients of myth: Paul Revere heroically and singlehandedly woke "every Middlesex village and farm"; George Washington owned up to his offense in the matter of the cherry tree; Abe Lincoln chased a customer through the mud to return a penny.

The important social function of these myths is to inculcate reverence and respect for core beliefs and values. Thus Hindu children of the higher castes learn that they are descendants of heroes of Vedic times and American children learn that their society was founded and maintained by men of great personal courage and honesty.

Myths most often express cosmology and values in symbolic form. Why is man the way he is? The Yanomamö Indians of southern Venezuela believe their ancestors originated in drops of blood from the leg of Kanaborama. They thus believe it in their very nature to be fierce and constantly at war.

The Dogon, with their reverence for "twinness," believe that they are descended from twins, brother and sister, created by the union of Amma, the high god, and the earth. Like all of humanity, this great deity was incomplete in himself and sought completeness in union with his mate. Dogon society retains this belief in the incompleteness of the lone individual, and also an interest in finding completeness through finding the lost twin. A man's ideal marriage partner is his mother's brother's daughter, a substitute for his own mother's daughter.

The more familiar story of Adam and Eve also encapsulates a view of the universe and a system of values. God created Adam, the father of humanity, in his own image and placed him in the Garden of Eden. He then created Eve from Adam's rib as a companion to him. Eve, however, succumbed to temptation and ate the forbidden fruit. She then seduced Adam to do the same. God drove them from Eden and man ever after must endure death, disease, toil, pain, and other forms of suffering. Through symbolic expression, this myth tells us of man's origin and place in the world. Created by God, man is the supreme creature on earth. Woman, however, is created from man, and is by nature subordinate to him. As Eve demonstrated by her fall, woman lacks man's strength but possesses cunning and guile that can corrupt man. Mankind's sorry lot on earth is the consequence of Adam's sin. Acting in obedience to God's will is the proper way to behave, because only thus can man be restored to His favor. Through myths such as this, each person learns to orient himself in the universe according to where he came from and what his basic nature is.

Ritual

Belief systems are more than values, myths, and a cosmology. A Christian does more than believe in Christ: he partakes in Communion and leads a Christian life. A Jew does more than believe the Torah: he keeps the Sabbath. A Muslim does more than revere Muhammad: he fasts at Ramadan. A Dogon not only believes each person is born with twin souls of the opposite sex: he circumcises boys and excises girls in order to remove the part of the body where the soul of the "wrong" sex resides. In short, a believer does more than believe, he acts—and he acts in a special, predetermined, stylized way. He carries out actions and makes use of objects that embody his concept of the universe and replicate the tenets of his beliefs.

A belief system is thus more than a system of beliefs; it is also a system of rituals and symbols to which the believer responds profoundly. According to Geertz (1965), a person does not hold such beliefs, but instead is held by them. Ritual symbolically recreates the incidents and values of the belief system, often in dramatic form. Thus, by taking communion, the Christian participates personally in the Last Supper. The ritual of the Passover seder states the point explicitly. "This is the bread of affliction, which our ancestors ate in Egypt," the leader says of the unleavened bread. By eating it, the celebrants *become* their ancestors, saying, "what the Lord did for *me* when *I* came out of Egypt."

The continuous repetition of rituals not only insures that traditional beliefs will be preserved and passed on, but it also allows the individual to participate in the group's shared belief system. This helps the individual find his own place in the group, and also helps the society as a whole express its unity and collective identity.

THE NATURE OF BELIEFS

Cultures construct belief systems on assumptions that are true by their very nature. The social experiences of members correspond to their beliefs and, from the inside at least, prove their validity. From the perspective of other cultures, however, these often appear to be accepted as true because of the force with which they are asserted rather than their inherent worth. Such forceful statements are, "There is no God but God, and Muhammad is his prophet" or, "I believe in God the Father Almighty, the creator of heaven and earth." Thomas Jefferson stated the assumptions of our belief systems with unusual bluntness when he wrote, *"We hold these truths to be self-evident:* that all men are created equal, that they are endowed by their creator with certain inalienable rights, that among these are life, liberty, and the pursuit of happiness."

In justifying the most radical step in English political history, Jefferson called on no higher authority than the shared beliefs of the colonists. In a profound sense, Jefferson was right; there is no earthly way to *prove* whether men are created equal or unequal, or whether or not their creator (of whose existence there is no proof) intended each of them to enjoy life, liberty, and the pursuit of happiness. The English king and the royal government, believing, with an equally strong and equally unprovable belief, that the colonists were inherently unequal to the king and that their proposed independence threatened the settled order of universe, resisted the colonists with force. Ultimately, of course, the accuracy or inaccuracy of Jefferson's stated "truths" was never established. The war for independence merely established the right of the colonists to base a society on their conceptions rather than the king's.

Regardless of their objective truth, Jefferson's words did come to form

Rituals depict beliefs and symbolically portray values. The annual dance performance of the Diablada (Devil Dance) on the Bolivian Altiplano reinforces the values of the Christian hierarchy in conquering the devils (pre-Christian deities). (courtesy of Arthur B. Hayes, III)

the basis of a new social order. As such, they repose in their original form, the hand-written Declaration of Independence, in a hushed marble hall in Washington, D.C. that thousands of reverent citizens visit annually.

This special treatment of the Declaration and other documents of the revolutionary period illustrates a further point about the basic beliefs of a culture and the rituals and objects embodying them. They are *sacred,* meaning, in anthropological usage, that they belong to a special realm separate from the everyday, charged with meaning and nearly inviolate. They may be questioned, altered, or criticized only with great difficulty. Visitors approach the case containing the Declaration with a deference and awe equal to that appropriate in a church. The very words and papers of sacred documents are themselves often sacred. Many Muslims believe, for example, that slips of paper containing lines from the Quran will guard their owners from harm or that recitation of Quranic quotations will forestall bad luck or illness.

Elevated to a level above that of ordinary discourse, sacred beliefs have another characteristic that separates them from the profane, or everyday world: they are impossible to prove or disprove absolutely. They form closed systems based on axioms of unassailable truth. Religions, for example, rest on the unreplicable experience of the divine; political and social ideologies

Praying fives times a day wherever they happen to be is an important ritual for Muslims. (courtesy of Claudia Crawford)

rest on essentially arbitrary assumptions about the nature of man; science on the unprovable assumption that the physical world is orderly. (If you have studied philosophy, you may recall the "evil demon" debates of the early modern period—could some malign force cause the sense data received by man to *appear* orderly when they were not?)

HOW BELIEF SYSTEMS WORK

Like the other systems composing a culture, belief systems operate by dividing a realm of experience into the items composing it, grouping the items into sets, and arranging the sets into patterns. The realm in question is, as we have seen, that of "reality"—cosmology, values, myths, and rituals—a realm seemingly infinitely vast and flexible. Cultures have given vastly different answers to the two questions: What kinds of beings are there? How should we act toward them? To the first question, Western rationalist culture answers: ourselves (humans), animals, plants, and maybe a residual category for such primitive beings as viruses. Western religion adds to this answer: God, angels, and maybe saints. (Most people put these last three kinds of beings in a different category from things that we can "see" or "know" to be there, even though most people have never seen a germ.)

But what is Islam's answer to the same question? The beings in their cosmology are: God, angels, men (who have souls), women (who don't), animals, plants, and *djinns.* Djinns are the creatures that are known to Westerners by the misnomer "genies"; we tend to dismiss them along with elves and leprechauns as mythical beings. To many Muslims, however, djinns are as real as viruses are to us. Composed of fire, they are invisible except at night, but we are visible to them. Djinns live under the earth, but in close proximity to people's houses, farms, or towns. There are good djinns and bad ones, just as there are good and bad people. Some do mischief to people; some leave man alone. All should be treated kindly and respectfully, for their power is considerable. The Quran mentions and describes them; they therefore must be real.

In spite of the djinns, the mental universe of Islam is close to ours; it springs from the same Middle Eastern cultural tradition that gave rise to our Western religions, and it even accepts the validity of Biblical prophets. What is the answer of a system different from ours? For example, Hinduism so differs from our mode of thought that not even the question "What kind of beings are there?" has the same meaning. If you are asking "What is real?" then one answer is appropriate; if you are asking "What do we see inhabiting the world?" then another is appropriate. Though short descriptions inevitably distort India's religious belief system, one might simply say that many Hindus believe in a *world soul,* that in some ways is the same thing as reality. The world soul can be known only on a spiritual level and only by certain beings of exemplary spiritual elevation. Surrounding the world soul is a false envelope of sense data, the creatures and things of the everyday world, which only imperfectly reflect or represent the true cosmic reality. The outer nature of these beings takes the form of people in all their variety, of spirits, gods, animals, plants, insects—all living things. The inner nature of all living things (except for plants) partakes of the same soul-stuff; the difference is that some beings are spending the present life at a higher level of purity than others. In a reborn future life, the positions will be rearranged, and some beings will rise in purity relative to others and some will fall. A few will reach the pinnacle of spiritual purity and unite themselves with the world soul, but most will continue on the cyclical round of repeated lives.

This short sketch only begins to suggest the points on which the mental universe of Hinduism differs from the world view familiar to us or to the Muslims. The differences continue. Instead of free will, *karma,* the combined weight of the actions of past and future lives, rules. Time is circular, instead of moving in a straight line from past to future. In place of a single, steadfast god, there are multiple manifestations of the divine that arise at different times. Instead of a single, eternal truth, there are multiple ways to approach the divine. Each of these different belief systems—the Western, the Muslim, and the Hindu—has a different set of beings in its cosmology and, consequently, a different set of values, myths, and rituals.

To reduce these differences to their most basic level, we recall that each system is a pattern constructed logically out of sets that in turn are composed of elements. If the set of beings capable of spiritual salvation includes only humans, as it does in the Western religions, then a certain pattern of action follows. If it includes only some humans (men but not women) but does include non-human terrestial beings (djinns), another pattern follows. If it includes all of the beasts of earth, air, and sea; if all of them are only ourselves to a greater or lesser degree, and if we ourselves are capable of salvation in different degrees, then an entirely different pattern follows.

To study belief systems, it is important to keep in mind a characteristic common to all systems of thought; they are based on categories that are accepted on their own terms and without proof. If you have studied geometry, you may remember meeting such statements, called axioms, on which the entire system of deduction is based. Because they may be based on entirely different axioms, the sets and patterns composing different systems may be entirely different, even when they refer to the same types of objects or behaviors. Thus, Christianity divides actions into the sinful and the non-sinful, and the former into various categories of sin. Islam divides acts into five categories: forbidden; discouraged; morally neutral; encouraged; and required. Hinduism divides actions into polluting and non-polluting, and organizes them according to a vastly complicated pattern of behavior suitable to persons of different castes. To understand more concretely how systems of belief operate, we will explore in detail two elaborated systems for handling one of every culture's everyday concerns: food.

Food and belief

Jewish ritual law divides all foods into two great sets: *kosher,* or "clean" and fit for the religious Jew to eat, and *traif,* or "unclean" and unfit to eat. Kosher foods meet certain specific requirements; all others fall into the residual category of traif. Kosher foods are further divided into three categories: milk, meat, and *parve,* or neither.

A complex and all-embracing pattern of behavior has developed around these sets. According to law, milk and meat foods may not be mixed—that is, eaten at the same meal; within several hours of each other; or even from the same plate, though at widely separated times. Parve foods, including fruits and vegetables, grains, starches, eggs, and fish, may mix freely with all others (except at Passover, when the additional categories *chometz* [leavened] and *Pesachdike* [kosher for Passover] apply). Further distinctions govern the handling of certain foods: kosher meats can be made only from the forequarters of animals that chew their cud, walk on cloven hooves, and are killed according to ritual law. To be kosher, poultry (a meat food) must also be killed according to religious law. Kosher fish are only those sea creatures that have scales and fins.

All cultural patterns relating to food service and preparation revolve around these rules. Special habits for handling dishes and utensils keep the meat and milk equipment separate. Menu planning reflects the split: there are two essentially separate repertories of foods. Kosher restaurants specialize in one or the other and serve no non-kosher foods.

Beyond this, the rules ramify into social patterns. Strictly observant Jews eat only from kitchens they consider reliable; thus, they restrict the number of restaurants and homes that provide acceptable meals. Dietary sets thus expand into social isolation.

To the observant Jew, the distinctions of *kashrut,* the dietary system, express the nature of the universe. The person "keeping kosher" can no more fail to notice the inherent "milkness," "meatness," or "parveness" of a food than an American can fail to notice a person's sex or race. Persons who unwittingly eat perfectly wholesome and hygienic but non-kosher foods sometimes become physically ill when they later learn the truth. Persons who are raised in kosher homes but later reject the practice often retain an insurmountable aversion to pork, lobster, and other inherently traif foods. As in all consistent systems of belief, the sets subsume reality and impose themselves upon it.

Another elaborated system for handling food is the ancient Indian medical system based on the Sanskrit *Ayurveda* ("knowledge of long life"), which relates food categories to a theory of body function, health, and disease. According to ayurvedic theory, the body consists of several "humors," or liquids, and several "fires" that provide the energy for various physiological functions. Good health depends upon a balance of these elements, and any condition that upsets normal balance causes illness or discomfort. The body may become too "hot" or too "cold", depending on the particular humor or fire that predominates. Fevers and childbirth, for example, represent an excessively "hot" body.

Foods play an important part in maintaining or restoring balance and, therefore, health. Ayurvedic theory divides foods into the sets of "hot," such as honey, fish, vegetable oil, millet and corn flour, raw sugar, and spices; and "cold," such as rice, milk, butter, vegetables, fruits, wheat flour, and refined sugar. Each type of food has a specific effect on the body. Thus, cold foods can counteract hot conditions and restore health. In addition, cold foods are believed to counteract the supposedly debilitating effects of sexual intercourse.

Considerations of health, therefore, often govern the foods people eat. A woman who has recently given birth, for example, avoids hot foods, as does a man attempting to build up his strength. Although in Western eyes this may lead to a diet that is nutritionally unbalanced, in the eyes of many Hindus any other approach would violate the true nature of the body and lead to bad health. Thus, by explaining how the universe works, belief systems indicate how individuals should act. If certain foods are unclean, then it is both unwise and unworthy to eat them. If certain foods contribute to health and strength, then the wise person eats them often.

TYPES OF BELIEF SYSTEMS

The belief system of a culture most often forms a seamless web: people visualize the nature of the world, the powers that govern it, man's relationship to reality, and the process of creation all as reflections of a single reality. Modern convention, however, commonly divides beliefs into a number of different areas: religion, magic, ideology, and science. One reason for this is that it permits easier study of the social institutions associated with each realm of belief. Another is that in complex societies people often harbor several separate pockets of inconsistent beliefs. At bottom, however, all these types of beliefs are not only composed of similar elements—cosmology, values, myths, and rituals—but also function in similar ways: they explain the nature of the world, its history, and man's place in it and they articulate values and guide behavior.

Roughly speaking, *religion* consists of beliefs dealing with the supernatural; *magic* with man's ability to control aspects of the supernatural; *ideology* with a non-supernatural explanation of the nature of society; and *science* with the empirical understanding of reality. All of these types of belief systems involve theories of cause and effect, acceptance on faith, and ritual behavior.

RELIGION

Why has religion survived for thousands of years and why does it still survive, even prosper, in the face of the scientific revolution? Why is it a nearly universal feature of human life found in almost every society, from the simplest to the most complex? The answers to these questions are important because they have to do with the most basic nature of man and society. To begin, we will define religion more precisely.

Religion has been defined in a variety of ways; it means one thing to a Yanomamö, another to an average American, and still another to a Muslim. At its core, religion involves belief in supernatural beings and in their ability to influence the world of man. Part of the problem of understanding religion lies in the fact that different cultures attribute different phenomena to supernatural causes. In other words, cultures define the limits of the supernatural and natural sets differently. To us, earthquakes and tornados do not express the supernatural; there are natural explanations involving the earth's crust and air currents. In many other societies, however, there are no "natural" explanations for these and similar phenomena—they are the province of superhuman beings. For example, among the Yanomamö, sickness is caused by demons stealing the victim's soul, while in the United States, sickness is caused by germs or viruses. Thus, the set of supernatural occurrences has an element for the Yanomamö that it does not have for the average American. The problem of distinguishing between the "supernatural" and the "natural" is an ethnocentric Western one. Many groups, including some religiously devout Westerners, do not emically divide up events into the categories of natural and supernatural; they simply accept them all as "real."

Another problem is that viewing religion as a separate, distinct way of thought is also very ethnocentric—a habit at once both modern and Western. European and North American societies remove considerations of the supernatural from public to private life; they divide church and state and relegate religious activity to church services. Many other societies, both primitive and complex, recognize no such distinction. Among great civilizations, neither the Muslim nor the Hindu worlds traditionally recognize religion as a distinct compartment of life. Orthodox Islam, for example, recognizes no secular realm nor any secular law. All human activities, public and private, civic and individual, ideally fall under the authority of God's law as revealed to the prophet Muhammad and interpreted by Muslim legal scholars. Such present day states as Saudi Arabia and Pakistan use religious law as a basis for their state legal codes. This close fit between religion and other aspects of life can generally be seen in American society only in relatively small, isolated communities of the type generally called "cults"—the Amish of Pennsylvania, the Hari Krishna community, Hasidic Jews, and Christian religious orders. The major ideology of American society has ceased to be, strictly speaking, religious.

A curer attempts to remove an evil spirit that caused illness from a man's arm. (courtesy of John Young)

Functions of religion

The reasons for the near universality of religion seem to lie close to the heart of individual psychology. Man seeks meaning and order, but day-to-day living is full of events that are neither meaningful nor orderly. Apparently incomprehensible problems continually arise—a healthy person suddenly takes sick; the hunt produces bounty one day and nothing the next; a car strikes and kills a child; a freak hailstorm destroys crops ready for harvest; the boy who cheats on his exam wins the scholarship.

Religion, however, can explain why these things happen and dispel some of the anxiety of daily living. It answers what the great nineteenth century sociologist Max Weber called the question of meaning—the explanation of events that lie beyond the power of the society's knowledge and technology. This is an important concept to grasp. It is not that people deny scientific or naturalistic explanations, it is simply that these don't always suffice. Understanding the biochemistry that caused his six-year-old child to die of leukemia does not answer the parent's agonized "Why?" Religion answers this "why." It offers a view of the world that explains all the perceived mysteries and ambiguities by explaining that it is God's incomprehensible will, Allah's anger, or the power of karma that causes the sick to suffer, the evil to flourish, the innocent child to die.

Religion is more than an explanatory mechanism, however. It also offers methods to alleviate problems. It tries to supply a prayer, ritual, or proper behavior for every circumstance; the gods are implored to aid their human

Culturally important items are used as offerings to insure a good coffee harvest. (courtesy of Daniel Early)

worshippers. Even if the rituals ultimately prove unsuccessful, it may comfort the sufferer to know that he has done everything humanly possible—the final outcome rests in the hands of the supernatural beings. Religion thus provides comfort and solace for the individual by helping him to understand and to do something about his problems.

A further function religion serves for the individual is to provide occasions for celebration. Through ritual and worship, religion permits beauty, mystery, awe, pomp, and exaltation to enter the worshipper's life. It ties the joys and sorrows of life to specific, stylized, and often deeply moving expressions of emotion and to a body of fellow worshippers.

Organization of religion

Religion appears to perform roughly the same functions everywhere. But how different are the divinities and the means used to deal with them! Nevertheless, the religious organizations of a number of cultures bear striking resemblances to one another. Anthropologists have devised a number of typologies to distinguish various types of religious groups and religious practitioners. In some groups all members take an equal or nearly equal part in ritual and worship: there are no religious specialists. In others, only persons possessing certain characteristics may validly communicate with the supernatural.

Religious specialists fall into two major types that derive their authority from different sources: one type of specialist derives his authority from his status as a member of an organized and legitimated religious institution; the other from his personal, ecstatic communication with the deity. Anthropologists distinguish these sources of power because they generally imply different social organizations, and often different values as well. A basic dichotomy separates the church-like religious group from the cult-like religious group. In the former type, an established organization channels religious feeling through an organization of office-holders; individuals achieve a position in this organization through a formal process of learning generally culminating with ritual acceptance into the position and conferral of powers by a superior. The holder of such a position is called, in anthropological terms, a priest. In the cult-like religious group an individual gains access to the divine through personal, usually ecstatic, experience, and validates his position by display of his powers, either by performing miracles or by stylized abnormal behavior. In some societies, such a person is called a *shaman.*

In the most highly developed religious traditions, church-type organizations often manage to subsume, or at least control, the potentially disruptive power of personal ecstasy. Within Islam, for example, the *Sufi* tradition of ecstatic mysticism exists alongside the austere, bookish tradition of orthodoxy. The holy man possessed of a personal tie to the divine is a commonly accepted figure throughout the Indian subcontinent. And Catholicism has, to some extent, bureaucraticized ecstasy by conferring sainthood on special, carefully documented cases. In the United States, most established Christian denominations have recently had to come to grips with the charismatic, or pentecostal, movement. Based on Biblical traditions, this movement centers around the ecstatic experience of speaking in tongues, which it regards as an overt sign of the coming of the Holy Spirit. Because believers who have achieved religious ecstasy can act as leaders and need no other specialists to communicate with the divine, the movement directly threatens the monopoly on access that is the basis of ecclesiastical control.

Content of religion

These differences in religious organizations and in the gods they serve are far from accidental. To understand the content of a particular belief system, it is helpful to study the social structure and ecology of the society in question. This goes beyond the simple observation that agricultural societies pray to rain gods and hunting societies to animal spirits. More profoundly, the content of a belief system depends upon the culture's basic view of man and society.

The Bible states that God created man in his own image, but anthropologists like to reverse this statement and show, instead, to what extent gods are reflections of the image of man. As the pioneer French sociologist Emile Durkheim (1965) observed a century ago, in worshiping the supernatural, man worships the collective image of his social reality. The supernatural beings recognized by members of a society tend to think and act as the human members do; in anthropological terminology they are, respectively, *anthropopsychic* and *anthroposocial.* For instance, the desires of gods differ from one another; some, like Allah, want their law spread by the sword and some, like the god of the Quakers, want total abstention from violence. These wishes tend to closely mirror the interests and values of the society in question.

The personalities of the gods also tend to reflect the interests and values of society. The results of a cross-cultural study done by Lambert, Triandis, and Wolf (1959) show a relationships between child-rearing practices and the character traits of gods. Societies that encourage harsh or punitive upbringing tend to believe in aggressive and malevolent gods; societies with gentler techniques tend to believe in benevolent deities. Similarly, Spiro and D'Andrade (1958) suggest that the god-human relationship mimics the parent-child one. If parents are nurturant, gods tend to be nurturant too; if parents are harsh and unpredictable, then gods behave capriciously toward humans.

As we have seen, social structures vary from egalitarian to highly stratified. Likewise, a cosmology may contain divinities that are ranked hierarchically or divinities that enjoy relative equality. Swanson (1960) has suggested an association between political complexity and types and ranks of gods. Monotheism, the idea of a single high god, exists in societies at all levels of political and economic organization, but the dispositions and activities of these high gods differ from society to society. In egalitarian societies, the high god usually creates the world and then leaves it alone, relegating intrusion into human affairs to a variety of lesser beings who work without supervision. Just as no leader controls the inhabitants of the human world, no god controls the inhabitants of the spirit world. But in stratified societies, the high god actively oversees and directs the lesser gods.

Swanson also found a relationship between the degree of divine intervention in human moral affairs and the distribution of wealth in society. In egalitarian societies, where wealth is equally distributed, religion is unimportant as a means of enforcing rules of conduct. But in stratified societies, where distribution of wealth is unequal, the gods take a much more active interest in individual thought and action; they intervene in human affairs by creating sanctions against "immoral" behavior. Nonconformity and disobedience result in divine, as well as human, punishment. This fusion of religion and morality appears to occur only in highly stratified societies with inequalities that threaten the ability of the political control system to maintain law and order. Thus, in stratified societies, religion does additional duty as a means of social control.

Nature of the supernatural

Beings with the ability to control the affairs of man need not, strictly speaking, be gods. Many societies cast dead ancestors in the role of guardian spirits who monitor day-to-day activities. The Dogon, for example, receive a portion of their *nyama* (vital force) from a recently deceased ancestor, their *nani.* Ancestor beliefs tend to occur in societies in which kin groups act as important decision-making entities. They function to assure the continued existence of the kin as a cohesive group, as well as to assure its continued adherence to traditional practices. A nani, for example, bestows a part of his nyama only on a child whose parents have closely followed established ritual practices. It remains the duty of the child, furthermore, to venerate his nani, and through the nani the entire kin group, throughout his life.

Although we are familiar with personified divinities, divine power need not take the form of a particular being. In some systems, religious power exists in impersonal form. In Polynesia, for example, spiritual power known as *mana* occurs in objects and people, giving them special abilities. It is a particular trait of the ruling families. Things heavily charged with mana are *tapu,* or untouchable. They are dangerous to the ordinary person and must be avoided. A somewhat similar concept, *baraka,* exists in North African Islam. The power to work wonders resides in certain holy men, in their graves, and in objects they have used or touched. It sets its possessors apart from the common run of humanity. Mana and baraka can be used by man but are not subject to his control.

MAGIC, WITCHCRAFT, AND SORCERY

Magic, witchcraft, and sorcery are related, but somewhat different, types of belief systems. Classifying these phenomena as a separate sphere is mainly a modern, Western practice; in other cultures and times such beliefs merely constituted a part of the common cosmology. Modern Europeans and Americans have banished them to a nearly forgotten corner of the mind.

Like religion, magic, witchcraft, and sorcery concern the supernatural. Unlike religion, they concern methods of compelling the supernatural rather than imploring it. If you think that this distinction seems shaky, you are in good company! Most of the cultures in which such beliefs occur do not make a clear distinction between magic and religion. Rather, the distinction is imposed on these cultures by Western thought. Keep in mind that one man's religion may appear to be another's magic. The origin of the expression "hocus pocus," for instance, is a Protestant parody of the holiest portion of the Catholic mass, the proclamation *hoc est corpus,* that the host has become the body of Christ.

Anthropology, however, has traditionally distinguished religion from magic on a number of grounds. Religion is viewed as encompassing the art, philosophy, and emotion of the supernatural world; magic the engineering. In religion, the worshiper comes to the supernatural to supplicate, worship, and adore. The power of man cannot approach that of the god, so he cannot force the desired outcome—he can only ask that his wish be granted. The magician, however, like the engineer, seeks a practical result. The magician knows the formula or ritual that will force the desired end. Supplicants often use the services of a practitioner of magic to solve specific problems in return for a specific fee, much as we use a doctor or lawyer. Thus, a person suffering from a disease, lacking rain for a crop, or hoping for a son, may engage a specialist in magical knowledge to effect the desired end. The goal is concrete, specific, and usually devoid of moral or ethical meaning; the performance may entail no more overriding significance than having a tooth pulled. In addition, the performance may take place whenever needed, and in private; there is usually no need to wait for a particular time of year or to gather a congregation of worshippers.

The anthropologist Bronislaw Malinowski (1954), one of the most acute students of magic, called magic "primitive science" because members of a primitive society used magic much as members of a complex society use science: to achieve control over events or objects. The tribesman performing a magic rite to bring rain is acting as rationally, within the terms of his culture's knowledge, as the pilot seeding the clouds to achieve the same end. Malinowski believed that the main difference between modern and primitve means of affecting outcomes lay in their efficacy, rather than in their intent.

Although enunciated 50 years ago, this view of Malinowski's is consistent with the concept of culture we have propounded in this book. It emphasizes that a culture's magical beliefs fit into a rational, integrated view of reality. Instead of attributing the role of invisible bearer of disease to germs, for example, a culture may cast malign spirits in the same role. In the absence of microscopes, either belief is as believable or as fantastic as the other; the difficulties experienced by Pasteur and other early proponents of the germ theory in persuading the medical profession of their theory's validity prove this quite convincingly.

In time of uncertainty, when direct control of events fails, people resort to the means they believe will bring results: either to "scientific" knowledge or equally rational "magical" knowledge. If your culture's cosmology includes sets such as germs and electrons, you will seek one pattern of aid;

if your cosmology includes sets such as spirits, ghosts, or djinns, you will seek another.

Malinowski observed that systems of magic appear to work by either of two natural laws. Under the *law of similarity,* the formulas used imitate the desired results. Thus, practitioners of voodoo pierce dolls with pins in parts of the body where they wish their enemies to suffer pain. Similarly, at an annual festival, the Aymara Indians of Bolivia buy miniature representations of all the things they wish to acquire during the coming year. Under the *law of contagion,* what happens to one object will happen to another one when the first is either ingested or touched. A rabbit's foot imparts luck simply by being handled or carried. A Polynesian sacred rock imparts the supernatural power *mana* to those who touch it. In our society belief in these same laws can be observed. The breakfast cereal, "Wheaties," has only to be ingested and one immediately becomes a champion, able to excel in diverse activities. Rock stars or their clothing have only to be touched and some of their mana will rub off. (This imparted mana seems only temporary and not too stable, however, and so the person thus touched is careful not to wash the affected area.)

If supernatural powers are used to harm enemies, to cause illness, or to bring bad fortune, the procedure is called witchcraft or sorcery. E. E. Evans-Pritchard (1937) distinguishes socery from witchcraft according to the nature of the practitioner, rather than the nature of the process. According to him, a sorcerer learns his trade much as a doctor might: he learns formulas, medicines, and spells. A witch, on the other hand, possesses inherent psychic powers, of which he may or may not be conscious, that permit him to do evil. Obviously, this distinction is not always clear in practice, but it does have an important side effect: though it is sometimes possible to find the props that a sorcerer uses, it is *impossible* to either prove or, more importantly, *disprove* an accusation of witchcraft.

Ordinarily feared, despised, and rejected, the witch or sorcerer is viewed as a dangerous enemy, intent on harming others. This belief has obvious social control functions; a deviant individual—one who doesn't cooperate or follow the rules—may be accused of being a witch. The accusation is almost impossible to disprove and the penalty for witchcraft is ostracism or death. The fear of this terrible charge, and of the punishment that follows, can act as a powerful incentive for members to conform to the norms of their society. The anthropologists Whiting (1950) and Swanson (1960) found, in fact, that beliefs in witchcraft and sorcery appear most often in societies lacking formal or judicial means of social control. Since all societies need to deter antisocial behavior and encourage conformity to cultural norms, these beliefs function to maintain order in societies lacking sufficient legal institutions to handle conflict. People may avoid alienating others in order to forestall accusations of witchcraft. Taking the opposite view, some anthropologists argue that belief in witchcraft is actually a source of conflict and discord because it creates suspicion and distrust within a community.

In evaluating the uses of witchcraft among the Navajo Indians of the Southwest, however, Clyde Kluckhohn (1962) concludes that, overall, witchcraft strengthens rather than weakens social harmony. Although it may increase fear, motivate occasional violence, and cause accusations against innocent persons, a belief in witchcraft also serves a number of positive functions. It levels the difference between rich and poor since, to avoid accusation, the rich tend to be generous. It insures support of the aged since they are believed to resort to witchcraft unless cared for by the young. It helps support the morals of the villagers since would-be adulterers are afraid of being called witches if they go out at night. It permits the discharge of hostile feelings and frustrations against distant and unrelated persons, who are those most commonly accused of witchcraft. This preserves harmony within a village or family group by providing both explanations and scapegoats when something goes wrong.

The provision of explanations and scapegoats is probably the most important function of a belief in sorcery or witchcraft from the standpoint of the individual. Why did this child sicken and die and not some other? Why, in Evans-Pritchard's (1937) vivid example, did a wooden granary collapse at precisely the moment that two Azande tribesmen were resting under it? The Azande knew full well that termites eating through the wood had "caused" the collapse of the structure, but this scientific explanation was not sufficient. Why had it collapsed at precisely the moment it did, and not 10 seconds earlier or two hours later? The answer was obvious—it had to be witchcraft. A theory of effectuated malign intent, coupled with a scientific cause, provides the Azande, and other peoples throughout the world, with a more complete, satisfying explanation of unhappy events than does scientific cause alone.

In summary, beliefs in religion, magic, and witchcraft, in recognizably human intention acting through supernatural means, provide needed explanations. They provide specific answers about the causes of one's troubles and specific means to attempt redress.

IDEOLOGY

As we implied earlier, in our discussion of Jefferson, belief systems may also concern the nature of power, government, and authority. Such considerations are called politics and ideology in Western cultures, but act like other belief systems. An excellent example of this is the social and political theory of communism.

Although a full description of the theoretic and social structure of communism is more appropriate to a political science course than an anthropology course, it is nonetheless germane to our concerns here to note how completely this "antireligious" system of thought fulfills the same social and psychological functions as religion. Like any religion, communism has a cosmology that includes explanations of the nature of the world and the forces affecting man. The irresistible force of history is believed to be aimed toward the inevitable triumph of communist society; the very nature of the universe propels events in this direction. Appropriate values emphasize the subservience of the individual to the interests of the state, which is the expression of irresistable history. Mythic and sacred figures, such as Marx, Engels, and Lenin, receive the veneration that other societies reserve for saints or holy men and serve as role models for youth. Each year, thousands of tourists visit the tombs of the community "holy men" for ritual celebration.

Political ideology is prominent in the belief systems of noncommunist societies as well. In the United States, a widely held set of beliefs, not usually considered as a single system, forms a significant part of the popular cosmology. This set of beliefs includes such tenets as the inherent rightness and invincibility of American intentions and the special interest of the deity in the welfare of the United States. This belief system also includes divinities such as the Founding Fathers and the martyred Lincoln; shrines; and holy days such as the Fourth of July, Veteran's Day, and Thanksgiving.

SCIENCE

Another highly influential modern belief system is science. Because of its extreme prestige in modern life, we do not tend to think of science as a belief system, but rather as an expression of the structure of the universe. Remember, however, that this "aura of absolute factuality" is part of Geertz's definition of a deeply held system of belief. Science, (or more accurately, the individual sciences) are, in part, elaborate systems for dividing the universe into sets to be used for analysis. Thus, in anthropology we group a large number of very disparate behaviors and concepts into a set called culture. Biology divides the world of living things according to several criteria to form species. Chemistry breaks down material objects into the elements and particles of which they are made.

The set-making feature of science is evident if we view a single object according to the perspectives of the various sciences. Take a certain individual—the person sitting next to you in class, for example. To the biologist he is a member of a certain species. The physical anthropologist sees him as a member of a particular breeding group or as a particular combination of body components. The cultural anthropologist sees him as a representative of a certain subculture; the sociologist as a member of a certain class or ethnic group; the chemist as a collection of chemical elements or processes; and the physicist as an object of a certain mass, weight, and volume. Seen by these different criteria, he is all these different things.

Scientists work by making a set of presumptions about the nature of the universe that includes the presumptions that it is orderly and predictable. Their combined work has provided us with a reasonably consistent cosmology, and, somewhat haphazardly, with a set of values. Science has its own peculiar rituals of observation and experiment and its myths of culture heros and villains. The search for knowledge for its own sake, however, is, as Galileo's adversaries perceived, as arbitrary a goal of human endeavor as the search for salvation.

Science does, however, differ from other belief systems in one respect— the method used in establishing the validity or invalidity of a particular belief. The scientific method consists of systematic observation, formulation of hypothesis, and controlled empirical testing. Most other belief systems rely on little testing of beliefs and, in fact, use faith to establish beliefs that cannot be tested empirically for truth or falsity. When viewed this way, it is possible to see why science will never completely supplant religion, for the two operate in different areas. Science does not investigate anything that cannot be studied empirically, and thus leaves out completely the realm of final causes, the empire of metaphysical "whys" that man is so fond of asking. To tell the Azandi tribesmen that "chance" caused the injury of their friends is neither emotionally satisfying nor intellectually complete. Humans continuously strive for more.

FIELD PROJECT: BELIEF SYSTEMS

I. COSMOLOGY

The cosmology of your group probably shares many elements with the general cosmology of the surrounding American culture. This is not always the case, however, especially if you are dealing with a deviant religious or political group.

A. What do members of your group believe to be the nature of the universe?

  1. What is the nature and form of the earth?

  2. What are the major forces that rule events on it?

  3. What are the major categories of beings that inhabit the world?

  4. What characteristics differentiate these categories?

  5. How do these categories relate to one another?

  6. Where do members of the group visualize themselves as fitting into the scheme of things?

  7. How much and what kind of control do people believe they exercise over their lives? How can this control be enhanced or strengthened?

  8. Is the universe basically congenial or uncongenial to members of your group? That is, do the forces that rule the universe treat them benignly, malevolently, or indifferently?

II. VALUES

Your group's values probably complement its cosmology. That is, their conceptions of good behavior are related to their view of the nature of the universe.

  1. What do members of the group view as the goal of human existence or human endeavor?

  2. Toward what ends do they believe people should work?

  3. What types of activities do they consider desirable?

  4. What types of activities do they consider undesirable?

  5. What traits do members of the group strive to adopt?

  6. List several traits they consider good and several they consider bad.

  7. Describe the ideal group member as visualized by the people themselves. What traits does he or she have? What traits does he or she not have?

III. MYTH
  A. Does the group have an origin myth? Ask one or more members to tell you the myth so that you can record a commonly accepted version. Ask yourself the following questions about the myth:
    1. According to the myth, by what means did the group come into being?
    2. What beings, forces, or people were instrumental in its establishment?
    3. Do these beings, forces, or people embody any of the virtues recognized by members of the group? Which ones?
    4. Did they overcome any circumstances the group considers undesirable?
    5. How do the founders' powers, characters, and motivations compare with those of present members of the group?
    6. Are members expected to model themselves on the founders?
    7. What features of the present-day structure of the group does the myth explain?
    8. Are these features considered desirable or undesirable?
    9. In what way do these features structure life within the group?

IV. RITUAL
Your group may well have rituals that commemorate important events in its mythical past and celebrate virtues the group admires.
    1. What ritual occasions does the group celebrate?
    2. Which of these relate specifically to the group?
    3. Do these occasions bear a relationship to important features of the group as it exists today?
    4. Does the ritual entail special behavior?
    5. How does this behavior relate to the incident being commemorated? For example, does it imitate the behavior of people in former times? Does it ritually glorify particular individuals? Does it recreate incidents in the past? Does it create a mood appropriate to the occasion?

Chapter 10

Culture and the Individual

In chapter 1, anthropology was broadly defined as the study of man. And yet, until now, this book has only analyzed the habits of *groups* of people. We have discussed anthropology's master concept, culture, in terms that seem to suggest that it exists apart from its carriers, as do phenomena such as electricity or cosmic rays. It is time to reintroduce the individual person into this seemingly mechanistic world of culture that appears to act independently of its individual members, precisely following its own rules.

Culture, of course, is not the same kind of phenomenon as cosmic rays or electricity. It is, after all, nothing more than an abstraction—a very useful abstraction to be sure, but something that has no existence outside the minds of its users. It cannot be measured like electricity; it will not activate any sensors as do cosmic rays. It no more corresponds to a physical reality than does a concept like "the twentieth century." Notwithstanding this, we have used the concept of culture to view human behavior, and we have found it so useful and revealing that it almost seems as though it must surely be a part of the physical world.

We know, however, that the concept is nothing more than a kind of shorthand used by anthropologists when they talk about human behavior. The fact remains that cultures don't do, make, believe, or feel anything; people do. So when we talk about culture patterns, we are really talking about the statistical propensity of the individual members of a society to behave according to certain patterns, or the likelihood that they will act in a particular way in certain situations. Cultural patterns exist only through cultural members. The relationship of the individual member to his culture is at once simple and subtle, obvious and profound. To the extent that a society is a collection of individuals, each person is one of a group of people, all of whom behave uniquely. To the extent, however, that cultural patterns guide his life, each person is in some sense a microcosm of his culture.

PERSONALITY AND CULTURE

Personality and culture are both abstractions but they exist at different levels. Culture considers the actions, thoughts, and feelings of people as members of groups, while personality considers the actions, thoughts, and feelings of people as individuals. The word "personality," like the word "culture," has several different uses, popular and technical, precise and imprecise. Our use of the term is technical though imprecise: we define personality simply as a given individual's characteristic approach to life. This definition postulates no particular theory of personality structure and has the further advantage of being fairly susceptible to external measurement. By "approach to life," we mean the characteristic way in which a person reacts to daily situations. Is he restrained or emotional, trusting or suspicious, energetic or lethargic, independent or dependent, optimistic or pessimistic, self-reliant or fatalistic, gloomy or cheerful? Does he anger quickly or slowly, rarely or often? Do his own internal opinions of himself motivate him more or less than opinions held by others? Does he seek to express his own feelings and desires or conform to group expectations? Does he face trouble serenely or anxiously?

A problem arises in deciding the exact relationship between culture and personality, however. How much of an individual's behavior is unique and independent, arising out of his own temperament? How much of it derives from culture, from what he has learned as a member of his group? Knowing that behavior is unconscious does not help us to answer this question: many studies have shown that dreams, which at one level can be viewed as the most intimate expression of an individual's wishes and drives, are nevertheless highly patterned by culture. The symbols, the language, even many of the events that occur in dreams are culturally derived. Although the emotions they express are those of an individual, even the emotions have been learned in a particular culture.

Perhaps a concrete example can make the problem clear. We have studied in some detail the stratification of an Indian village and have observed that the members of the various caste groups generally accept their positions in village society. Such a system depends, after all, on large numbers of people accepting and acting on the assumption that they are inherently inferior to other people. Why don't Indians feel the conviction that most Americans feel and believe to be instinctive, that "I'm as good as the next guy?"

We can approach the question on at least two levels. On the level of social structure, we can answer that as members of different strata, members of the various castes carry out the behavior appropriate to their position in society. Or, on a different level, we can answer that the members of different caste groups act differently because their personalities are different. G. Morris Carstairs, (1961), a psychiatrist and anthropologist who studied this question in an Indian village, treated social position mainly as a point of difference between individuals. He noted that members of the same caste group tended to display similar combinations of emotions and general responses to everyday life, and that these combinations differed from caste to caste. Thus, the social structure and the individual person interact in the personality.

If you have thought about personality, you have probably observed that traits do not appear to be distributed randomly. Rather, clusters of people tend to show the same traits. You've probably heard people say things like, "All the Jones women are high strung," or "The Smiths are very ambitious." These observations are often generalized to much larger groups as well: "The Irish love to talk and are very outgoing"; "Spaniards take offense easily." Statements of this kind have a puzzling aspect, however. Certainly there are some taciturn Irishmen and some forgiving Spaniards; surely some members of the Smith family are lackadaisical and some female Joneses are serene. But you may also notice that something is wrong with the following sentences: "The English are so emotional"; and "The Italians are very reserved." Although you can also cite individual exceptions to these rules, in general the statements still seem incorrect. They should be reversed—right?

What we are talking about here is the general tendency for people in a given culture to display certain personality traits. Surely no one could document a statement that all Italians are emotional, but the general impression of people who know Italy is that emotionalism predominates over calm and reserve. This bit of folk knowledge gives some insight into the field of culture and personality, in which anthropologists investigate the effects of culture patterns on the personality and behavior of the individual in a society.

A concern with the relationship between culture and personality has been prominent in American anthropology for at least 50 years, though anthropologists in other countries have shown less interest in it. A number of different approaches to the field have consequently developed in the United States. Although they follow a rough historical progression, their actual dates overlap somewhat. Interest first grew in the 1920s and 1930s with the works of Edward Sapir, Ruth Benedict, and Margaret Mead. Then the insights of Freudian psychology were applied to culture and personality. During the fifties and sixties the field of culture and personality became more empirical.

Early studies: Margaret Mead

Many people associate the study of culture and personality with Margaret Mead. Although she was not the first investigator interested in the field, she did become its greatest popularizer. In books that have been best sellers for 50 years, Mead brought the concepts of culture and personality, along with those of anthropology in general, to millions of readers. Her early research, on which two significant books were based, attempted to determine the relative strength of biological, or genetic, inheritance versus that of culture in determining individual behavior.

In *Coming of Age in Samoa* (1928), a study of adolescence in a Pacific island society, Mead sought to find out whether the rebellion and travail of the teenage years in American society resulted from physiological changes associated with puberty or from some other, cultural, cause. She observed that Samoan youths seemed to pass through adolescence without the psychic turmoil of their American counterparts. She therefore concluded that the storms of the postpuberty years in America do not arise from physiological factors. Rather, she concluded, it is because American culture has elongated adolescence and institutionalized it as an intermediate status that the adolescent years are full of contradiction. The characteristic teenage rebellion, self-doubt, and worries over career choices are, in Mead's view, direct responses to specific cultural pressures.

Sex and Temperament in Three Primitive Societies (1935) asks similar questions about the characteristic personalities of the two sexes. Does the American pattern of dominant, aggressive men and subordinate, passive women derive from innate physiological differences between the sexes? Mead presents three New Guinea cultures that, combined, stand the American pattern on its head. Among the gentle Arapesh, both men and women are passive, cooperative, conciliatory—perfect examples of American-style femininity. Among the fierce Mundugamor, both sexes are aggressive, competitive, active, and belligerent—just like an American he-man. And the Tchambuli reverse our pattern completely—the men are vain, gossipy, nervous, retiring, and dependent upon the steady, reliable, practical women whose work provides the basis of the economy.

Mead's striking studies show the malleability of biology. She concludes that culture, rather than genetics or physiology, mold psychology and temperament. The studies were not without methodological problems, however. Her research techniques lacked some of the refinement that more recent anthropologists have come to demand. She generalized from her own impressions, largely ignoring variations within a group. In addition, she depended on only a few informants rather than on a representative sample of a society and she tended to view the testimony of all informants as equally valid. Nevertheless, her vividly written, impressionistic accounts remain among the most widely read works in the field.

Early studies: Ruth Benedict

One of the earliest theoretical statements about the relationship of culture to personality came from Ruth Benedict. Her classic book, *Patterns of Culture* (1934), was not only an academic trailblazer but a popular best seller as well. Benedict wrote not so much about personality *and* culture, but rather about personality *of* culture. She observed that particular cultures appear to express dominant themes, or "configurations," as she termed them, around which they are structured. Culture, in this formulation, is an integrated whole, somewhat like a large individual personality. It has a dominant configuration that shapes all cultural traits and social institutions such as religion, the arts, and economics, and influences the personalities of individual members.

Benedict also described specific cultural groups in configurational terms. She contrasted the "Apollonian" Zuni with the "Dionysian" Kwakiutl. The Apollonian group, she claimed, exhibited the traits and attitudes consistent with the values of moderation, rationality, and control—the Greek "golden mean." The title Apollonian, in fact, refers to the Greek god Apollo, who epitomized these traits in Greek mythology. The Dionysians, on the other hand, expressed the values associated with the orgiastic Greek god Dionysus: extremism, excitement, ecstasy, and gratification of the senses. According to Benedict, all the institutions of the two societies, and all the cultural patterns, express the appropriate theme and encourage and reward appropriate behavior.

Benedict's moving prose and striking examples gained wide attention for the book, but other anthropologists have criticized it on a number of scientific points. Most importantly, Benedict totally ignored the question of variability within the culture. How many Zuni actually exhibit, and to what extent, the so-called Apollonian traits enumerated? How many members of either group show personalities markedly different from the ideal model? How do societies change if configurational culture only allows certain types of behaviors and not others? In what sense can a culture have a personality? How does it in actuality transmit this to individuals? Information from subsequent fieldwork even suggests that some of Benedict's facts were wrong. It cannot be denied, however, that Benedict's work has a core of truth. Some societies do seem violent and extremist, while others appear calm and moderate. It is true that some societies do encourage and reward certain personalities, and that the desired personality characteristics vary from society to society.

A second, more sophisticated approach to the problems of culture and personality, views culture not in individual psychological terms, as if it were one big personality, but as the source of common characteristics found in each member of society. This idea culminated in the national character studies so prominent during World War II and in the 1950s; in the theory of basic personality structure, developed by Abram Kardiner; and in the empirically-based modal personality theory elaborated by Cora DuBois and Anthony F. C. Wallace.

Freud's influence on culture and personality studies

In order to understand this general approach, however, it is necessary to step aside for a moment to consider the vast influence of Sigmund Freud

Early childhood experiences are critical in personality formation. (courtesy of John Landgraf)

The mother-child relationship is one of the most important of the primary institutions. (courtesy of John Landgraf)

on the intellectual life of the time. According to Freud, the experiences of early childhood exert a decisive and indelible influence on personality. Factors such as amount and kind of contact with the mother, timing and emotional overtones of weaning, severity of bowel training, and resolution of the Oedipal conflict with the parent of the same sex determine for all time the basic features of individual personality. Strict Freudians maintain that personality is irrevocably set by as early as age three.

Anthropologists, influenced by Freud, began to observe that childrearing practices vary markedly in different cultures. In some, the infant is suckled generously whenever he cries; in others, he is left alone for hours on end.

In some, the child evicts the father from the mother's bed for a year or longer, and then in turn is abruptly evicted himself when the father reclaims his wife; in others, the child never sleeps with his mother at all. In some, bowel training is swift and severe; in others, almost haphazard. In some cultures the child is bound tightly to a cradle board and in others he is encouraged to move his limbs, to crawl and to explore. In some, the baby's genitals are stroked or fondled to still his crying, and in others they are totally ignored. If Freudian findings have any validity, these differences in childrearing practices should express themselves in differences of personality. And since, furthermore, the major childrearing practices tend to be applied quite consistently within a given culture, the features associated with those practices must be widespread.

The second major effect of Freud's work was to call attention to the way that *psychophenomena* (the unconscious defenses against anxiety or unconscious responses to forbidden material) appear, more or less disguised, in religion, humor, art, and other expressive aspects of a culture. Freud argued that certain cultural patterns and institutions are in reality expressions or projections of unconscious psychic processes of individuals within society.

Freud believed in uniform human psychic processes. He developed the main outlines of his thought some time before an understanding of culture existed. Thus, some critics maintain that he ignored the influence of his own Viennese cultural milieu on his theories. For example, Freud presented the Oedipal conflict, in which the young boy resolves his hatred for his father as the competitor for the mother's love, as a universal human process. Bronislaw Malinowski (1953) argued from his research in the Trobriand Islands that this conflict arises from a specific cultural situation; that is, the patriarchal family in which the father represents discipline. Among the matrilineal, matrilocal family of the Trobriands, the mother's brother, rather than the father, represents the discipline and responsibility of the family. Malinowski discovered that among the Trobriands the Oedipal conflict, as Freud elaborated it, does not exist.

National character studies

National character studies attempted to use Freud's insights to discover the basic personality types of people in modern nation-states. A number of anthropologists had attempted similar investigations within primitive cultures, but World War II necessitated an understanding of the behavior to be expected from enemies such as Japan and Germany, and allies such as Russia. In these studies, the supposed results of various childrearing practices were projected onto the society at large and made to account for behavior patterns and themes in religious, symbolic, and fantasy life. One of the best known of these studies is Ruth Benedict's *The Crysanthemum and the Sword* (1946). Though many have called this the single best introduction to the people and culture of Japan, it nonetheless relied on some questionable Freudian hypotheses. Benedict believed that the Japanese practice of severe early toilet training produced a compulsive personality preoccupied with order, ritual, and cleanliness. Furthermore, the aggression and rage produced by this strict toilet training was of necessity suppressed in the unconscious while growing up, but found expression in the adult pattern of brutal warfare. Subsequent research has called into question this stereotyped compulsion.

In another well-known example, Geoffrey Gorer (1949) related the wide mood swings supposedly characteristic of the Russian people to the custom of swaddling, in which the child is alternately bound tightly and permitted freedom. Specifically, Gorer said, the swaddling experience of early childhood produced adults with manic-depressive personalities. They were given to drinking bouts, which replicate the food and love that accompanied release from the infant bindings; to confessions of uncommitted sins, which assuage the unconscious guilt arising out of rage over being bound; and to a strong need for authority, which replaces the bonds of infancy. Among the many problems with this theory is the fact that drinking bouts, extreme guilt, and submission to authority exist in cultures that lack the custom of swaddling. And Gorer never established exactly what percentage of Russian infants did in fact experience swaddling.

We have cited Gorer's work because it clearly exemplifies some of the major weaknesses of national character studies. The assumption that there exists a single character trait, or a small group of them, related to a given culture assumes: first, that all parents apply these childrearing practices in essentially the same manner (which few people would concede, in a large, complex society); and second, that all children react to them in the same way. It further assumes that the largely intuitive analysis of a few anthropologists can accurately discover the effects of given childhood training on adult behavior and cultural institutions. The methodology has been criticized as a mere hunt in the inventory of a society's habits for two that appear related. Many have called this approach a misapplication of Freudian techniques of psychoanalysis, which are intended to study the psychological history of a given individual in great depth over an extended period of time. By the late 1950s, studies of national character had, for all practical purposes, been abandoned.

Basic personality structure

At a series of seminars held at Harvard during the late 1930s and early 1940s, Abram Kardiner and Ralph Linton proposed a far more sophisticated theory of the relationship between culture and personality. Kardiner believed that the bulk of a society's members share a *basic personality structure* based on common early experiences. The basic personality structure functions within the society's institutions, which he defines as constellations of functionally related behavior patterns. Kardiner discerns two types of institutions. The *primary institutions* are those patterns of thought and behavior that act on a child early in life, such as family organization, feeding, weaning, sexual training, and subsistence practices. *Secondary institutions* are those adult modes of behavior that help maintain society, and include the expressive institutions such as art and religion.

Kardiner argued that individuals, by adapting to the primary institutions common throughout the society, acquire common personality traits; he labelled the totality of the traits derived from contact with the primary institutions the *basic personality structure.* Secondary institutions, in turn, arise from, reflect, express, and require the personality type provided by the primary institutions. In many religious systems, for example, the gods act in a way that conforms to the members' basic personality structure, which was formed in the first place largely by the parents' treatment of the child.

Kardiner's work logically extends that of both Benedict and Freud. Instead of the rather vague cultural configuration concept that Benedict proposed, it is the basic personality structure that binds the culture together by standing at the intersection of societal institutions and personal experience. Freud's influence is obvious in Kardiner's belief in the extreme importance of early experience and in his perception of secondary institutions as projections of the basic personality structure.

For all its sophistication in dealing with society, however, Kardiner's theory takes a rather simplistic view of individuals. It postulates a closed, circular core of personality that can be changed only by external pressure, not by internal growth. More importantly, his model allows little room for individual variation. Kardiner realized that variation exists within every group, but his theory only accounted for a single basic personality type within a given society, produced by homogeneous primary institutions bearing on all the society's members.

Modal personality

Regardless of its theoretical merit, a theory that reduces every individual to a single personality violates common sense and experience. In part to clarify this problem, Cora Dubois, and later Anthony F. C. Wallace, developed the concept of *modal personality.* This approach recognizes the wide variation among the members of a single cultural group and attempts to discover the personality type that represents the group's statistical *mode,* or single most common personality class. In a pioneering study in 1952,

Wallace tested the concept on the Tuscarora Indians of upstate New York. Using the Rorschach inkblot test as his measure of personality types, Wallace divided the Indians into a number of personality classes and then determined by statistical means which of these was the modal, or most frequently seen, class. Interestingly, he found that 37 percent fell into the modal class, 23 percent clustered around it, and 40 percent belonged to personality classes unrelated to the mode. In other words, although most prevalent, the modal type was far from predominant: nearly half the Indians showed no modal personality characteristics at all!

The modal personality approach thus solved many of the methodological problems that had bedeviled earlier culture and personality work. It produced results that had an objectivity and statistical validity far greater than previous attempts. But it did little to advance understanding of the relationship between culture and personality. If anything, it ignored culture in its search for objectively verifiable results. Although recognizing the methodological soundness of the approach, some anthropologists questioned its ultimate usefulness in answering the questions that prompted the study of culture and personality in the first place. How useful is a modal category if only a third of the group's members belong to it?

The modal personality studies of the 1950s signalled a trend away from interest in large questions of causality and relationship to much smaller-scale studies of particular aspects of culture in relation to personality. Anthropologists felt that the old whole-culture stereotypes were in a sense true—Italians *are* different from Englishmen—but attempts to describe these differences in terms that permitted variation within groups did not prove fruitful. The characterizations were too gross to permit the discovery of useful relationships.

Anthropologists thus turned more and more to studies of single-dimensional relationships. The quality of anthropological research improved as anthropologists undertook specifically problem-oriented fieldwork, using objective techniques such as the Rorschach, TAT (Thematic Aperception Test), and similar instruments. Limited comparisons of personality traits to social or ecological variables demonstrated some important relationships.

Personality as adaptive mechanism

To say that there are problems with the "typical personality" approaches, however, is not to say that they were abandoned completely. Although Kardiner's theory that a single personality type characterizes the members of a society came under attack, his insight that personality is an important adaptive mechanism still holds true.

The individual's personality—his characteristic approach to life—is probably his most important adaptive tool. Every cultural system represents a system of opportunities, rewards, and challenges which, if mastered, permit the individual to survive and even prosper. Making his way within his culture requires each person to respond appropriately to the circumstances that befall him. And because the pattern of opportunities available within a given culture tends to make similar demands on a whole group of people, the personality characteristics appropriate to meeting them tend to be widespread too. As we mentioned earlier, culture is an apparatus for making people do what they have to do.

The institutions of culture work throughout the individual's life, forming the perceptions that are the basis of his characteristic approach to life. Through the interaction of his experience and his inborn temperament, the individual develops methods of dealing with his surroundings. He thus evolves emotional responses so deeply based as to appear instinctive, but yet well suited to the survival of his group. The adaptive utility of personality has been approached from two points of view: adaptation to social conditions and adaptation to ecological surroundings. The individual survives by extracting what he needs from both the social structure and the physical environment.

Adaptation to social structure. Some of the most famous theories based on the postulate that personality is an adaptation to social environment are concerned with changes in predominant personality type as a function of general social change. A celebrated theory developed by Max Weber and Tawney (1926) links the so-called Protestant Ethic, which emphasizes thrift, hard work, discipline, and initiative, and the independent, aggressive, compulsively success-oriented personality that embodies it, to the rise of capitalism, an economic system that demands just such traits. David Riesman (1950) suggested that subsequent social change in America no longer favored this personality drived by inner compulsion, which he called "inner-directed," but favored, instead, a personality based on the need for approval from one's peers and the ability to function smoothly within a group. Reisman called the latter type "other-directed," and argued that it arose from the spread of large organizations at the expense of individual free enterprise. The personality traits that had accounted for the success of the early capitalists were, he argued, an impediment to the individual trying to make his way in a large corporate or government bureaucracy.

In relatively simple societies, the institutions and experiences that bear on any individual bear simultaneously on many, perhaps most, members of his group. In complex societies, however, various segments of the society live radically different lives. Responding to different experiences and demands, members of a sub-group develop characteristic personalities. A famous exchange between the writers F. Scott Fitzgerald and Ernest

Hemingway illuminates this point. Fitzgerald stated, "The rich are different from you and me." To which Hemingway replied, "Yes, they have more money."

But Fitzgerald meant more than that. He expanded his idea in a celebrated story that began, "Let me tell you about the very rich. They are different from you and me. They possess and enjoy early, and it does something to them, makes them soft where we are hard, cynical where we are trustful, in a way that, unless you are born rich, it is very difficult to understand."

Fitzgerald meant that the very rich, as a class, have a different approach to life than the rest of us. In the terms we have been using, they have a different personality, derived from their early experiences. Each of the major social classes in the United States seems to display typical personality traits that are so well known as to be stereotyped in films and stories. There is the self-assured, superior upper class, the self-disciplined high achievers of the upper-middle class, and the earnestly respectable, obedient, lower-middle class. We do not mean to suggest that all members display these characteristics, just that they and the values they represent tend to dominate in the groups in question. Studies show that values and childrearing practices differ among American social classes because different traits are adaptive for the individuals within them.

Carstairs (1961) made similar observations within the rigidly caste-segmented Indian village he studied. The Rajputs, descendants of warriors and rulers, emphasize personal aggressiveness, courage, and subordination in their children. The Brahmins, hereditary priests whose traditional function is the careful performance of religious ritual, emphasize self-restraint and formal relationships. The Bania merchants, while professing a deep regard for spiritual values, in practice prize wealth and accept ruthless business competition. Although Carstairs warns that these sketches must not be taken as indicative of all individuals in each of these castes, he implies that in general they reflect the situation in the village. Thus, in even so small a society as a rural village, different personality traits are adaptive for different castes.

E. Terry Prothro (1961) came to a similar conclusion in his study of personality differences among various religious groups in Lebanon. In addition to differing in religious affiliation, these groups also differ in social position. The Armenian Christians are urban merchants; the Arab Muslims, village farmers. The Arab Christians are intermediate between the two—somewhat more urban than the Muslims but less commercial than the Armenians. Prothro found that by age five children exhibited marked differences in their attitude toward discipline and achievement and performed differently on certain psychological tests. He was also able to relate these differences to both social position and childrearing practices.

Achievement was valued most by the highly urbanized Armenians, who consistently rewarded it from babyhood on. The Arab Muslims scored lowest on achievement motivation; largely tradition-oriented peasants, they also showed the least interest in rewarding achievement and independence. The Christian Arabs, who fall between the others in socioeconomic position, also fell between them in personality traits and childrearing practices.

Adaptation to environment. Personality traits and the childrearing practices intended to produce them are adaptive in other ways as well. Numerous cases show the adaptive utility of certain personalities in particular ecological situations. The Arabian Bedouin, for example, who inhabits a fiercely hostile natural environment populated with almost as hostile competing tribes, develops a fanatical loyalty to his patrilineal kin group and an iron discipline in the face of pain. Both these traits, loyalty and discipline, result from stern training over many years; the young man must submit to many painful trials such as saber cuts or knife stabs that build his endurance and test his courage.

On the other hand, Latin American peasants tend to have personalities that are highly individualistic and they tend to be suspicious of neighbors and even relatives. The anthropologist George Foster (1967) attributes this behavior to the world view he calls "the image of limited good." Foster believes that this image, although never expressed and possibly even unconscious, crucially influences personality and behavior; peasants respond to what they perceive to be the true nature of the world. They believe, Foster argues, that all desirable goods in the village community—goods such as land, wealth, love, and social status—exist in finite quantity, in amounts insufficient to supply everyone. Because of this scarcity, each individual can increase his share only at the expense of someone else. Although the means by which they rob their neighbors may be so devious as to be invisible, individuals who improve their standing must necessarily be hurting other members of the community. Peasants therefore learn to think first of themselves and their immediate families, in contrast to the Bedouins, who learn to subordinate their personal interests to those of their extended kin.

In general, desirable personality traits seem to reflect a society's basic ecological orientation. In a 1959 study, Barry, Child, and Bacon found that agricultural and herding societies tend to stress obedience and responsibility, while hunting societies tend to stress self-confidence, independence, and achievement. They reasoned that societies depending on large supplies of accumulated resources could not afford departures from established routines because experimentation might jeopardize the long-term food supply. Populations with little accumulated food could not suffer this loss, and might benefit from innovation and independence. Robert Edgerton (1971) found related differences between East African farmers and herders. The

The harshness of the Bolivian Altiplano fosters the stoicism reflected in the face of this Quechua Indian. (courtesy of Arthur B. Hayes, III)

farmers valued hard work and consulted a good deal with their neighbors, but meanwhile covertly mistrusted them and often visited sorcerers. The herders had less respect for hard work, acted more independently, and were more overt in their aggression. In personality terms, the farmers were indirect, abstract, anxious, given to fantasy, and less able to control their impulses. The herders were more direct, concrete, and open, and showed better control over their emotions.

Studies showing clear-cut relationships between personality and ecology suggest that the Freudian theory of personality formation may be too limiting. Not only childhood experience, but life-long experience in a specific economy, ecology, and social structure influence personality development.

NORMAL VS. ABNORMAL

When studying the relationship between personality and culture, it is important to realize that the definition of "normal" personality is *culturally* defined. Characteristics that one culture or subculture assumes are normal aspects of human personality may fall very far from the norm in other cultural settings. A less obvious, but equally significant conclusion, is that "abnormal" personality is therefore also culturally defined. Group consensus is the only measure of mental illness and mental health.

To take an example, suppose a young woman petitioned to see the president of the United States because she had been told by celestial beings that she alone could lead the armed forces to victory over their enemy. Imagine the reaction she would get! She would actually be imitating very closely the career of the revered Saint Joan of Arc, the patroness of France, but the changes in Western culture since Joan of Arc's time have totally changed social reaction to this type of behavior. Joan of Arc's contemporaries believed she was inspired either by God or by the devil. Her modern imitator's contemporaries would believe the girl was inspired by schizophrenia—or just plain crazy.

The ability or tendency to see visions, fall into trances, and communicate with invisible spirits is not highly valued by most Americans. In other times and places, however, possessors of these abilities have received their culture's highest honors. In many societies, shamans owe their influential and respected positions to their ability to fall into trances and receive spiritual visitations. In India, and in the Sufi tradition throughout the Muslim world, holy men undertake special exercises and disciplines to achieve a state of detachment from worldly affairs that in Western society is deemed evidence of mental illness. A substantial proportion of the wandering holy men of India probably are, in American terms, psychotics. Nonetheless, these men are honored in their countries as holy representatives of the highest form of religious endeavor.

Among the Plains Indians of North America, the ability to see visions was the most important prerequisite for admission to full manhood. During late adolescence, the young would-be warrior set out on a series of trials that he hoped would result in a visit from a divine personage. For a number of days the boy lived alone in the forest, without food or sleep, spending his time in painful exercises to prove his courage and devotion. At last a spirit would take pity on him and appear to him; this spirit then became the boy's lifelong supernatural protector. On his return to the settlement, the boy related his conversation with his guardian spirit and thereby gained acceptance as a warrior and a full man. Those boys who failed this test were forever excluded from full manhood in the tribe; no one could hope for success in the manly pursuits of hunting and warfare without the help of a spirit guide. Anthropologists believe that the reports of successful vision quests are completely sincere: the young men did see spirits.

Studies indicate that it is not difficult to achieve ecstatic trancelike states or visions under the right circumstances. The proper combination of fatigue, hunger, and sense deprivation will produce such a state in many people. Various Sufi mystical orders have developed reliable techniques of whirling, dancing, or gyrating that consistently send their members into trances. What is important is not how members of other cultures achieve these states, but that they wish to achieve them. Far from viewing trance-like states as dangerous or weird, they view them as high achievements— something desirable that should be actively sought. This is very unlike the American viewpoint that anything that cannot be seen, measured, and controlled is highly suspect.

Forms of mental illness

We don't want to give you the impression that no mental abnormality occurs in other cultures. Most societies recognize certain behaviors as aberrant, though the cultural explanations given for these states vary. Some cultures ascribe them, for example, to spirit possession. But we must not think that ours is the only culture to have developed a systematic explanation of mental abnormality.

A particularly enlightening example is given by the Iroquois, who developed a theory of personality centuries before modern psychiatry developed. According to the Iroquois, the mind consists of two parts, one conscious and the other unconscious. Both parts have wishes and desires that the individual must meet in order to prevent harm from befalling him. Only the desires of the conscious mind, however, make themselves directly known to the individual. The unconscious mind expresses its desires symbolically in dreams. The individual may ignore these desires only at his peril, because the unconscious mind may force him to foolish behavior if it does not have its way. Discovering the true meaning of dreams is far from easy, however, and the Iroquois frequently consulted wisemen who specialized in interpretation. The similarity to Freudian theory is striking enough to give pause to those who would assert the superiority of Western views of mental illness, especially since the Iroquois had the idea first!

The behavior of the mentally disturbed often appears so aberrant that many people assume it is random. Good evidence exists, however, that both the content and form of mental illness are culturally determined. In many cases, the themes of a mental disturbance reflect the themes of a culture or the strains in its pattern of interpersonal relations. In the United States, for example, many mild, and even some severe, disturbances among men center around sexuality and sexual performance. In India, however, educational or career success is a far more prevalent theme. In the United States, the most important relationship of the adult man (or the young man who hopes soon to become an adult) concerns the wife or other female partner. The man's adequacy in these relationships defines, to a large extent, his adequacy as an adult. In India, however, the emotional significance of the relationship with the wife pales beside the relationship with the parents, who remain dominant figures as long as they live. Parental demands center not on sexual prowess, but rather on career success in a highly competitive labor market. An Indian man's inability to achieve success in school or on the job undermines his central relationship with his parents as surely as an American man's failure as a sex partner harms his relationship with his wife.

The cultural hold on the abnormal mind is also clear from the fact that fantasies and delusions generally exploit symbols known in the culture in question. Members of Western culture, for example, may suffer delusions that they are Jesus Christ, John the Baptist, or the Virgin Mary. They rarely imagine themselves as the Prophet Muhammad, the Emperor Asoka, or other figures who lack symbolic importance in Western culture.

Morris Opler's (1959) study of patients in American mental institutions demonstrated that members of different ethnic minorities displayed different symptoms for the same illness. Italian-American schizophrenics, for example, tended to be talkative, emotive, and expressive, while Irish-American sufferers of the same disease were depressed and guilt-ridden.

Not only the content, but also the form of mental illness, the expression of the abnormality, seem to be to a large extent culturally patterned. Particular mental abnormalities show a tendency to appear in certain societies. Individuals in certain sub-artic American Indian tribes, for example, sometimes suffer from the Wiitiko psychosis, during which they imagine that the spirit of a cannibalistic giant, or Wiitiko, possesses them. They suffer from hallucinations and a desire to commit cannibalism. Arctic hysteria, or *pibloktoq,* occurs in Greenland, mainly among Eskimo women. They run or wander about in a state of high excitement, often throwing off their clothing. A somewhat similar manifestation is *amok* of Malaysia, New Guinea, and Indonesia. The victim of amok is usually a man; he first suffers depression and withdrawal and then an episode of frantic excitement during which he becomes violent and destructive.

Anthropologists have long discussed the genesis of these conditions. At least two, Wiitiko psychosis and Arctic hysteria, have been attributed in part to physiological causes. Anthony F. C. Wallace (1961 b) linked *piblokotq* to calcium deficiency; Ruth Landes (1938) claimed that Wiitiko psychosis is associated with anxiety and fear of starvation. Other convincing theories, however, propose that Arctic hysteria and amok are means of demanding and receiving solicitude and attention. Amok, in particular, permits a man to withdraw from some of the heavy social responsibilities he may have acquired, while still retaining some honor in the society.

Regardless of their ultimate origin, these conditions interest the anthropologist because they are examples of culturally patterned abnormality. Although it has been suggested that they are merely specific cultural manifestations of more widespread illnesses, they are not known to appear in precisely the same form in other societies.

The role of the deviant

The treatment accorded the abnormal person varies from culture to culture. Many cultures provide a socially accepted, or at least recognized, role for the deviant. The young Plains Indian who fails at his vision quest, or doesn't wish to go to war and fight, can nonetheless achieve adulthood through the institution of the *berdache,* which permits him to formally adopt the clothing, status, and activities of an adult woman. Because he is strong and willing to work, he is often sought as a marriage partner by men, usually as a second wife. Plains Indian society regards the transvestite with acceptance, not with the horror traditional in Western society. Because the requirements of manhood are so stringent, it is possible that some boys will find them unattainable. To meet this contingency, the society provided these boys with an acceptable outlet.

Plains Indian society is by no means unique in sanctioning the fulfillment of the social role of one sex by people physically members of the other. Some societies permit both sexes to fulfill the opposing sex's social role. An exclusively female transvestism of sorts occurs among the Blackfoot. The *minauposkinzapxpe,* or "manly-hearted women," although not strictly transvestites, function in normally masculine spheres of their culture. Although Blackfoot women can own, inherit, and dispose of property, the strong masculine emphasis of the culture forestalls any culturally approved way of gaining distinction on female terms.

The manly-hearted woman, a person of high abilities, therefore distinguishes herself on male terms. She occupies a unique position in society, formally recognized as different from the general run of women. Wealthy, prominent, married, and mature (often over 60), they enjoy the rights to dress more elaborately and less modestly than other women, to head a household, to use "dirty" language in argument, and to compete on equal terms with men. Manly-hearted women do not enjoy complete social approval, but they enjoy respect based on their economic talents.

SEXUAL PERSONALITY

We have arrived at one of the most significant, but as yet inconclusive lines of anthropological study of personality—that of the relationship of sex to personality. In her classic book *Sex and Temperament in Three Primitive Societies,* discussed previously, Margaret Mead attempted to prove that sexual personality is culturally determined.

Many societies rear boys and girls somewhat differently, generally in hopes of producing somewhat different results with each. Barry, Bacon, and Child (1959) found a statistically significant tendency for childrearing practices applied to females to foster the traits of nurturance, obedience, and responsibility, while male enculturation practices stress achievement and self-reliance. Few cultural groups distinguish as sharply between the sexes in social roles and expectations as do the Arab Muslims, and their childrearing practices show an equally sharp distinction. Boys are nursed on the average twice as long as girls, and are indulged and cherished by their mothers and female relatives more than their sisters are. Young girls shoulder household responsibilities earlier than boys, and learn during childhood that they must cater to men and boys. In mid-childhood, boys pass into the world of men, where they learn the elements of the culture that "matter," such as business, politics, and religion. Once a girl passes puberty she is restricted both physically and mentally to a completely feminine world; the only men she meets are members of the family.

Nearly all societies differentiate the roles and modal characteristics of men and women. But the expectations of various societies are not the same. In some, such as the traditional Arab Muslim, women ideally live totally removed from affairs of business of finance, except for keeping household accounts. In others, such as parts of West Africa, women form the backbone of the market merchant class. Some societies, such as Mediterranean Europe and the United States, expect the male sex drive to be stronger than the female; others, such as high-caste India or present-day Sweden, view the woman as the demanding sex partner. Some societies, such as those of the West, expect women to develop the skills of flirtation and seduction necessary to catch a man on the open marriage market. Others, such as Indian and Muslim societies quash any tendency toward flirtatiousness.

In all known societies, men dominate women; it appears that true matriarchy never existed. But to say that women are ideologically subordinate does *not* imply that women in all societies are subordinate in all aspects of life, that their personalities reflect this subordination, or that this subordination arises out of a natural anatomical or physiological inferiority. Much evidence exists that economy and ecology play an important part in determining the status of women in a society. When the survival of the group depends significantly upon the contributions of women, women occupy positions of greater equality and influence than when they depend wholly on men for their support. Among hunters and gatherers, for example, the two subsistence practices are divided between the two sexes—men hunt and women gather. The group could no more survive without the vegetable food provided by women that it could without the animal food provided by men. Women in these societies occupy a social position that reflects their economic indispensability and their personalities do not reflect strict subordination. Even in Muslim societies, in which inequality of the sexes rests on foundations of religious law, tradition, and world view, the position of women depends upon their economic contribution. In rural areas, where they contribute indispensable labor in the fields, women enjoy a much freer social position than do the secluded women of prosperous urban families. The latter contribute nothing to the family's income so their position consequently suffers.

As Marvin Harris (1975:610) states,

> Males are not born with an innate tendency to be hunters or warriors or to be sexually or politically dominant over women. Nor are women born with an innate tendency to care for infants and children and to be sexually or politically subordinate. Rather, it has been the case that under a broad but finite set of cultural and national conditions certain sex-linked specialities have been selected for in a large number of cultures. As the underlying demographic, technological, economic, and ecological conditions to which the sex-linked roles are adapted change, new cultural definitions of sex-linked roles will emerge.

ART

Emotion speaks not only in the spontaneous voices of everyday life; for people in many cultures, the profoundest and most resonant expressions of feeling, the truest and most revealing glimpses of their hopes and fears, take the shape of structured, highly formal performances. The various endeavors that Western societies lump together under the rubric of the arts strive to make concrete some of the deepest feelings and meanings implicit in a culture. The power of these performances to move, incite, inspire, enrage, sadden, gladden, and transport leaves no doubt that they speak to people at levels beyond the rational.

But artwork that enthralls members of one culture can appear to be nothing but random actions or nonsensical objects to members of another. Poems that raise an Arab audience to a frenzy are gibberish to a foreigner. The majestic grandeur of a Beethoven symphony is a deafening cacophony (and off-key besides!) to many Chinese, who use a different scale. The emotional power of the arts is obviously culture bound.

Any discussion of expressive behavior must begin with the ambiguous and much-debated question, "What is art?" Determining the artistic merits of particular works, or even discovering criteria for doing so, is obviously beyond the scope of this book. A number of the world's cultures have developed large literatures on this subject. It is well within our scope, however, to discuss the position of the artwork and the artist in society.

First we must observe, in agreement with Marvin Harris, that art, in the sense of a separate category of endeavor, is an emic distinction peculiar to the modern West. As Harris points out, activities like painting, singing, acting, dancing, musical composition, carving, and poetry recitation exist in many cultures. The concept that some of the products of these activities are "art" while the rest are "non-art" exists only in a few. In American culture, the major distinction between "art," which is "serious," and "non-art," which is not, lies not in the nature of the performance, but in the nature of its treatment by the professional organizations and individuals designated as "the art world." Thus, when an anonymous industrial designer devised the Campbell's soup can, the product ranked not as art, but as commercialism. When Andy Warhol created an oversized facsimile of the very same can, the acclaim of the art profession guaranteed its acceptance as art. This crucial factor of professional acceptance explains the phenomenon of the "lost" artist whose work receives little attention and then is later "discovered."

This feature of Western society complicates discussions of creative endeavor on a cross-cultural basis. In many cases, the individual creating objects that modern Western society would consider "art" views himself (or herself, since many artisans are women) as producing objects to serve the gods, glorify the ruler, enhance the magical potency of the possessor, fulfill the obligations of kinship, or just supply the mundane needs of the household. Even in Western society until the renaissance or even later, most objects and activities now considered "art" were created to please God. The anonymous artisans who erected and decorated the cathedrals that are one of the glories of Western art did not intend to create "art for art's sake," but to win God's favor by glorifying him. These artists were in harmony with the ideology of their culture. The view of the artist as possessing a special sensibility at odds with that of his age and society is a product of, and revolt against, industrialization and the standardization it brings. For many centuries, in the West and in other advanced cultures, the finest works of the creative individual served to strengthen and express the ruling ideology.

An illuminating example of the difference between Western and non-Western concepts comes from Zaire, where the government recently gathered a collection of fine tribal objects for a national art museum. The owners of many of the objects, however, viewed them not as "works of

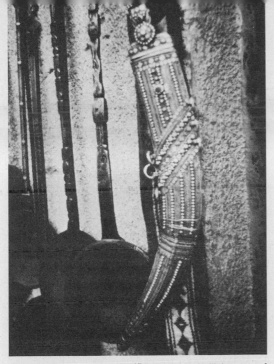

This Arabian dagger typifies the embellishment of utilitarian objects. (courtesy of Claudia Crawford)

art," but as repositories of spirits. This threatened to stall the project. Not even for the price of the bicycle offered in exchange for their objects would they risk angering the spirits by sending them off to a museum. The government, however, was finally able to acquire its collection by making replicas of all the objects in question. The owners then enticed the spirits to move into the replicas, thus freeing their former abodes to be displayed to museum-goers as works of tribal "art."

Aesthetic values

Although few cultures recognize our emic distinction between art and non-art, nearly every culture recognizes aesthetic standards, or a concept of beauty. This concept imposes limits on the producer who would have his or her work considered admirable, and guides other members of the culture in evaluating the work. In some complex societies, including our own, several standards exist. Russel Lynes (1949) characterized them as high-brow, or the standards of the professional art community; middle-brow, or the standards of the educated nonspecialist; and low-brow, the standard of the mass of the common people. In simpler societies, however, a single aesthetic standard tends to be shared by most or all members. Everyone readily agrees on which objects or performances are beautiful.

Aesthetic standards tend to emphasize virtuosity and originality. These two features may at first appear contradictory. Technical mastery of a medium generally requires a lengthy apprenticeship and an ability to produce at the highest standard objects or performances or works like those produced by previous masters. The creative ability to produce works that differ significantly from those of one's predecessors, on the other hand, requires a disregard for the very masters who serve as one's models.

The factor that makes virtuosity and originality combine to produce work of a high order is *style*. This is the characteristic selection of elements that gives a work or a body of work its distinctive flavor and places it in a cultural tradition. Aesthetic creation involves, in the first place, selection among the almost infinite components that could compose a work; only those deemed appropriate gain a place. It further involves the arrangement of those appropriate elements in a pattern characteristic of the type of work at hand. A woodcarver making a box among the Northwest Coast Indians, for example, considers animal forms to be the most appropriate content of his work. He further selects among the various possible methods of representing animals, choosing to depict them as closed oblong forms with few sharp corners. He then arranges these forms symmetrically so that they cover the entire field while emphasizing the middle. A woodcarver among the Dogon of Africa, on the other hand, also selects animal forms as appropriate content, but chooses to represent them by use of a larger variety of forms. In addition, he leaves a large portion of the field empty of decoration, and is not bound by rigid symmetry.

Within the boundaries of a style, virtuosity and originality can combine without conflict. The gifted producer remains close enough to the tradition not to violate its canons and at the same time arranges the elements of his work into a combination never seen before. By his respect for tradition, the producer allows his public to understand and evaluate the work with relative ease and strengthens the tradition itself.

Probably for these reasons, truly popular work, in both simple and complex societies, is generally highly traditional. In the United States, for example, popular music, fiction, painting, and drama hew closely to the harmonies, plot lines, and representational devices that have been traditional for centuries. Works of the professional avant garde, on the other hand, break stylistic rules and thus become difficult for the nonspecialist to appreciate. Twelve-tone music, theater of the absurd, and minimalist painting, for example, neither move nor satisfy people who have not devoted special study to understanding them. Created out of different aesthetic standards, they cannot speak to people devoted to traditional art.

In many cultures, music, painting, sculpture, dance, and other works tend toward traditionalism for another reason. They express the values and institutions of a relatively static society and thus strive for a fixed aesthetic ideal over a long period of time. In such cases, the work's continuity with tradition overrides the importance and identity of its individual creator; the work blends into a body of works by many different creators.

Art as a reflection of culture

As well as providing a standard for the judgment of specific pieces of work, aesthetic values in some sense express and enrich the emotional life of society, just as aesthetic creation expresses and enriches the emotional life of the individual creator. A good deal of decorative work appears to serve little or no strictly practical function. To a certain extent, the impulse to embellish daily and ritual life—the home, the human body, tools, weapons, vehicles, public places, and houses of worship—appears to exist in itself; it is a specifically human striving for an aesthetic ideal. But aesthetic endeavors also express the basic themes or emotional overtones of a culture, both in their content and in their style. The anthropologist Claude Levi-Strauss (1963), for example, suggests that mythology expresses in veiled form some of a culture's basic emotional conflicts. Similarly, various studies have attempted to relate stylistic similarities in several arts to features of personality and social structure. Raphael Patai (1973) argues that the tendency of Arab artists to compose architectural designs, poems, and musical pieces out of many similar small elements relates to a cultural emphasis on ideal forms and concepts rather than on reality.

John Fisher (1961) attempted a more ambitious comparison of artistic styles with social organization in a number of cultures. He concluded that egalitarian societies emphasize symmetry and repetitive motives while tolerating substantial areas of empty space. Stratified societies, on the other hand, appear to combine various dissimilar elements into asymmetrical, enclosed patterns with little empty area. He argues that style is a vision of social reality projected into the abstract. He views the small, repetitive elements surrounded by open space as representing a society of equals relatively isolated from outsiders. The highly integrated patterns of unlike elements represent the interdependent strata of an unequal society.

Levi-Strauss argues, however, that a certain type of strict symmetry found in cultures as disparate as the ancient Chinese, the Indians of the Northwest Coast, the Maori of New Zealand, and the Cadunes of South America, corresponds to specific features of social stratification and, presumably, of attitudes to man and nature. Split representation, the style in which a creature appears divided into two profiles, joined at the beak or nose and perhaps the tip of the tail, characterizes the products of all these cultures. Levi-Strauss believes that this style derives from the importance of masks in these societies, in which they serve to indicate and validate social status. He maintains that in these situations of competitive stratification according to ancestry, the importance of specific facial decorations or masks in asserting primacy leads to the detailed patterning of the split representation.

It is often unsafe to make cross-cultural generalizations about art, however. "The more horrible this world is," Kamal Boullata (1973) quotes the painter Paul Klee as saying, "the more abstract our art, whereas a happy world brings forth an art of the here and now." Such a statement might validly describe Western painting, but other traditions address realism from their own points of view. The Muslim tradition, for example, emphasizes abstraction in part because of a religious proscription on representation of living beings. Muslim artisans sometimes introduce intentional imperfections in their designs so as not to challenge the primacy of the sole perfect creator, God.

Although studies relating style to other aspects of culture have yet to yield fully satisfactory results, the truth of their central insight seems clear. The products of creative artisans and craftsmen express, at a deep and significant level, some of the central psychic and cognitive concerns of a culture. For this reason, their products take on meaning far beyond their physical reality. And possibly from this, too, comes the apparently universal impulse toward embellishment and imaginative representation.

FIELD PROJECT: CULTURE AND THE INDIVIDUAL

I. MODAL PERSONALITY
  A. Can you discern one or more personality traits or clusters of traits characteristic of your group? How would you define these traits or clusters of traits?
  B. How are these personality traits distributed in the group? Do many or most members display them? Do more members display these traits or cluster of traits than any other combination of traits?

II. BASIC PERSONALITY STRUCTURE
  A. Why are these personality traits characteristic of your group? What features of the group's social, economic, or political structure permit or encourage them? For example, does physical separation encourage independence? Does differential access to power encourage differential self-confidence? Attempt to ask similar questions appropriate to your group's structure. Carefully define the traits you believe characteristic of your group and attempt to relate each to a specific feature of the group.
  B. Do different segments of your group display different characteristic personality types? Can you relate these traits to specific features of the life situation of members of the segment?

III. CULTURE AND PERSONALITY
  A. How do these personality characteristics develop? That is, do members display them before they join the group or do they develop them while they are members?
  B. Do certain features of your group attract persons who display particular personality characteristics? Which features of your group attract which particular personality characteristics?
  C. Do the experiences of individuals as members of the group encourage them to develop certain personality traits? Which particular experiences encourage which particular personality traits?

Chapter 11

Culture Change

Our discussion of culture is nearly complete. We have defined culture, examined its major components, and considered their interrelationships. We have, as it were, gotten everything ready for a play: we have erected the scenery, dressed the actors in costume, placed them on the stage, and assigned them their roles. But you have probably noticed an important oversight that makes for an unsatisfying, and ultimately untrue, performance. We have not yet developed the plot that will carry the action forward. Our discussion of culture is still incomplete because we have not permitted change.

Culture is in a state of constant change. Change may well be the very essence of life; certainly, in medical terms, an organism is considered alive only as long as bodily functions, which are organic changes, can be discerned. The same is true for groups of people. People carry out their daily activities, changing in response to the seasons. People are born and people die, and in between they pass through the various stages of life. From time to time exceptional circumstances arise and people devise novel ways to deal with them. Different generations face different challenges and respond to them in ways that will alter the lives of their descendants. All life is motion and change.

If anthropologists hope to understand, and ultimately to predict, human behavior, they must study change. But how can sociocultural models account for change? Our model thus far has emphasized balance and equilibrium, the interrelationship of the counterpoised parts that compose a culture. How can we modify the model so that it tells us where changes originate and in what direction they will go? The problem, in simple terms, is how do societies maintain their integration and yet change at the same time?

TYPES OF CHANGE

Our first task in studying change is to define precisely what we mean by the word. You may have noticed that we have called two different kinds of processes by the single term "change." We said, "People carry out their daily activities . . . people pass through the various stages of life." We also said, "People devise novel ways to deal with new circumstances . . . different generations face different challenges and respond to them in ways that alter the circumstances of their descendants." These two types of change are usually referred to, respectively, as *maintenance changes* and *systemic changes.*

Maintenance change

The first type of change, maintenance change, might be described by the old French saying, "The more things change, the more they remain the same." These are the changes that occur so that things may remain the same. Thus, for example, a person must ingest and digest food and excrete the waste products daily, or nearly so, if he is to remain alive. These activities of course involve changes, but they are not changes that imply any alteration in the basic nature of the organism. Likewise, children are born, grow up, and ultimately die, but this change in personnel does not imply any necessary change in the basic nature of the society; new generations are required to replace the people who are constantly dying. We may say that maintenance changes do not imply any alteration in the sets and patterns composing a cultural system.

E. R. Leach (1954) discerned a complicated pattern of maintenance changes among the Kachin of Burma. Political organization among this group tends to fluctuate between a democratic *(gumlao)* and an aristocratic *(gumsa)* form of government. Neither form endures permanently, however, in part because both contradict elements of the marriage system, which is a truly basic element of Kachin society. Leach indicates that the gumsa order usually comes into conflict with norms governing relationships with the wife's family. Because of the functional importance of the marriage system, this conflict contributes to the disintegration of the aristocratic regime. As the pendulum swings toward the democracy and social equality of the gumlao order, however, Kachin norms requiring that the wife's family outrank the husband's come under attack. Dissolution of the gumlao order is thus also related to saving the marriage system. Leach concludes that great changes in Kachin society do occur, but they are largely alternating cyclical changes that serve to preserve the culture's basic norms.

A more contemporary example of maintenance change is provided by the generation that came to their majority in the second half of the 1960s. This group entered adulthood to the accompaniment of loud hosannas from social prophets who saw them as harbingers of drastic social change who would overthrow traditional American values and social structure. In the widely read book, *The Greening of America* (1970), Charles Reich of Yale University predicted that a revolutionary new consciousness rejecting materialism and competition and emphasizing self-expression would spread from college youth to all of society. More skeptical and ultimately more acute social analysts such as Peter and Bridgette Berger (1972) argued that the so-called new consciousness would affect particular individuals far more than it would affect the structure of society. If, the Bergers argued, the sons and daughters of the upper-middle class rejected the elite positions they traditionally would have taken, then the sons and daughters of the lower-middle class would rise to fill them. The structure of society, they argued, would remain basically unchanged. American industry would not grind to a halt because Yale graduates refused to take jobs in management. Industry would get along perfectly well with Fordham graduates, they said. Rather than representing a revolutionary change in social and economic structure, the process the Bergers called the "bluing of America," because of the potential use of youths from blue collar families, represented a new example of Pareto's nineteenth century idea of the circulation of elites, which stated that one elite group is simply replaced by another, without change in the basic social structure. Thus, the "revolutionary" generation of the 1960s proved to be a temporary variation rather than a long-term trend. The youth of the 1970s have "reverted" to competition and materialism in their search for good jobs rather than good highs.

It is often helpful to analyze the types of changes by the use of models. Maintenance changes may be visualized as cycles; that is, they are balanced and repetitive. Particular cultural states alternate, but ultimately do not change the nature of the society. Thus Kachin society, according to Leach, alternated between a gumsa and a gumlao political order.

Systemic change

Some changes, on the other hand, resemble a spiral: the trajectory doubles back toward its origin, but does not pass through the same point. We can analyze the social organization of the Makrani herdsmen of Pakistan, studied by Stephen Pastner (1974), in terms of a spiral. In times of drought, the Makranis, nomadic pastoralists who ordinarily travel in small family bands, regroup into new, larger bands so that they can maximize the limited resources of their environment. They pool their smaller herds into groups that need fewer herdsmen. Some herdsmen can then seek work among settled populations and contribute their earnings to the group at large. They attempt to ride out the drought, in this way keeping sufficient head of livestock alive to permit their return to full-time herding when conditions allow. When normal weather returns, they break up into smaller bands once again, and all return to full-time herding.

We can observe a cyclical trend in the social organization of the Makrani as times of drought alternate with times of adequate rainfall. A particularly severe drought, however, may so strain resources that it permanently alters the cycle. Some herdsmen, forced to sell off their animals or even to eat them, find it impossible to reestablish themselves as herdsmen once the emergency has passed, and must move permanently to the town. Such a change produces a long-term alteration in the structure of society. We may call it a spiral, rather than a cyclical change, because the society moves to a different equilibrium.

Conservatism and change. The Makrani example gives us an important insight into social change. As a rule, people attempt to change just enough to remain the same. Makrani herdsmen change so that they may reestablish themselves as herdsmen when conditions improve; they do not abandon herding in favor of permanent employment in town unless forced to by external circumstances. Even in societies like our own, in which technology is increasing geometrically, people attempt to respond to industrialization in ways that protect the social and cultural forms they are used to. Business concerns introduce new technology in an attempt to retain or improve their position in competition with other companies assumed to be doing the same; they do not seek to set off large-scale cultural trends. Even technological changes as massive as the adoption of agriculture generally begin as a means of achieving marginal improvements that would maintain or slightly improve the current society. It is unlikely that the generation that adopted the automobile foresaw the immense effects it would have on the moral, legal, economic, and geographical patterns of society. They thought they were dealing with a slightly better horse carriage.

Anyone who has changed jobs, schools, or homes knows that change is difficult. It requires taking risks, learning, and being flexible. People, individually and in groups, generally strive to retain part of their familiar, psychologically comfortable past, even while they are coping with changed circumstances requiring new responses. As we saw in our study of belief systems, the symbolic and valuational aspects of culture can remain unchanged for a very long time. Despite the widespread propaganda that "progress [usually defined as technological change] is our most important product," even American society shows a marked tendency toward *homeostatis*, the maintenance of internal stability in the face of external disturbance. Many theorists agree that the more a potential change affects the *cognitive*, or ideological aspect of life, rather than the material or technological, the more difficult it is to achieve.

APPROACHES TO CHANGE

If analysis of the concept of culture change requires lengthy discussion, imagine how much more complicated the empirical study of the phenomenon is. Anthropology has yet to develop a comprehensive theory of social and cultural change, but it has developed a number of approaches that have yielded significant results. In general, anthropologists have attempted to deal with the problem by studying change at three different levels: (1) the individual; (2) social groups composing either parts or the whole of societies; and (3) human society generally. The first type of study attempts to pinpoint what motivates individuals to change their habits; cultural change, after all, is in one sense nothing more than the adoption of new modes of life by many individuals. The second set of studies considers the structural features of a social organization that encourage or hinder the spread of new ways. The third set attempts to discern general trends in the development of all human societies and to derive principles that appear to explain these trends.

CHANGE AT THE LEVEL OF THE INDIVIDUAL

Studies of social and cultural change at the individual level attempt to answer two related questions. How do individuals develop cultural innovations? How do individuals decide to adopt them once developed? Homer Barnett, in his book *Innovation: The Basis of Cultural Change* (1953), emphasizes the role of the single innovative person as the ultimate source of variation within a culture. The process of innovation, Barnett says, consists of the recombination of existing cultural elements into a new synthesis. The innovator reorganizes one or more of the sets or patterns of his culture to produce something new. Innovations do not therefore represent a complete break with the cultural past so much as a reorganization of parts of that past.

In Barnett's analysis, the process of innovation consists of three steps. First comes the *analysis*, breaking down a problem or situation into its component parts. In the second, the *identification* stage, the innovator recognizes similarities between components of two heretofore unrelated phenomena, objects, or behaviors. Finally, the *substitution* stage transfers a component that existed in a different context into the original problem. Thus, for example, a Pacific islander may recognize as a problem the economic and social disarray of his people after the departure of American troops. His analysis of the problem indicates that the people's suffering began when the supplies of American goods, brought by plane, stopped flowing. He then proceeds to identify elements common to the American soldiers and the spirit ancestors of his people: both have the power to fly through the air, both have the power to bring prosperity to the people. Substitution of the ancestors for the Americans is not then a difficult step; if the American soldiers have gone forever, taking their planes full of bounty with them, then surely the ancestors will be able to take their place. The result of this thinking might be a cargo cult such as we discussed in chapter 1.

In another example, a South Arabian herdsman may analyze the problem of transporting goods in the desert. The problems arise, he finds, because the most common means of transport, the mule-drawn cart, often bogs down hopelessly, and the mule needs to drink too frequently to make it across waterless stretches of desert. He then identifies the similarities between two disparate cultural elements, the mule-drawn cart and an animal previously used only for milk, the camel. Both are able to carry hundreds of pounds of cargo; both travel at an acceptable speed; both are readily available. The camel, however, can travel long distances over desert terrain without stops for water. It is then a simple step to substitute the camel for the cart and mule. The result may not be only a more effective means of desert transport, but ultimately an entirely new social structure.

Note that in both these cases we said "might." A new idea does not necessarily become a cultural innovation. The crucial difference between an idea and an innovation is acceptance by other members of the group. Each borrower of the idea passes through roughly the same process as the original innovator, recognizing a problem to which the innovation may serve as a solution, assimilating the idea into his mental framework, and finally adopting it in action. Various factors may influence the borrower's ultimate decision to accept or reject the innovation, and he may not adopt it in exactly the same form that the innovator originally developed. Thus, he may modify or reinterpret it, accepting part and rejecting part, or perhaps even changing its function.

An American woman living in a tropical Latin American country, for example, was distressed to see a local woman with her hair always in rollers. The American deduced that the extreme humidity made the woman's kinky hair very difficult to manage. She suggested that her friend wear one of the inexpensive synthetic wigs then coming into use in the United States. The local woman responded enthusiastically, and on a trip home the American purchased a wig and brought it to her friend. The woman was delighted; she would no longer have to go around with her kinky hair always in rollers! To her great pleasure, and the American's equally great dismay, she now went around with the smooth, shiny hair of the *wig* always in rollers. To her, the American learned, the rollers were a hair style rather than a treatment for kinky hair. So the different analyses of the situation produced different uses of the innovation.

Such individual differences in perception and thought are crucial, according to Anthony F. C. Wallace's theories of cultural change. Wallace (1961 a) argues that each individual possesses a *mazeway,* a unique conceptual and cognitive map of the world around him. Because each individual's life experience is unique, no two mazeways are identical. Furthermore, every individual possesses only a part of his group's culture; no one possesses all of it. Thus, although the mazeways of members of the same cultural group concur in many respects, because these varied mazeways guide individual behavior, variations in behavior exist. According to Wallace, these variations are a major source of potential cultural change. As each individual makes decisions based on the options that appear open to him from the perspective of his own mazeway, clever or original solutions arise that provide the material for cultural variation and change.

Acceptance of innovation. Everett Rogers (1967) attempted to discover the social and psychological factors that make some individuals innovators but not others. Research in Colombia, South America, showed that innovators tended to be less fatalistic, more confident in the possibility of human control over events, wealthier, and more literate than non-innovators. But Rogers ran into trouble when he tried to explain why certain villages were more receptive to innovation than others. Nearly every village had a few highly innovative individuals; the receptivity of the innovators' neighbors, however, made the difference between villages that modernized and those that remained traditional. Villages that modernized accepted their innovators as leaders, while those that remained traditional rejected them as undesirable deviants.

Frederick Barth's (1963) study of Norwegian fishing villages attempted to address this problem. Like other investigators, Barth assumed that cultural change occurs as a result of rational decision-making by individuals. But he further demonstrated that acceptance of innovations depends on the particular circumstances of a community. He suggests, for example, that situations of ambiguity promote acceptance of innovation, while situations with well-defined norms tend to discourage it. The isolated Lapp villages that Barth studied were anxious to join the modern world but lacked the know-how to make the transition. These conditions created a place for entrepreneurs, who mediated between outside institutions and those of the village. Entrepreneurs shared a lack of commitment to existing village ways, a strong commitment to personal profits, and a willingness to take risks to achieve them. Because of the function they served in bringing the modern world to the villagers, the entrepreneurs were accepted as filling a particular need of the people, who followed their example.

CHANGE AT THE LEVEL OF THE SOCIETY

The approaches thus far described focus on individuals and deal with relatively short time periods. They attempt to understand how people innovate and to discover the strategies they use in making personal choices to accept or reject particular innovations. Basically, they seek psychological explanations for processes that lie beneath all human change. At the level of a group or a whole society, studies of change concentrate on the structure of the group rather than the structure of human cognition and personality. The dynamics of social structure and organization, not of individuals, is the focus of these studies.

There are two basic approaches anthropologists have emphasized in studying change at the societal level. The first, *acculturation,* involves changes that occur as a result of contact between two cultures; the second, *specific evolution,* or adaptive change, looks at change as a mechanism to help a particular group survive in its physical or social environment.

Acculturation studies

Contact between cultural groups has been a major cause of change, particularly in the centuries since the expansion of European culture to other continents through exploration and conquest. When previously unassociated cultures meet, the opportunities for change are many and far-reaching. What are the specific changes that may take place? Which particular aspects of culture are most susceptible to change? Which of the two cultural groups changes, or which segments of them? How does change come about? Anthropologists studying acculturation have developed a large literature on these questions.

Observation of societies all over the world has yielded certain generalizations. Two distinct factors may account for the degree of change that takes place during culture contact: first, the flexibility of internal behavioral structures and norms; and second, the openness of the group. To exemplify the first, one can look at the Shiite Muslims, for whom flexibility of behavioral norms is a matter of religious doctrine. The Shiites began as a political minority within Islam and survived under hostile regimes in many countries. Their doctrine of *taqiyya,* or religious dissimilation, has helped them adapt. According to this teaching, a Shiite may, and in case of personal danger must, hide his true beliefs and religious practices from outsiders; he may adopt the outward forms of the people he lives among in order to protect his safety. Shiites thus have no strong sanctions against adopting, at least outwardly, the forms of other groups while safeguarding their own inner beliefs in order to escape persecution.

A similar flexibility of behavior, though lacking any religious justification, has been observed in India. A number of writers have remarked on the widespread Indian ability to compartmentalize roles and behavior, which permits one individual to carry out different, even contradictory, behavior in different social situations. The commonest example occurs among the modern, educated city dwellers who follow two different sets of social norms, one relevant to their work lives and one to their home lives. Modern business and professional life has made strict observance of caste distinctions impossible. Members of various castes mingle relatively freely in their work lives, talking and even eating together as if India's formal abolition of caste represented a true social reality. As long as Indian workers wear Western clothes and are at their places of employment, they observe norms in line with "modern" ideas. At the end of the work day, however, when they return to their homes, many resume traditional dress and nearly all resume their traditional caste attitudes. A business associate who is a perfectly acceptable luncheon companion might be a totally inappropriate guest at home because of the possibility of caste defilement. Indians do not view this behavior as hypocrisy; unlike Chinese culture, which emphasizes consistency of personal behavior across a variety of roles, Indian culture emphasizes behaving appropriately in the particular situation in which one finds oneself.

The degree of change resulting from intergroup contact is also determined by the "openness" of the group, or the permeability of its boundaries. Japan, for example, has been very receptive to foreign ideas throughout its history. The Old Order Amish, on the other hand, reject as ungodly all innovations, including such seemingly innocuous ones as zippers. Boundaries may be maintained by cultural phenomena as diverse as language, patterns of interpersonal relationship, and ideology.

Of course, even in a relatively closed society a conscious manipulation of symbols by someone in power can influence the acceptance of things from the outside. In Saudi Arabia, one of the most conservative of Middle Eastern societies, religious leaders opposed the introduction of television. The king, however, wanted television for his country. He arranged for religious leaders to see a television program consisting of readings from the Quran, the holy scripture of Islam, and completely disarmed them. How, after all, could a device that can transmit the word of God be ungodly!

Because acculturation concerns contact between cultural groups, political or military factors sometimes figure more prominently than do features of internal structure. Put more simply, the stronger group can often force acculturative changes on the weaker. The best-known example of this type of change is colonialism. Even seemingly simple decisions by colonial authorities have had far-reaching consequences for colonial populations. The imposition of money taxes by Europeans, for example, forced thousands of native Africans out of subsistence farming and into jobs in mines to earn the necessary cash to pay their taxes.

In addition to studying the causes and processes of acculturation, anthropologists study the fate of specific acculturative changes. How does the culture absorb the new item? How does the culture become reintegrated around the new item? In probably the simplest process of absorption, the new item is simply added to the cultural inventory of the society as one of a number of possible choices. We might think, for example, of the worldwide influence of Coca cola as one of many beverages available, or of television in Saudi Arabia. In a more complex situation, the new item takes the place of an existing item with the same function. The sewing machine, one of the most widely accepted items of material culture, has replaced hand sewing in cultures all over the world.

A yet more complex form of absorption blends the new cultural element or elements with preexisting ones to produce a new synthesis unlike anything in either of the original cultures but combining features of both. This process is known as *syncretism.* Some of its most intriguing examples come from the world of religion. In many parts of the world, elements of Christianity have combined with elements of preexisting religions to produce local forms of Christianity. For example, in Mexico, and elsewhere in Latin America, native peoples, with at least the tacit approval of Catholic missionaries, associated Christian saints with their indigenous gods. Recent research has shown that many churches built by Indian laborers during the early years of the Spanish colonial period incorporate Aztec and other religious symbolism in their decorative carvings. Whether or not the missionary priests knew the meaning of the designs their workmen created is not known; it is clear, however, that the workmen vividly combined their old and new religious faiths.

Finally, a culture may accept new items on top of old and keep both, even if they conflict, by compartmentalizing thought and behavior. As in our example from India, modern life and traditional life may exist in two separate compartments, such as home and work or city and village. Each type of behavior retains its validity within the appropriate realm.

All cultural elements do not change at the same rate. (courtesy of
Leonard J. Gallagher)

Adaptive change

At the level of whole societies, some anthropologists have studied change
that occurred in the absence of contact with foreign cultures. This approach, probably most forcefully propounded by Julian Steward and
Marshall Sahlins, concentrates on the specific changes or evolution of a
particular cultural group over a relatively short period of time. These studies stress the adaptation of a culture to its specific physical and sociocultural environment and examine in detail the processes of change causing
the evolution of the culture.

Robert Hackenburg's (1962) comparison of the Pima and the Papago,
two tribes living in the same arid environment, typifies this approach to
cultural change. Before the advent of the Spanish in what is now Arizona,
both tribes practiced horticulture along with some hunting and gathering.
The Papago, not fully sedentary, lived in extended family groups whose
headmen had little authority. The groups were widely dispersed over the
land and derived no more than 25 percent of their food from domesticated
plants such as corn, beans, and squash.

The Pima, on the other hand, exploited horticulture more fully. They
depended on domesticated plants for more than 60 percent of their food.
Completely sedentary, they lived in permanent villages under a headman
who directed activities and organized the fairly extensive irrigation works.
Even during droughts, which occurred approximately every five years, the
Pima did not abandon their villages. At these times they depended on wild
foods, using their villages as a center for hunting and collection.

Of the two groups, the Pima found themselves in a far more favorable
position to make use of the wheat introduced by the Spanish. Wheat proved
a valuable supplement to their diet. A winter crop, it provided a relatively
reliable food supply for the summer months, when the Pima had previously
depended on wild foods while cultivating their corn. The new crop consequently allowed them to abandon hunting to a much greater degree than
before. The cultivation of wheat increased the importance of cooperation
among villagers, particularly in regard to irrigation, and thus the increased
food supply resulted in a more developed and integrated political structure

This Bolivian father and son demonstrate that changes in material items often occur by simple substitution. (courtesy of Arthur B. Hayes, III)

and even the beginnings of social differentiation. At about the same time, the invading Apaches began to arrive in Pima and Papago territory. Their raids further increased the importance of cooperation for mutual defense and enhanced the advantage of nucleated villages.

The Papago, meanwhile, found themselves unable to take advantage of wheat. Dispersed and semi-nomadic, they could not develop the irrigation works required, nor could they defend themselves as effectively against the Apache. Thus, these two culturally similar, neighboring Indian groups, because of small differences in their original ecological adaptation, evolved along separate lines by reacting very differently when two new elements, wheat and raiding Apache bands, were introduced to their environment.

Hackenburg's study, and others following the same approach, study the processes of cultural change in terms of the ecological adaptation of the society. Marvin Harris (1975), whose model of society we discussed in chapter 2, and other anthropologists working in this vein, believe that the technical and ecological adaptation of a society forms the mold into which the rest of the culture fits. Social and political organization, and ultimately ideology, belief systems, and the arts, will change as the ecological and technological mold changes. Harris asserts that the technical and environmental level of culture is more "basic" than the rest, and that change flows up from the base rather than down from the higher levels. That is to say, a change in environmental adaptation, whether caused by the adoption of wheat among the Pima or drought among the Makrani tribes, brings to bear a greater influence on social structure and belief systems than a change in

An individual adopts those innovations he considers most useful. (courtesy of Claudia Crawford)

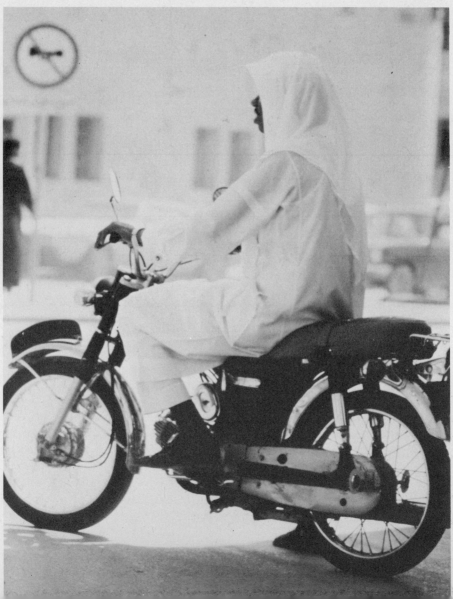

Syncretism is illustrated by this Catholic priest in Bolivia who has permitted the incorporation of Indian beliefs into Christian practice. The Indians believe that a deceased person, whose skull is kept in the church wall, is needed to protect the village. (courtesy of Arthur B. Hayes, III)

either of the other can bring to bear on ecological adaptation. Indeed, a change in either social organization or belief systems is unlikely to occur in the absence of an environmental change.

Cultural lag and social movements. To state that change in ecological adaptation causes change in social, political, and belief systems is not to state that all these changes occur at once. Technological change usually happens first—often abruptly. Social, political, and especially belief and value changes often lag far behind. A culture might suffer for some time from a disjuncture between two or more of its systems. Technological change, for example, forces people to carry out new roles before the appropriate statuses have been formulated and widely accepted and before the basic value system can change to support the new reality.

Research into this situation of disjuncture—appropriately called cultural lag—has shown that a culture can tolerate only so much friction from ill-fitting parts rubbing against one another. The culture must attempt to bring the pieces into harmony once again or it will disintegrate. Anthropologists have suggested that social movements may be an effective way of playing "catch-up ball." A social movement can lead to the widespread and rapid acceptance of a new belief system that is more appropriate to the changed social structures, thus allowing for the continuation of the society. Anthony F. C. Wallace says that social movements allow people to "resynthesize their mazeways." In the language we have been using throughout this book, a social movement might permit people to reformulate the system of sets and patterns they use to organize cultural components, or perhaps even to perceive some new components. In other words, people achieve a new perception of reality that accomodates their situation more easily.

The case studied by Mary Gallagher (1972), the women's movement of the late 1960s, appears to confirm this view. By the 1960s, the objective situation of women was radically different from the situation assumed in the widely accepted belief system. In other words, there was an incongruity between the social structural and the ideological levels of the society. The parts no longer "fit" together. Rather than working primarily as housewives and mothers, women had increased their average educational level and had taken a significant place in the employment market. Women no longer worked at jobs for "pin money" until they had children. Instead many, even mothers of preschool youngsters, worked to provide income that was deemed essential for the family standard of living or that formed the sole support of their families. The ideological system, however, with its images of the "little woman" happily scrubbing, serving, baking, and shopping; its belief that children reared in day care centers suffer irreparable harm; and its negative evaluation of working women, had not changed in generations.

A major function of the women's movement was to leapfrog the national belief system forward to encourage both men and women to change their ideas, values, and images of the appropriate status for women. The movement also justified a shift in the sets "women's work" and "men's work." It expanded the former to include almost any type of gainful employment. Coal miners and sailors had to relinquish their superstitutions about the unlucky presence of women in the work place. The movement also expanded the set "men's work" to include more housework and child care than had previously been deemed appropriate.

In a similar vein, another student of social movements, Eric Wolf (1951), has suggested that the Muslim religious belief system was also a form of cultural catching up. The ministry of the Prophet Muhammad, Wolf argues, coincided with important social and economic changes in Western Arabian society and Muhammad's teachings meshed perfectly with social trends already underway. In the late seventh and the early eighth centuries, Wolf says, increased dominance of trade by the merchants of Mecca was moving society away from the traditional tribal organization based on personalized loyalties and toward a unified state system based on loyalty to a single overarching central authority. The worship of many tribal gods, each responsible for a specific kinship group, supported the old system of loyalties. Muhammad, however, brought the message of a single God who required the loyalty of all people, regardless of tribe. The believers, or Muslims ("those who submit"), are joined in a single, egalitarian community of Islam ("submission"). While not suggesting that the revelation of Muhammad was in itself a product of social change, Wolf notes that monotheistic prophets occurred elsewhere in Arabia at about the same time and that Muhammad's religious movement encouraged, and indeed consummated, the social changes already underway.

Adaptive changes as reflected in material culture. When either systemic or maintenance change takes place within a cultural system, it is visible in many facets of the culture at once. We have shown how ideas (as components) and things (as other components) interact within the total pattern and reflect each other. Thus, the hair curlers reflected one idea in one culture but a totally different one in another culture; the "ancestor component" was represented by a spirit in one case and an airplane in another. In cultures that have become extinct, it is often possible to deduce the idea from the thing and to determine how a piece of material reflects a *conceptual pattern* (a set of ideas). This area of study has traditionally belonged to the archaeologist.

James Deetz (1967), an archaeologist whose interest spans prehistoric and historic aspects of American culture, determined that there had been a change in the social structure of the Arikara Indians based on his analysis of components of their material culture, in this case types of pottery.

Deetz found that the pottery from an Arikara site in South Dakota could be readily sorted and divided into three different sets. However, when he tried to sort the sets further, according to certain attributes of the pottery, Deetz found that while the earliest set could be broken down into typological groups, the two later sets showed an increasing lack of common attributes. In fact, none of the attributes used for typing the earliest set could be distinguished in the latest set, leaving only random association as a means of further classification.

An investigation of Arikara history and ethnography revealed the reasons for this change in pottery style. The Arikara Indians were originally located in northeastern Nebraska, where they were organized into large families and practiced matrilocal residence in permanent communities. The women produced the majority of the food and lived together in matrilineal families that their husbands joined upon marriage. Since they were relatively isolated from other groups and yet shared their innovations among one another, the women of each family group produced similar pottery.

But the Arikara later migrated north into South Dakota. Since their new environment was not as favorable as their old one, the Arikara found it necessary to migrate every five or 10 years in order to obtain necessary resources. During this period, the Arikara came in contact with other groups of people, such as the Dakota Indians and European settlers. While these contacts meant the establishment of trade between the groups and occasional warfare for the Arikara, they also meant the exposure of the Arikara people to previously unknown diseases. An epidemic of smallpox swept through the group and greatly reduced their population.

All of these factors combined to break down the original Arikara social system. The large families and matrilocal groups were broken up, and the women were often forced to live with families other than their own. With all the intermingling among groups, the women producing pottery began to assimilate other's ideas. There no longer were isolated groups of women making pottery.

These breakdowns in the Arikara social structure help to explain both the shift in their pottery styles and Deetz's subsequent difficulties in finding common attributes within the later sets. When the families were large and isolated from other family groups, the pottery each woman produced was distinctive, yet it shared some attributes of other pottery made by members of the same group. However, when the Arikara were exposed to other cultures and lost their strong, isolated family groups, the pottery became less distinctive and the attributes of many styles tended to blend together. Thus, the change in the Arikara social structure is reflected in the material culture that they have left behind for the archaeologist.

CHANGE AT THE LEVEL OF CULTURE IN GENERAL

Although many anthropologists content themselves with studies of specific changes in particular cultures, some ambitious scholars attempt to discover laws that underlie social change in human societies generally. They search for trends and mechanisms common to all cultures and attempt to discern the processes that animate the trends. Indeed, curiousity about these questions motivated some of the very first anthropological writings during the nineteenth century.

As part of the general intellectual excitement surrounding Darwinian evolution, scholars began to ruminate on the direction of change in human societies. No notion even vaguely resembling the modern concept of culture existed in those days, and the scientific world was overwhelmed with the concept of evolution. What could be more natural, therefore, than to erect a theory of the evolution of human societies, based on the best notions of the time?

A theory of general evolution developed, usually associated with the names Lewis H. Morgan and Edward Tylor. It proved vastly influential in anthropology, to both the good and the detriment of the field. These social theorists entirely missed the basic point of Darwinian theory, which was that species evolve in response to specific local conditions; instead they began with the assumption that there existed a single, unilineal trend in human society. The goal of this trend was the "highest" form of social life which, coincidentally, happened to be British and American life of the period. The "lowest" form of society was also presumably the oldest, that which nineteenth century evolutionists called "savagery" and which we have called hunting and gathering. The basic trend of human life, this theory taught, was to move from the "lowest" form to the "highest." To do so, societies were thought to pass in a single, unilineal direction from "savagery" through "barbarism" (or village farming) to "civilization." The various societies existing around the world could therefore be arrayed on a scale of advancement, depending on their similarity to the pinnacle of human existence, Victorian Britain. The greater the similarity, the greater was their advancement; the greater the differences, the greater their backwardness.

Anthropology was so young that decades had to elapse before the ethnocentrism of this approach became obvious. Nor were contradictory cases well known. How, for example, could this theory explain the Maya, who lapsed from civilization to "barbarism"; how could it explain the Plains Indians, who, in abandoning sedentary life for the nomadic existence of horse-mounted buffalo hunters, lapsed from "barbarism" to "savagery"? How, indeed, could it explain the Dark Ages in Europe?

The reaction to nineteenth century evolutionism, when it finally occurred, brought a revulsion so profound that for generations any evolutionary study was suspect. It is only in the last decade or two that anthropologists have begun to admit that certain general trends do appear to occur in most societies when given the chance.

Raoul Naroll (1970) has summarized these main patterns of change. He observed, in agreement with Leslie White (1949), that in a general way, societies tend to move toward higher levels of energy use and capture. Cultures move in the direction of greater specialization when ecological conditions permit. Social organization becomes less egalitarian as wealth accumulates; elites grow in power, riches, and means of exploitation. Leadership tends to become less consensual and more authoritarian. Despite contrary cases, societies generally have appeared to move away from nomadism and toward more and more complex sedentary organization. Warfare tends to lose its association with personal revenge and to become associated instead with political ends such as acquiring territory or resources; the warring unit tends to change from a kinship group to a division of the state.

All these trends involve movement toward greater complexity. Marshall Sahlins and Ellman Service (1960), among others, suggest that more complex societies are more adaptive than simpler ones. A larger, more complexly organized society brings greater diversity to bear on problems. More possible solutions are available: more skills, more manpower, more innovators, more effort. Sahlins and Service believe, therefore, that a complexly organized group has, other things being equal, a greater chance to survive a disaster or change in conditions than a simple group committed to a single solution.

David Kaplan (1960) has summarized this view in his law of *cultural dominance,* which states that a cultural system that more effectively exploits the energy resources of a given environment will tend to spread in that environment at the expense of less effective systems. Agriculturalists, therefore, tend to spread at the expense of hunters and gatherers, and industrial systems at the expense of peasant agriculturalists.

Kaplan's formulation, however, is not without problems. We all know the sad story of the dinosaurs, great dominant beasts that became so finely adapted that they could not survive when change overtook their environment. Like an organism, a society may become so specialized or delicately adapted that it is vulnerable to environmental change. The culture of the Plains Indians, for example, depended so heavily on the buffalo that it died when the great herds did. Ellman Service's *law of evolutionary potential* attempts to account for this possibility. The more specialized an organism or society, he states, the less likely it is to be the foundation or source of important evolutionary changes. The highly specialized system has less flexibility for coping, and less likelihood of developing major evolutionary advances.

Kaplan's theory and Service's refinement reestablish the intellectual validity of studies of general social evolution. Unlike nineteenth century theorists, they do not claim that evolution must proceed in a single, unilineal direction, nor that it must necessarily be cumulative. Rather than map out the course cultures have travelled, anthropologists attempt to discover the forces that fueled the trip. They assume that certain regularities exist because cultures themselves act fairly regularly. This, indeed is the assumption on which all of anthropology is based.

ANTHROPOLOGY AND ETHICS

Throughout this book we have presented anthropology as a "pure" science. Like most other pure sciences, however, it has its engineering arm. Not all members of the profession spend their time gathering knowledge for its own sake. Some attempt to apply this knowledge to achieve practical ends. We cannot close a discussion of cultural change without mentioning efforts of anthropologists to use their knowledge to direct change. We must also consider the ethical problems these efforts may cause. It is also possible, with openly published research, that someone other than the researcher may put the information to practical use, and not always to uses the researcher might choose. This possibility also raises ethical problems.

The history of *applied anthropology,* as efforts to put anthropological knowledge to practical use are called, is almost as long as that of anthropology itself. Anthropologists served as advisors to, and even members of, colonial administrations. Later they worked in the same roles in government-sponsored schemes to bring economic and social change to so-called developing countries. Anthropologists who carried out such activities generally viewed themselves as impartial scientific advisors whose responsibility was to help power holders make wise policy choices rather than to create policy themselves. As such, they sometimes saw their knowledge put to uses they did not favor or approve.

Direct academic involvement in fostering social change began in 1948, when a group from the University of Chicago undertook what they termed "participant interference" or "action anthropology" among the Fox Indians of Iowa. These anthropologists attempted to help the Fox locate and solve their problems. Mainly through education, they attempted to help the Fox make their own informed decisions about adaptation to the white world surrounding them. The Chicago group exercised no authority over the Fox, however.

A much more elaborate and structured scheme was the famous Vicos project undertaken by Cornell University in Peru in 1952. In cooperation with an agency of the Peruvian government, Cornell took a five-year lease on the hacienda of Vicos, hoping to undertake a "research and development" project among its 1700 Quechua Indian inhabitants. The anthropologists hoped to interfere in social life in specific, goal-oriented ways and to study the results of their interference. They hoped to induce changes in

Vicos that would help the inhabitants achieve a life of greater social, political, and economic independence than was possible under their former cultural conditions as serfs to a succession of *mestizo* landlords. Using profits that formerly went to the landlord, Cornell invested in education and health care on the manor itself. Anthropologists also taught the Indians new and more productive agricultural techniques and a variety of other useful skills.

The Cornell experiment was such a success that when the university's lease expired the community petitioned to buy title to the manor. Over the strenuous and concerted opposition of much of the local power structure, the community was finally able to negotiate terms for a sale and in 1962 the Vicosinos took control of their own community.

Not all academic attempts to intervene in social change have met with such success, however, The disastrous Project Camelot, undertaken by the Special Operations Research Office under contract with the United States Army, was intended to develop means that would "make it possible to predict and influence politically significant aspects of social change in the developing nations of the world." That is, the Army wished to predict possible social change so that it could intervene where necessary to further what it viewed as American interests. Undertaken in the 1960s, Project Camelot was a product of the "counter-insurgency" approach to violent political change that had occurred in a number of countries.

Officials selected Chile as the first study site. Although the true aims of the project were known in the scientific community, their public disclosure in Chile, following the arrival of an anthropologist who claimed to belong to the project, created an international scandal. The project was cancelled after a Congressional investigation, but not before it had gravely damaged the reputation of American social science in many of the Third World countries. Later, during the Vietnam war, further controversy developed over revelations that American social scientists, including anthropologists, had cooperated with the army in studies of insurgency in Thailand.

These disclosures galvanized organized anthropology to make a serious study of the ethical questions involved in anthropological research. Among the results of this effort were the creation of a standing committee on ethics in the American Anthropological Association and the adoption of a code of ethics in 1970. This code emphasizes the overriding obligation of the anthropological investigator to the people he studies. He must never use the information he has gained from them, often through confidential relationships, for any purposes detrimental to their well-being. He must place their welfare above his own gain or personal advancement. He must openly inform them of the aim of his study and protect their confidence throughout the gathering and publication of his material. He should never cooperate in the accumulation of secret or classified information about the group he is studying.

The anthropologist further owes an obligation to the public and to his colleagues to conduct his research and publish his findings openly and without bias. He should be frank about his sources of financial support. He should also satisfy himself that he is aware of the source of funds given him by sponsors and should retain full control over the substantive content of his work and the ethical questions relating to it.

FIELD PROJECT: CULTURE CHANGE

Because your field study has lasted only one semester, it may not be possible for you personally to observe any significant changes in your cultural system. Therefore, you may have to depend on the longer-term observations of informants to gather this material.

I. If you believe that you have witnessed a change within your group, specify the cultural pattern or patterns you believe to be involved. Describe this pattern as it existed before the change, and describe it now.
   A. Does this change involve a systemic change in the sets or patterns of your group's culture, or is it a maintenance change?
   B. If you have witnessed a maintenance change, explain the way in which this process functions to maintain the cultural system as a whole.
   C. If you believe you have witnessed a systemic change, list the old sets and patterns and compare them with the new ones.
   D. What do you think "caused" the change? In terms of Harris' model of the three levels of a sociocultural system, attempt to explain the change by referring to changes in the next lower level. For example, explain a change in values or beliefs (ideology) by correlating it with a change in the sociopolitical organization, or explain a social or political change by showing its relationship to a change in the ecology or demography of the group.

II. If you have not witnessed any significant changes, ask one, or preferably several, long-term members of the group to name patterns that they believe have changed. Try to get several people to talk about the same patterns.
   A. Obtain descriptions of a particular pattern as it existed in the past. Attempt to isolate the most significant features of that pattern.
   B. From your own observation, describe a corresponding present-day pattern. For example, you might compare today's dating behavior with that of 50 years ago, or the accounting procedures of a modern store with those used during the 1950s.
   C. List the most important difference in the two patterns. Is this a maintenance change or a systemic change?
   D. Try to think of reasons to explain these changes. What do you think caused the changes? In terms of Harris' model of the three levels

of a sociocultural system, attempt to explain the change by referring to changes in the next lower level.
E. What further changes have been effected in your group as a result
of the change you observed? For instance, how have other aspects
of the group accomodated themselves to the new situation?

References

Ardrey, Robert. 1961. *African Genesis: A Personal Investigation into the Animal Origins and Nature of Man.* New York: Atheneum Press.

———. 1966. *The Territorial Imperative: A Personal Inquiry into the Animal Origins of Property and Nations.* New York: Atheneum Press.

Barnett, Homer G. 1953. *Innovation: The Basis of Cultural Change.* New York: McGraw Hill.

Barry, Herbert, Child, I. L., and Bacon, M. K. Relation of child rearing to subsistence economy. *American Anthropologist* 61 (1959): 51–63.

Barth, F. 1963. *Role of the Entrepreneur in Social Change in Northern Norway.* Bergen, Norway: Norwegian Universities Press.

Benedict, Ruth. 1934. *Patterns of Culture.* Boston: Houghton Mifflin.

———. 1946. *The Chrysanthemum and the Sword: Patterns of Japanese Culture.* Boston: Houghton Mifflin.

Berger, Peter L. and Brigitte. 1972. The bluing of America. *Contemporary Society* by John A. Perry and Murray Seidler. San Francisco: Canfield Press.

Birdwhistle, Ray L. 1970. *Kinesics and Context.* New York: Ballantine Books.

Bohannon, Paul. 1960. *Social Anthropology.* New York: Holt, Rinehart & Winston.

Bott, Elizabeth. 1957. *Family and Social Networks.* London: Tavistock.

Boullata, Kamal. Classical Arab art and modern painting: A study in affinities. *Muslim World* 63 (1973): 1–14.

Brown, Roger and Ford, Marguerite. Address in American English. *Journal of Abnormal Psychology* 62 (1961): 375–385.

Bulliet, Richard W. 1975. *The Camel and the Wheel.* Cambridge, Mass.: Harvard University Press.

Carstairs, G. Morris. 1961. *The Twice-Born: A Study of a Community of High Caste Hindus.* Bloomington: Indian University Press.

Carroll, John B., ed. 1956. *Language, Thought and Reality: Selected Writings of Benjamin Lee Whorf.* New York: Wiley.

Deetz, J. F. 1967. *Invitation to Archaeology.* Garden City, N.Y.: Natural History Press.

Dubois, Cora. 1960. *The People of Alor: A Social-Psychological Study of an East Indian Island.* Cambridge, Mass.: Harvard University Press. (First published in 1944.)

Dundes, Alan. 1968. The number three in American culture. *Every Man His Way: Readings in Cultural Anthropology.* Edited by Alan Dundes. Englewood Cliffs, N.J.: Prentice Hall.

Durkheim, Emile. 1965. *The Elementary Forms of the Religious Life.* Translated by Joseph Ward Swain. New York: Free Press. (First published in 1915.)

Edgerton, Robert. 1971. *The Individual in Cultural Adaptation: A Study of Four East African Peoples.* Berkeley: University of California Press.

Ember, Carol R. and Ember, Melvin. 1973. *Cultural Anthropology.* New York: Appleton-Century-Crofts.

Evans-Pritchard, E. E. 1937. *Witchcraft, Oracles and Magic Among the Azande.* Oxford, England: Clarendon Press.

———. 1941. *The Nuer.* Oxford, England: Clarendon Press.

Fischer, John. Art styles as cognitive maps. *American Anthropologist* 63 (1961): 79–84.

Foster, George M. 1967. *Tzintzuntzan: Mexican Peasants in a Changing World.* Boston: Little Brown.

Fried, Morton. 1967. *The Evolution of Political Society: An Essay in Political Anthropology.* New York: Random House.

Gallagher, Mary F. Women's liberation: Social movement in a complex society. Unpublished Ph. D. dissertation. University of Colorado, 1972.

Gellner, Ernest. 1969. *Saints of the Atlas.* Chicago: University of Chicago Press.

Geertz, Clifford. 1960. *The Religion of Java.* Glencoe, Ill.: The Free Press.

———. 1965. Religion as a cultural system. *Anthropological Approaches to the Study of Religion.* Edited by Michael Bantom. London: Tavistock.

Goodenough, W. H. Residence rules. *Southwestern Journal of Anthropology* 12 (1956): 22–37.

Gorer, Geoffrey and Rickman, J. 1949. *The People of Great Russia.* London: Cresset.

Gough, E. K. The Nayars and the definition of marriage. *Journal of the Royal Anthropological Institute* 1959: 23–34.

Hackenburg, Robert A. Economic alternatives in arid lands: A case study of the Pima and Papago Indians. *Ethnology* 1 (1962): 186–195.

Hall, Edward T. 1959. *The Silent Language.* Garden City, N.Y.: Doubleday and Co.

Harris, Marvin. 1975. *Culture, People, Nature.* Second edition. New York: Thomas Y. Crowell.

Hill, James N. 1968. Broken K. Pueblo, patterns of form and function. *New Perspectives in Archaeology.* Edited by S. R. Binford and L. R. Binford. Chicago: Aldine.

Hoijer, Harry. Cultural implications of some Navaho linguistic categories. *Language* 27 (1951): 111–120.

Holloway, Ralph. 1968. Human aggression: The need for a species-specific framework. *War: The Anthropology of Armed Conflict and Aggression.* Edited by M. Fried, M. Harris, and R. Murphy. New York: Natural History Press.

Holmberg, A. R. The changing values and institutions of Vicos in the context of national development. *American Behavioral Scientist* 8 (1965): 3–8.

Horowitz, I. L., ed. 1967. *The Rise and Fall of Project Camelot: Studies in the Relationship Between Social Science and Practical Politics.* Cambridge, Mass.: M.I.T.

Hymes, Dell H. 1962. The ethnography of speaking. *Anthropology and Human Behavior.* Edited by Thomas Gladwin and William C. Sturtevant. Washington, D.C.: Anthropological Society of Washington.

Kaplan, David. 1960. The law of cultural dominance. *Evolution and Culture.* Edited by Marshall D. Sahlins and Elman R. Bernice. Ann Arbor: University of Michigan Press.

Kardiner, Abram, ed. 1939. *The Individual and His Society.* New York: Columbia University Press.

Kluckhohn, Clyde. 1949. *Mirror for Man.* Connecticut: Fawcett Publisher.

Kluckhohn, Clyde and Leighton, Dorothea. 1962. *The Navaho.* Garden City, N.Y.: Natural History Library. (First published in 1946.)

Kluckhohn, Clyde and Kroeber, A. L. 1963. *Culture: A Critical Review of Concepts and Definitions.* New York: Vintage.

Lambert, William W., Triandis, Leigh Minturn, and Wolf, Margery. Some correlates of beliefs in the malevolence and benevolence of supernatural beings: A cross-societal study. *Journal of Abnormal and Social Psychology* 58 (1959): 162–169.

Landes, Ruth. The abnormal among the Ojibwa. *Journal of Abnormal and Social Psychology* 33 (1938): 1–14.

Leach, E. R. 1954. *Political Systems of Highland Burma.* Cambridge, Mass.: Harvard Press.

Lee, Richard B. What hunters do for a living, or, How to make out on scarce resources. *Man the Hunter.* Edited by R. B. Lee and I. De Vore. Chicago: Aldine Press.

Levi-Strauss, Claude. 1963. *Structural Anthropology.* Translated by Claire Jacobson and Booke Grundfest Schoepf. New York: Basic Books.

Lorenz, Konrad. 1966. *On Aggression.* New York: Harcourt, Brace, and World.

Lutfiyya, Abdulla M. 1966. *Baytin, A Jordanian Village: A Study of Social Institutions and Social Change in a Folk Community.* The Hague: Mouton.

Lynes, Russell. 1949. *The Tastemakers.* New York: Grosset and Dunlap.

Malinowski, Bronislaw. 1922. *Argonauts of the Western Pacific.* London: Rutledge.

———. 1931. Culture. *Encyclopedia of the Social Sciences,* Vol. 4. New York: Macmillan.

———. 1953. *Sex and Repression in Savage Society.* London: Rutledge and Kegan Paul.

———. 1954. *Magic, Science, and Religion.* New York: Anchor Books.

Mead, Margaret. 1928. *Coming of Age in Samoa.* New York: William Morrow and Company.

———. 1935. *Sex and Temperament in Three Primitive Societies.* New York: William Morrow and Company.

Morgan, Lewis Henry. 1870. *Systems of Consanguinity and Affinity in the Human Family.* Washington, D.C.: Smithsonian Institution.

———. 1877. *Ancient Society.* Henry Holt and Company.

Naroll, R. What have we learned from cross-cultural studies? *American Anthropologist* 72 (1970): 1227–1288.

Opler, Marvin K. Cultural differences in mental disorders: An Italian and Irish contrast in the schizophrenias. *Psychiatric Quarterly* July 1959.

Pastner, Stephen L. Cooperation in crisis among Baluch nomads. Unpublished manuscript, 1974.

Patai, Raphael. 1973. *The Arab Mind.* New York: Charles Scribner's Sons.

Polyani, Karl. 1944. *The Great Transformation.* New York: Holt, Rinehart & Winston.

Pouissaint, Alvin F. A Negro psychiatrist explains the Negro psyche. *The New York Times* August 20, 1967: Section 6, 52 ff.

Prothro, E. Terry. 1961. *Child Rearing in Lebanon.* Cambridge, Mass.: Harvard University Press.

Rappaport, Roy. 1968. *Pigs for the Ancestors: Ritual in the Ecology of a New Guinea People.* New Haven: Yale University Press.

Reich, Charles. 1970. *The Greening of America.* New York: Holt Rinehart.

Rhoads, Robin E. and Thompson, Stephen I. Adaptive strategies in alpine environments: Beyond ecological particularism. *American Anthropologist* 2 (1975): 553–554.

Riesman, David, Glazer, Nathan, and Denney, Rueul. 1950. *The Lonely Crowd: A Study of the Changing American Character.* New Haven: Yale University Press.

Sahlins, Marshall. The segmentary lineage: An organization for predatory expansion. *American Anthropologist* 63 (1961): 322–45.

––––––. 1965. On the sociology of primitive exchange. *The Relevance of Models for Social Anthropology.* Association of Social Anthropologists Monographs, Vol. 1. New York: Praeger.

Sahlins, M. and Service, E. R., eds. 1960. *Evolution and Culture.* Ann Arbor: University of Michigan Press.

Sapir, Edward. Conceptual categories in primitive languages. *Science* 74 (1931): 578.

Simmons, Leo W., ed. 1963. *Sun Chief: The Autobiography of a Hopi Indian* (revised edition). New Haven: Yale University Press.

Spiro, Melford E. and D'Andrade, Roy G. A cross-cultural study of some supernatural beliefs. *American Anthropologist* 60 (1958): 456–466.

Swadesh, Morris. 1971. *The Origin and Diversification of Language.* Edited by J. Sherzer. Chicago: Aldine-Atherton.

Swanson, G. E. 1960. *The Birth of the Gods: The Origin of Primitive Beliefs.* Ann Arbor: University of Michigan Press.

Tawney, Richard H. 1926. *Religion and the Rise of Capitalism: A Historical Study.* New York: Harcourt Brace.

Turnbull, Colin M. 1961. *The Forest People.* New York: Simon and Schuster.

––––––. 1968. *The Lonely African.* New York: Simon and Schuster.

Tylor, E. B. 1871. *Primitive Culture.* London: J. Murray.

––––––. On a method of investigating the development of institutions applied to the laws of marriage and descent. *Journal of the Royal Anthropological Institute of Great Britain and Ireland* 18 (1888).

Vayda, Andrew. 1967. Hypotheses about functions of war. *War: The Anthropology of Armed Conflict and Aggression.* Edited by Morton Fried, Marvin Harris, and Robert Murphy. New York: Natural History Press.

Van Gennep, A. 1960. *The Rites of Passage.* Chicago: Phoenix Books.

Wallace, Anthony F. C. 1952. *The Modal Personality of the Tuscarora Indians, as Revealed by the Rorschach Test.* Bulletin 150, Bureau of American Ethnology. Washington: United States Government Printing Office.

———. 1961 a. *Culture and Personality.* New York: Random House.

———. 1961 b. Mental illness, biology, and culture. *Psychological Anthropology: Approaches to Culture and Personality.* Edited by Francis L. K. Hsu. Homewood, Ill.: Dorsey Press.

Weber, Max. 1920. *The Protestant Ethic and the Spirit of Capitalism.* Translated by Talcott Parsons. London: G. Allen and Unwin.

White, Leslie A. 1949. *The Science of Culture.* New York: Farrar, Straus and Co.

Whiting, Beatrice B. Paiute Sorcery. *Viking Fund Publications in Anthropology* 1950, number 15.

Whiting, J. W. M. 1964. Effects of climate on certain cultural practices. *Explorations in Cultural Anthropology: Essays in Honor of George Peter Murdock.* Edited by W. H. Goodenough. New York: McGraw Hill.

Wilson, Monica. 1963. *Good Company: A Study of Nyakyusa Age-Villages.* Boston: Beacon Press.

Wolf, Arthur P. Childhood association, sexual attraction, and the incest taboo: A Chinese case. *American Anthropologist* 68 (1966): 883–898.

———. Adopt a daughter-in-law, marry a sister: A Chinese solution to the problem of the incest taboo. *American Anthropologist* 70 (1968): 864–874.

Wolf, Eric R. The social organization of Mecca and the origins of Islam. *Southwestern Journal of Anthropology* 7 (1951): 329–356.

Young, J. M. United States Air Force study. Personal communication, n.d.

Glossary

Acculturation: The process that produces changes in a culture as the result of contact with another culture.

Achieved status: A social status that can be gained by an individual's efforts.

Adaptation: The means by which a species derives the requirements of survival from its ecological niche.

Affines: Kin related through a marriage link.

Agricultural society: A society whose economy is based on large-scale food cultivation involving the use of domesticated animals. An agricultural society can support a large, dense population and full-time specialists.

Allophone: One of several sounds composing a single phoneme.

Ambilineal descent: A kinship system that traces a single line directly to the apical ancestor using links through both males and females but not simultaneously or equally.

Ascribed status: A social status that is assigned to an individual for reasons other than his or her own achievements.

Balanced reciprocity: Exchange of goods or services of equal value between persons of equal status.

Basic personality structure: In Abram Kardiner's theory, the totality of traits derived from contact with the primary institutions of a culture.

Bilateral descent: A kinship system that recognizes equally both the mother's and the father's line of descent.

Caste: A stratum or status group within a stratified society, in which membership is determined by birth. Marriage must be between members of the same caste. Movement between castes is not possible.

Class: A stratum or status group within a stratified society, in which membership is determined by economic standing and style of life. Marriage need not occur between members of the same stratum, and individual movement between strata is possible in a class society.

Cognate: A kinsman related to ego through a blood relationship.

Cognitive: Relating to the ability to learn, understand, or perceive.

Cultural lag: A discrepancy between two aspects of the same culture created when one aspect changes more rapidly than the other.

Cultural relativism: The anthropological philosophy that a particular custom or belief of a culture should be understood within the context of that culture rather than in comparison with the patterns of another culture or with universal ideal patterns.

Ecological niche: Elements of a species' environment that permit the harmonious relationship between the species and the physical environment required for the continued success of that species.

Ecology: The dynamic relationship between a species and its natural (both physical and social) environment.

Egalitarian society: A society that lacks social differentiation except for age and sex; one that makes all achieved statuses equally available to all adult members.

Emic: Relating to the array of cognitive categories and their relationships, as seen by a member of that culture; that is, the native's, or insider's, perspective.

Enculturation: The process of learning a culture.

Ethnocentrism: The belief that one's own culture is superior to others.

Ethnography: The systematic, complete description of a particular culture.

Ethnology: The theoretical and comparative study of cultural groups.

Etic: Relating to the array of cognitive categories and their relationships, as seen by one who is not a member of the culture; generally speaking, *etic* refers to the categories used by social scientists.

Generalized reciprocity: Gift giving without expectation of immediate or equal return, in the context of a continuing relationship.

Glottochronology: In historical linguistics, the study of the rate of change of a language.

Homeostasis: A balanced relationship between a population and its environment.

Horticultural society: A society that derives its food from naturally occurring plants and animals.

Infanticide: The practice of killing new-born infants, usually as a means of population control.

Kinesics: The study of the cultural meaning of bodily postures and gestures.

Lexicostatistics: See glottochronology.

Lineage: A unilineal descent group traced from a known ancestor.

Maintenance change: Change that occurs within a cultural system in order to permit the preservation of the system's basic patterns.

Mechanical solidarity: An interdependence among the members of a society that derives from the fact that they all perform the same work and share the same values and beliefs. The members have a high degree of self-reliance but can depend upon one another when necessary.

Monogamy: A marriage system that permits having only one spouse at a time.

Morpheme: The smallest unit of a language that has meaning.

Negative reciprocity: Exchange of goods or services of unequal value, taking advantage of one party involved.

Network: An ego-centered set of interpersonal relationships and interactions.

Nomadic society: A small society that moves periodically in pursuit of natural resources.

Norm: A culturally shared standard of behavior.

Organic solidarity: An interdependence among the members of a society that derives from the fact that members perform specialized work and can not survive without the other members.

Participant-observation: A type of anthropological fieldwork technique in which the anthropologist immerses himself in the group he is observing and, usually, attempts to become a member of the group.

Pastoral society: A society that derives its subsistence from animals it raises. Pastoralists are nomadic insofar as they must follow their herds.

Personality: The characteristic approach to life of an individual.

Phoneme: The array of sounds that is recognized as constituting a single category by a given language.

Polyandry: A marriage system that permits a woman to take more than one husband at a time.

Polygamy: A marriage system that permits a person to have more than one spouse at the same time.

Polygyny: A marriage system that permits a man to take more than one wife at the same time.

Proxemics: The study of the cultural uses of space.

Rank society: A society that allows for distinctions between people based on prestige or social standing but not on wealth.

Role conflict: The situation in which the demands of a person's different roles conflict with one another.

Role equipment: The people, things, knowledge, and skills that enable a person to perform a role.

Segmentary lineage: A unilineal descent group that consists of a number of progressively larger lineages that are mobilized in times of conflict.

Slash-and-burn: A horticultural system in which gardens are permitted to lie fallow for a number of years after losing their fertility and are later cleared and reclaimed for further use.

Society: A group characterized by a distinctive culture.

Subculture: A group within a society, some of whose values and beliefs differ from those of the larger, predominant culture.

Swidden: See slash-and-burn.

Systemic change: A change in a cultural system that alters one or more of the system's basic patterns.

Unilineal kinship: A kinship system that recognizes only one line of descent. The kinship connection may be either exclusively female links (matrilineal descent) or male links (patrilineal descent).

Index

Ability, division of labor and, 104
Abnormal personality, 234–237
Acculturation, 253–255
Achieved status, 128–129
Adaptive change, 256–262
Adaptive mechanism, personality as, 229–233
Address, forms of, 64–65
Adulthood, initiation into, 127–128
Aesthetic standards, 241–242
Affinity, 142, 164
African culture:
    food collection, 88
    languages, 57, 59–60
    personality, 232–233, 238
    social system, 136
Age, division of labor and, 104
Age-grading, 139
Age set system, 178
Aggression, 184–186
    See also Warfare
Agriculture, 31–32, 92–93, 95
Allomorphs, 60
Allophones, 58–59
Ambilineal descent, 155, 156, 157
American Anthropological Association, 266
American culture:
    art, 240–242
    ascribed status, 129–130
    belief system, 199–200
    change, 248, 259
    child care, 98–99
    control system, 172–175
    division of labor, 100–105
    eating pattern, 36
    groups, 132–133
    homeostasis, 250
    housework, 98–99
    individual territoriality, 71–72
    initiation rites, 127–128
    kinship, 144, 161–164
    language, 60–63
    marriage, 27–28
    mental illness, 235–236
    myths, 197
    networks, 135
    nuclear family, 144–145, 161
    ownership, 105, 106
    personality, 236
    role equipment, 123
    social stratification, 138–139
    spatial patterns, 35
    "three patterning," 38
    values, 196
    wedding ceremony, 125–127
    women's movement, 259
Amish culture, 206, 254

281

Amok, 236, 237
Anglo-Saxon culture, 155
Animal domestication, 90–91
Anthropology, 17–52
    applied, 265
    characteristics of, 19, 21–24
    defined, 18
    emics, 23–24, 46–48
    ethics and, 265–267
    etics, 23–24, 46–48
    explanations in, 44–50
    field projects, 50–52
    subfields of, 18–19
    systems approach to behavior, 44–46
Applied anthropology, 265
Arab culture:
    art, 239, 243
    change, 251, 254–255
    division of labor, 100, 103
    initiation rites, 127
    networks, 135
    See also Bedouin cultures; Muslim
        culture
Arabic, 58, 59
Arapesh culture, 222
Archaeology, 18–19, 74–75
Arctic hysteria, 236, 237
Ardrey, Robert, 185
Argonauts of the Western Pacific (Mali-
    nowski), 111
Arikara Indian culture, 261–262
Armenian culture, 231
Art, 239–244
Ascribed status, 129–132
Ashanti culture, 146
Australian aborigine culture, 83–84
Avunculocal residence, 148
Ayurvedic theory, 204–205
Azande culture, 214
Aztec language, 66

Bacon, M. K., 232, 238
Balanced reciprocity, 108–109
Baluchi culture, 87
Bands, 175–177, 186–187
Barnett, Homer, 250–251
Barry, Herbert, 232, 238
Barth, Frederick, 252–253
Basic personality structure, 227–228
Bedouin culture:
    desert adaptation, 87
    division of labor, 100, 103
    home territory, 33
    kinship system, 144, 158, 159
    leadership, 178

    pastoralism, 93
    personality, 232
    rank society, 137
    warfare, 187, 190
Behavioral meaning, 75
Behavioral patterns, see Patterns of
    behavior
Belief, cognitive systems of, 195
Belief systems, 193–218
    cosmology, 194, 195–196
    defined, 195
    elements of, 195–199
    field project, 217–218
    food, 203–205
    ideology, 200–201, 205, 214–215
    magic, 205, 211–214
    myths, 197–198
    nature of, 199–201
    operation of, 201–205
    religion, see Religion
    ritual, 198–199
    science, 205, 215–216
    sorcery, 211–214
    types of, 205–216
    values, 196–197
    witchcraft, 211–214
Benedict, Ruth, 222, 223–224, 227
Berber culture, 175
Berger, Bridgette, 248
Berger, Peter, 248
Bifurcation, 164
Bilateral descent, 154–155, 157, 160, 161
Bilocal residence, 148
Birdwhistell, Ray, 76
Black English, 61
Blackfoot Indian culture, 237
Body posture, 70, 76–78
Bohannon, Paul, 112
Bolivian Indian culture, 47
Bott, Elizabeth, 134
Boullata, Kamal, 244
Boundaries, 32
    material, 71–75
    speech patterns and, 65–66
British culture:
    ownership, 106
    role equipment, 123
Brown, Roger, 64
Bulliet, Richard W., 87

Cadune culture, 243
Carroll, John B., 68
Carstairs, G. Morris, 121, 221, 231
Caste system, 39–40, 105, 122, 138
Category, defined, 132

Chagnon, Napoleon, 187, 188
Change, 246–269
    acculturation studies, 253–255
    adaptive, 256–262
    approaches to, 250
    conservatism and, 249–250
    cultural lag, 259–261
    ethics and, 265–267
    field project, 268–269
    at individual level, 250–253
    at level of culture in general, 262–265
    maintenance, 247–248
    at societal level, 253–262
    systemic, 248–250
Chicago, University of, 265
Chiefdoms, 180–181
Child, I. L., 232, 238
Chinese culture:
    art, 243
    change, 254
    marriage, 153
Chomsky, Noam, 8–9, 61–62, 68
Christianity, 198, 199, 203, 209, 255
Chrysanthemum and the Sword, The
    (Benedict), 227
Churchill, Winston, 123
Clan, 159
Class societies, 138–139
Cognatic descent, 154–156, 160
Collateral kin, 64
Colombian culture, 252
Coming of Age in Samoa (Mead), 222
Communication systems, 55–80
    ethnolinguistics, 66–68
    field projects, 79–80
    historical linguistics, 62–63
    kinesics, 70, 76–78
    language structure, 57–62
    nonverbal communication, 55–56,
        68–78
    proxemics, 70–75
    sociolinguistics, 64–66
    symbols, 56
Communism, 215
Complex kinemorphic constructions, 76
Components, 10–14, 36–38, 40
Conceptual pattern, 261
Conflict:
    role, 124–125
    See also Aggression; Warfare
Conservatism, change and, 249–250
Contagion, law of, 213
Control systems, 171–190
    aggression, 184–186
    bands, 175–177, 186–187
    chiefdoms, 180–181

field project, 191–192
functions of, 171–175
institutional differences in, 172–175
the state, 181–184, 189–190
tribes, 177–180
warfare, see Warfare
witchcraft and, 213–214
Conversation, topics of, 65
Cornell University, 265–266
Cosmology, 194, 195–196
Crane, Hart, 120
Crawford, Claudia, 14, 72, 87, 103, 182,
    201, 241, 258
Cree Indian culture, 32
Crow Indian culture, 167–168
Cultural anthropology, 18
Cultural construction of reality,
    see Reality, cultural construction of
Cultural dominance, 264
Cultural influence of language, 66–67
Cultural lag, 259–261
Cultural patterns, see Patterns of behav-
    ior
Cultural relativism, 16
Cultural systems and subsystems, 17,
    48–49
Culture, concept of, 7, 48
Culture change, see Change
Cuna Indian culture, 107

D'Andrade, Roy G., 210
Deetz, James, 75, 261–262
Descent, principle of, 142
Descent rules:
    cognatic, 154–156, 160
    unilineal, 156–160
Dialogue of the Two World Systems
    (Galileo), 193
Dinka culture, 180
Distribution of goods and services, 107–
    117
Division of labor, 100–105
Dogon culture:
    art, 242
    belief system, 195–196, 198, 211
    initiation rites, 127
Dominance, cultural, 264
DuBois, Cora, 224, 228
Dugum Dani culture, 187, 189
Dundes, Alan, 38
Durkheim, Emile, 209

Early, Daniel, 86, 92, 122, 123, 208
Eating patterns, 36, 37

Ecological systems:
    field project, 97
    technology and, see Technology
Economic systems, 98–119
    distribution of goods and services, 107–117
    division of labor, 100–105
    field project, 118–119
    functions of, 99–100
    ownership, 105–107
Edgerton, Robert, 232–233
Egalitarian societies, 89, 136–137
Ego-centered group, 155
Ember, Carol R., 88
Ember, Melvin, 88
Emics, 23–24, 46–48
Endogamy, 153
Enforcement control, 181
Engels, Friedrich, 215
Environment:
    adaptation to, 232–233
    technology and, 86–87, 95
Eskimo culture, 11, 88
    control system, 175, 177
    kinship terminology, 165–166
    language, 66
    mental illness, 236
    technology, 84
Ethics, 265–267
Ethnocentrism, 15, 16
Ethnography, 18, 44
Ethnolinguistics, 66–68
Ethnology, 18
Etics, 23–24, 46–48
Evans-Pritchard, E. E., 159, 213, 214
Evolutionary potential, law of, 264
Exclusive groups, 133
Exogamy, 153–154
Extended family, 145

Facial expressions, 76
Facteme, 75
Faisal, King, 182
Family:
    extended, 145
    joint, 145
    nuclear, 144–145, 160, 161
    polyandrous, 146
    polygynous, 146, 147
    See also Kinship systems
Father, physiological, 151
Field projects, 50–52
    belief systems, 217–218
    change, 268–269
    communication systems, 79–80

control systems, 191–192
ecological systems, 97
economic systems, 118–119
kinship systems, 170
patterns of behavior, 53–54
personality, 245
social systems, 140–141
Fiscal control, 181
Fischer, John, 149–150
Fitzgerald, F. Scott, 230–231
Food:
    belief and, 203–205
    collecting, 87–91
Food-producing technologies, 90–94
    agriculture, 92–93, 95
    horticulture, 91–92
    pastoralism, 93–94
Ford, Marguerite, 64
Formal bodies, 133
Foster, George, 232
Fox Indian culture, 265
Free goods, 100
French culture, 34–35
Freud, Sigmund, 224–226
Fried, Morton, 181
Functional meanings, 75

Galileo Galilei, 193–194, 196
Gallagher, Leonard J., 256
Gallagher, Mary, 259
Gathering societies, 89–90, 175, 186–187
Geertz, Clifford, 65, 195, 198
Gellner, Ernest, 180
General purpose money, 114–117
Generalized reciprocity, 108–109
Generation, kinship terms and, 164
Genitor, 159–162
Genitrix, 152
Gireaudou, Jean, 190
Glottochronology, 63
Goodenough, Ward, 149–150
Goods:
    distribution of, 107–117
    free, 100
Gorer, Geoffrey, 227
Gough, Kathleen, 150
Grammar, 60–61
    transformational, 61–62
Greening of America, The (Reich), 248
Greeting behaviors, 36–37, 42
Groups, 132–134

Hackenburg, Robert, 256–257
Hall, E. T., 71–72

Hari Krishna culture, 206
Harris, Marvin, 46–49, 154, 188–189, 239, 240, 257–258
Hawaiian culture, 166
Hayes, Arthur B., III, 20, 47, 93, 200, 233, 257–258, 259
Hemingway, Ernest, 230–231
Hill, James N., 75
Hindu culture:
    belief system, 202–203, 206
    construction of reality, 9
    myths, 197
Hinduism, 202–203, 206
Historical linguistics, 62–63
Hoijer, Harry, 66–67
Holism, 21–22
Holloway, Ralph, 185
Holt, Ruth Ann, 77
Homeostasis, 250
Hopi Indian culture:
    initiation rites, 127
    language, 68
Horticulture, 91–92
Household forms, 144–147
Hunting societies, 89–90, 175, 186–187
Hurwitz, Geoffrey, 5, 129
Hymes, Dell H., 64

Ideology, 200–201, 205, 214–215
Incest taboo, 152–154
Incongruity, 42–44
Indian culture:
    Ayurvedic theory, 204–205
    caste system, 39–40, 105, 122, 138
    change, 254
    construction of reality, 9
    exchange system, 111–112, 116–117
    households, 145–146
    mental illness, 236
    personality, 231, 234, 236, 238
    sacred cow, 46–48
Indochinese languages, 59–60
Indonesian culture, 236
Industrial society, 94–95
Initiation rites, 127–128
Innovation, 250–251
Innovation: The Basis of Cultural Change (Barnett), 250–251
Integral contacts, 130
Involuntary groups, 133
Iroquois Indian culture:
    kinship terminology, 166–167
    personality, 235
Islam, 32, 198, 202, 206, 209, 211

Japanese culture, 27
    change, 254
    personality, 227
    prisoners of war, 13, 15, 16
    spatial patterns, 33–34
Javanese culture, 65
Jefferson, Thomas, 199–200
Joint family, 145
Judaism, 198, 199, 203–204
Judicial control, 181

Kachin culture, 247–248
Kaplan, David, 264
Kardiner, Abram, 224, 227–228, 229
Karimojong culture, 178
Keller, Helen, 56
Kinemes, 76
Kinemorphemes, 76
Kinesics, 70, 76–78
Kinship systems, 83–84, 135, 142–170
    classificatory, 162–163
    cognatic rules, 154–156, 160
    defined, 142
    descriptive, 162–163
    ecology and, 160–161
    field project, 170
    functions of family, 147–148
    household forms, 144–147
    kinship bonds, 154–161
    marriage, see Marriage
    principles of, 163–165
    residence patterns, 148–150
    status and, 143, 161
    terminology systems, 165–169
    terms, 161–169
    tribal, 177–180
    unilineal rules, 156–162
Klee, Paul, 244
Kluckhohn, Clyde, 7, 13, 214
Krober, A. L., 7
!Kung Bushman culture, 176
Kwakiutl Indian culture:
    personality, 223
    social stratification, 137–138

Labor, division of, 100–105
Labor sets, 102–105
Lambert, William W., 210
Landes, Ruth, 236–237
Landgraf, John, 37, 151, 224, 225
Language structure, 57–62
Latin American culture:
    change, 255
    individual territoriality, 72
    personality, 232

Leach, E. R., 247–248
Leadership:
  bands, 176
  chiefdoms, 180–181
  tribes, 177–178
Lee, Richard B., 89
Levi-Strauss, Claude, 8–9, 243
Lexicostatistics, 63
Life crises, 125
  initiation rites, 127–128
  wedding ceremony, 125–127
Lineages, 158–160, 178–180
Lineal kin, 164
Linguistics, 19
  ethnolinguistics, 66–68
  historical, 62–63
  language structure, 57–62
  sociolinguistics, 64–66
Linton, Ralph, 227–228
Lorenz, Konrad, 185
Lutfiyya, Abdulla M., 135
Lynes, Russel, 241

Magic, 205, 211–214
Maintenance change, 247–248
Makrani culture, 249
Malaysian culture, 236
Malinowski, Bronislaw, 22, 110–111, 153,
  212–213, 226
Manankabau culture, 146
Maori culture, 243
Market exchange, 112–114
Marriage, 150–154
  incest taboo, 152–154
  patterns, 27–28
  roles, 150–152
  wedding ceremony, 125–127
Marshall, Alfred, 107–108
Marx, Karl, 215
Mater, 152
Material culture:
  adaptive changes as reflected in,
    261–262
  study of, 71–75
Material tools, 69–70
Matrilineal descent, 156–158, 160–161
Matrilocal residence, 148
Mazeway, 252
Mbuti Pygmie culture, 88
Mead, Margaret, 128, 222–223, 238
Mechanical solidarity, 102
Menger, Karl, 107–108
Mental illness, 235–237
Methodology, 22

Mexican culture:
  change, 255
  ownership, 106
Modal personality, 228–229
Money, general purpose, 114–117
Monotheism, 210
Morgan, Lewis Henry, 162, 263
Morphemes, 59–60, 61–62
Muhammad, 17, 206, 261
Multiplex roles, 101
Mundugamor culture, 222
Murdock, George Peter, 145
Murngin culture, 186–187
Muslim culture:
  art, 244
  belief system, 200–203, 206, 260–261
  change, 253–254, 260–261
  marriage, 153
  networks, 135
  ownership, 106–107
  personality, 231–232, 234, 238, 239
  roles, 122, 124
  sexual segregation, 13, 14, 238, 239
  status, 130
  wedding ceremony, 127
Myths, 197–198

Naroll, Raoul, 263–264
National character studies, 226–227
National frontiers, 32–33
Navajo Indian culture:
  language, 66–67
  witchcraft, 214
Nayar culture, 150
Negative reciprocity, 108–109
Neolocal residence, 148
Network analysis, 134–135
Networks:
  defined, 134
  social, 134–135
New Guinea culture:
  mental illness, 236
  personality, 222
Nomadic pastoralism, 93–94
Non-market economies, 110–112
Nonverbal communication, 55–56, 68–78
  kinesics, 70, 76–78
  proxemics, 70–75
Northwest Coast Indian culture, 242,
  243
Norwegian culture, 252–253
Nuclear family, 144–145, 160, 161
Nuer culture, 180
Number, rules of, 35, 37–38
Nyakyusa culture, 139

Omaha Indian culture, 167
Opler, Morris, 236
Order, rules of, 35, 37
Organic solidarity, 102
Ownership, 105–107

Pakistani culture, 103–104
Papago Indian culture, 256–257
Participatory observation, 22–23, 29
Passage, rites of, 125–128
Pastner, Stephen, 87, 249
Pastoralism, 93–95
Patai, Raphael, 243
Pater, 152
Patrilineal descent, 156, 157, 158, 160,
    162
Patrilocal residence, 148
Patterns of behavior, 10–14, 26–44
    analysis of, 39–42
    congruity, 42–44
    difference between sets and, 38
    field project, 53–54
    number, rules of, 35, 37–38
    order, rules of, 35, 37
    participatory observation and, 29
    repetitive nature of, 27–28
    selection, rules of, 35–37
    space and, 32–35
    time and, 29–32
Patterns of Culture (Benedict), 223
Patterns of speech, 64–66
Personality, 219–245
    as adaptive mechanism, 229–233
    art, 239–244
    basic personality structure, 227–228
    defined, 220
    deviant, role of, 237
    early studies, 222–224
    field project, 245
    Freud, 224–226
    mental illness, 235–237
    modal, 228–229
    national character studies, 226–227
    normal vs. abnormal, 234–237
    sexual, 238–239
Phonemes, 57–59
Phratry, 159
Physical anthropology, 18
Physiological father, 151
Physiological tools, 69–70
Pigs for the Ancestors (Rappaport), 189
Pima Indian culture, 256–258
Plains Indian culture, 234–235, 237
Polanyi, Karl, 108
Political ideology, 214–215

Polyandrous family, 146
Polygynous family, 146, 147
Polynesian culture:
    belief system, 211, 213
    chiefdoms, 181
    social stratification, 136
Population control, 181
Positive/negative reinforcement, 77–78
Poussaint, Alvin, 64–65
Primary institutions, 228
Primary relationships, 131
Project Camelot, 266
Protestant Ethic, 230
Prothro, E. Terry, 231–232
Proxemics, 70–75
Psychophenomena, 226
Purdah, 103
Pygmie culture, 185
    control system, 176
    food collection, 88

Quechua Indian culture, 265–266

Ramadan, 32
Rank societies, 137–138
Rappaport, Roy, 189
Reality, cultural construction of, 1–17
    components, 10–14
    concept of culture, 7
    cultural relativism, 16
    ethnocentrism, 15, 16
    Hindu, 9
    learned nature of, 14–16
    multiple conceptions of reality, 4–9
    patterns, 10–14
    sets, 10–14
    shared, 16–17
    society and, 17
Reciprocity, 108–111
Redistribution, 109–112
Reich, Charles, 248
Relative age criterion, 164
Relativism, cultural, 16
Religion, 200, 205–210
    content of, 209–210
    defined, 205, 206
    distinguished from magic, 212
    functions of, 207–208
    nature of, 200–201
    operation of, 202–205
    organization of, 208–209
    ritual in, 198–199
    See also Belief systems

Residence patterns, 148–150
Rhoades, Robin E., 86
Rhythm, patterns of behavior and, 29–32
Riesman, David, 230
Rites of passage, 125–128
Ritual, 198–199
Rogers, Everett, 252
Role conflict, 124–125
Role equipment, 122–124
Roles, 120–121
    control system, 172–173
    deviant, 237
    groups, 132–134
    kinship, 161–169
    marriage, 150–152
    multiplex, 101
    parenthood, 151–152
    simplex, 101
    social networks, 134–135
    social stratification, 135–139
    wedding ceremony, 125–127
    See also Status
Russian culture, 227

Sahlins, Marshall, 108–109, 159, 180, 256, 264–265
Samoan culture:
    personality, 222
    unilineal descent, 156
Sapir, Edward, 67, 222
Sapir-Whorf hypothesis, 67
Saud, King Abd al Aziz al, 182
Saudi Arabian culture, 254–255
Science, as belief system, 205, 215–216
Secondary institutions, 228
Secondary relationships, 131
Segmental contacts, 130
Segmentary lineages, 159–160, 178–180
Selection, rules of, 35–37
Service, Ellman, 264–265
Services, distribution of, 107–117
Sets, 10–14, 36–38, 40, 56
    labor, 102–105
    phonemes, 57–59
    work, 101–102
Sex:
    division of labor and, 102–104
    of ego, 165
    kinship terms and, 164
    taboo, 128
Sex and Temperament in Three Primitive Societies (Mead), 222, 238
Sexual personality, 238–239

Shiite Muslim culture, 253–254
Similarity, law of, 213
Simmons, Leo W., 127
Simplex roles, 101
Sinhalese culture, 146
Skill, division of labor and, 104–105
Smith, Joseph, 17
Social anthropology, 18
Social class, 105, 138–139
Social group, defined, 51
Social movements, 259–262
Social networks, 134–135
Social organization, technology and, 86–87
Social segments, 75
Social stratification, 135–139
Social structure, 120–125, 230–232
Social systems, 120–141
    field project, 140–141
    groups, 132–134
    rites of passage, 125–128
    roles, see Roles
    social networks, 134–135
    social stratification, 135–139
    status, see Status
Societies:
    class, 138–139
    culture and, 17
    defined, 132
    egalitarian, 89, 136–137
    rank, 137–138
    See also Control systems
Sociocultural systems, model of, 49–50
Sociolinguistics, 64–66
Sorcery, 211–214
South African culture:
    caste system, 138
    languages, 57
Southern dialect, 60–61
Space, 70–75
    patterns of behavior and, 32–35
    status and, 71
    territory, see Territory
Spanish language, 58, 59, 60, 63
Special Operations Research Office, 266
Speech patterns, 64–66
Spiro, Melford E., 210
Standard Average European (S.A.E.), 68
State, the, 181–184, 189–190
Status, 120–121
    achieved, 128–129
    ascribed, 129–132
    defined, 120–121
    groups, 132–134
    kinship systems and, 143, 161

rites of passage, 125–128
sexual personality, 238–239
social networks, 134–135
social stratification, 135–139
space and, 71
symbols, 123
See also Roles
Stern, Henry, 28, 124, 161, 184
Steward, Julian, 256
Stratification, social, 135–139
Style, 242
Subculture, 17
Subsociety, 17
Sudanese culture, 168–169
Supernatural:
    magic, 205, 211–214
    nature of, 211
    religion, *see* Religion
    sorcery, 211–214
    witchcraft, 211–214
Supply and demand, law of, 107–108
Swadesh, Morris, 63
Swanson, G. E., 210, 213–214
Syncretism, 255
Systemic change, 248–250
Systems approach to behavior, 44–46

Taboo:
    incest, 152–154
    sex, 128
Tanzanian culture, 147
Tawney, Richard H., 230
Tchambuli culture, 222
Technology, 81–97
    agriculture, 92–93, 95
    defined, 82
    environment and, 86–87, 95
    food collecting, 87–90
    horticulture, 91–92
    importance of, 81–83
    industrial society, 94–95
    levels of, 83–86
    pastoralism, 93–94
    social organization and, 86–87
    symbolic communication and, 82–83
Territory:
    body posture and, 76
    material boundaries, 71–75
Thompson, Stephen, I., 86
Time, patterns of behavior and, 29–32
Tiv culture:
    control system, 174, 175
    market exchange, 112–114

Toda culture, 146
Transformational grammar, 61–62
Transvestism, 237
Triandis, Leigh Minturn, 210
Tribes, 177–180
Trobriand culture:
    exchange system, 110–111
    marriage, 151
    personality, 226
Trukese culture:
    kinship system, 158, 159
    residence pattern, 149–150
Tsembaga Maring culture, 187
Turnbull, Colin M., 176, 183
Tuscarora Indian culture, 229
Tylor, Edward, 154, 263

Unilineal descent, 156–162
Unilocal residence, 160
Usufruct tenure, 106
Uxorilocal residence, 148

Values, 196–197
Van Gennep, A., 125
Vayda, Andrew, 189
Vicos project, 265–266
Virilocal residence, 148
Voluntary groups, 133

Wallace, Anthony F. C., 224, 228–229, 252, 259
Warfare, 184–190
    change and, 264
    causes of, 188–189
    defined, 185
    among horticulturalists and pastoralists, 187–188
    among hunters and gatherers, 186–187
Weber, Max, 207, 230
Wedding ceremony, 125–127
White, Leslie, 264
Whiting, Beatrice B., 213–214
Whiting, John W. M., 128
Whiting, Marjorie Grant, 183
Whorf, Benjamin Lee, 67, 68
Wiitiko psychosis, 236–237
Wilson, Monica, 139
Witchcraft, 211–214
Wolf, Arthur P., 153
Wolf, Eric R., 260
Wolf, Margery, 210

Work sets, 101–102
World view, 194, 195–196

Yanomamö culture, 12, 185
   belief system, 197–198, 206

horticulture, 91
   warfare, 187, 188, 189
Young, John M., 4, 19, 23, 74, 113, 207

Zuni Indian culture, 223